A Rumour of Spring

A Rumour of Spring

South Africa after 20 Years of Democracy

MAX DU PREEZ

ZEBRA PRESS

Published by Zebra Press
an imprint of Random House Struik (Pty) Ltd
Reg. No. 1966/003153/07
Wembley Square, First Floor, Solan Road, Gardens, Cape Town, 8001
PO Box 1144, Cape Town, 8000, South Africa

www.zebrapress.co.za

First published 2013
Reprinted in 2014 (twice)

3 5 7 9 10 8 6 4

Publication © Zebra Press 2013
Text © Max du Preez 2013

Cover photographs © Michelly Rall/Wirelmage/Getty Images/Gallo Images

PUBLISHER: Marlene Fryer
MANAGING EDITOR: Robert Plummer
EDITOR: Bronwen Leak
PROOFREADER: Lisa Compton
COVER DESIGNER: Angela Tuck
TEXT DESIGNER: Jacques Kaiser
TYPESETTER: Monique van den Berg
INDEXER: Sanet le Roux

Set in 10.5 pt on 14 pt Minion

Printed and bound by Paarl Media, Jan van Riebeeck Drive, Paarl, South Africa

ISBN 978 1 77022 543 5 (print)
ISBN 978 1 77022 544 2 (ePub)
ISBN 978 1 77022 545 9 (PDF)

Contents

Preface

The year 2014 marks the twentieth anniversary of South Africa's democracy and will undoubtedly be a crucial year for the country. Indications are that we will have reached a tipping point – if we survive 2014 with our stability, our democracy and our freedom intact, the future will look a lot brighter.

My publishers and I agreed that it would be a good idea to take stock of where South Africa is after two decades of democracy. I had just completed a vast body of research on the political processes leading up to the settlement of 1994 for the South African Democracy Education Trust's Road to Democracy series, and had started working my way through the developments and trends of every year since then.

It was going to be a monstrous book, a magisterial and wannabe definitive body of work.

I ended up dissecting more than a few dozen books and collecting many thousands of documents, speeches and newspaper clippings. After working my way through several weighty contemporary political biographies and books such as Hein Marais's awe-inspiring 600-page *South Africa Pushed to the Limit*, R.W. Johnson's contrarian 700-page *South Africa's Brave New World* and Susan Booysen's excellent 500-page *The African National Congress and the Regeneration of Political Power*, I realised that I might as well abandon my efforts at academic prowess.

(I also remembered how annoyed I always am when I see a book I think I should read and, when I take it off the bookshelf, it weighs two kilograms. Come on, who has time to read two kilograms of dense writing? Life is too short!)

I realised that I should be suitably humble and concentrate on my strengths: simplifying things, explaining things, telling stories, making difficult reading accessible to concerned citizens with limited time. It did, of course, help that this is exactly what I do on a daily basis as a columnist for three newspapers, a public speaker and an analyst for commercial clients.

It was quite a relief that I wouldn't have to compete for the nod of approval of the academic world or those who call themselves political analysts.

So here's the product: my understanding of where we are as a nation twenty years after our liberation and my reading of what the future could hold. A guide, if you will, to help South Africans better understand their society, government, political processes and interactions, and the economy at a time of uncertainty, confusion and anxiety.

My thanks to my advisor-in-chief and the designer of this book's cover, my wife Angela Tuck; to all the politicians, colleagues and friends I consulted during the writing process; and to Robert Plummer and his very able colleagues at Zebra Press.

MAX DU PREEZ
OCTOBER 2013

Abbreviations and acronyms

AMCU: Association of Mineworkers and Construction Union
ANC: African National Congress
APLA: Azanian People's Liberation Army
ASGISA: Accelerated and Shared Growth Initiative for South Africa
AWB: Afrikaner Weerstandsbeweging
AZAPO: Azanian People's Organisation
BBBEE: broad-based black economic empowerment
BBC: British Broadcasting Corporation
BEE: black economic empowerment
BRICS: Brazil, Russia, India, China and South Africa
CASAC: Council for the Advancement of the South African Constitution
CDE: Centre for Development and Enterprise
CONTRALESA: Congress of Traditional Leaders of South Africa
COPE: Congress of the People
COSATU: Congress of South African Trade Unions
DA: Democratic Alliance
DRC: Democratic Republic of the Congo
EFF: Economic Freedom Fighters
FRELIMO: Mozambique Liberation Front
FVB: Federale Volksbeleggings
GDP: gross domestic product
GEAR: Growth, Employment and Redistribution
HSRC: Human Sciences Research Council
IDASA: Institute for Democracy in South Africa
IFP: Inkatha Freedom Party
IMF: International Monetary Fund
IPID: Independent Police Investigative Directorate
ISASA: Independent Schools Association of Southern Africa
JSC: Judicial Service Commission
KGB: Committee for State Security (Soviet Union)
LSM: living standards measure
MEC: member of the executive council

MERG: Macroeconomic Research Group
MK: Umkhonto we Sizwe
MP: member of Parliament
MPLA: People's Movement for the Liberation of Angola
NAT: Department of Security and Intelligence
NDP: National Development Plan
NDR: National Democratic Revolution
NEEDU: National Education Evaluation and Development Unit
NGO: non-governmental organisation
NIA: National Intelligence Agency
NP: National Party
NPA: National Prosecuting Authority
NPC: National Planning Commission
NUM: National Union of Mineworkers
NUMSA: National Union of Metalworkers of South Africa
OBE: outcomes-based education
PAC: Pan Africanist Congress
POPCRU: Police and Prisons Civil Rights Union
RDP: Reconstruction and Development Programme
SABC: South African Broadcasting Corporation
SACP: South African Communist Party
SADC: Southern African Development Community
SADF: South African Defence Force
SADTU: South African Democratic Teachers Union
SAIRR: South African Institute of Race Relations
SANDF: South African National Defence Force
SAP: South African Police
SAPS: South African Police Service
Stasi: East German Ministry for State Security
SWAPO: South West African People's Organisation
TRC: Truth and Reconciliation Commission
UCT: University of Cape Town
UDF: United Democratic Front
UDM: United Democratic Movement
UN: United Nations
UNESCO: United Nations Educational, Scientific and Cultural Organization
UNISA: University of South Africa
UNITA: National Union for the Total Independence of Angola
VOC: Dutch East India Company
ZANU-PF: Zimbabwe African National Union – Patriotic Front

Introduction

Spring? What spring?

The title of this book, *A Rumour of Spring*, emerged from my own (rather schizophrenic?) analysis that I regularly dish out as a columnist and political commentator.

I am always conscious of the need for hope, and of the tendency among so many South Africans to focus on the negative. So I try, sometimes almost against my own better judgement, to be upbeat, to see the good in government and society, and to record and acknowledge our achievements.

After the African National Congress (ANC) elective conference in Mangaung in December 2012, I told my readers and listeners that we had witnessed something of a turning point. Compared to the ANC's previous conference at Polokwane five years earlier, Mangaung reflected a more disciplined and focused ANC. The sensible and ambitious National Development Plan (NDP) was formally accepted without much resistance as the blueprint for development towards 2030; the impressive Cyril Ramaphosa was elected as deputy president; strong statements were made that corruption would henceforth be tackled with vigour; a nail was finally driven into the coffin of the nationalisation debate; and the rowdy, reckless ANC Youth League was effectively put in its place.

I confronted my audiences, especially those where most members were white: You guys looked at Julius Malema, former leader of the Youth League, and thought to yourselves, 'Well, that's the real face of the ANC'. When he insults and threatens and foams at the mouth, you think he represents who black South Africans really are. *En kyk hoe lyk hy nou* (And look at him now): marginalised, humiliated, on trial for corruption and racketeering.

Perhaps, I said many times, we've seen the worst of the ANC in the period between Polokwane and Mangaung. Perhaps the pendulum is now swinging back. Perhaps we can start taking the rumours of a new spring of hope and growth seriously.

Over the past few years, a lot of commentators here and abroad had warned that South Africa was facing its own Arab Spring, referring to the revolutionary protests and uprisings in the Arab world that toppled the governments of Tunisia, Egypt, Libya and Yemen and plunged Syria into a devastating civil war. This prophecy of doom got more traction after the Marikana mining massacre in August 2012 and the violent strikes on farms around De Doorns almost at the same time.

No, I said, this is an inappropriate comparison. The citizens of these Arab countries lived in dictatorships and had very little freedom of speech and association. South Africans live in a legitimate democracy with all the freedoms they need. If enough of them are unhappy with their government, they can vote them out at the next general election. The one thing we have really done right since 1994 is to hold credible elections that have not been questioned by anyone.

We had our Arab Spring in the 1980s, I said. The United Democratic Front (UDF) mobilised the majority of citizens very effectively against the apartheid government. Mass protests, marches, strikes and 'rolling mass action' by trade unions almost paralysed the country. Thousands of people were in detention without trial under state-of-emergency regulations, and apartheid dirty tricks and death squads like the police's Vlakplaas unit and the army's Civil Cooperation Bureau and Directorate Covert Collection were rampant.

But South Africa's political leadership eventually rose to the occasion and started a process of negotiation that defused the conflict and brought us a democracy, thus avoiding the fate that has befallen Syria and Egypt, I told audiences.

Um, sorry, I was wrong.

A few weeks after the Mangaung conference, vicious power struggles in the ANC again bubbled to the surface and it did not take long for President Jacob Zuma to start a purge of opponents.

It also very quickly became clear that the conference's acceptance by consensus of the NDP meant nothing. First, some Congress of South African Trade Unions (COSATU) affiliates such as the National Union of Metalworkers of South Africa (NUMSA) rejected virtually all of it, calling it a 'cut and paste of DA [Democratic Alliance] policies', and then the South African Communist Party (SACP) ripped the guts out of it by rejecting the proposals on labour and the economy, and downgrading the plan to a discussion document.

There was no evidence whatsoever in the months after Mangaung that the ANC was serious about fighting corruption – in fact, it appeared that the problem was getting worse.

In June 2013 Malema walked back onto the national stage and launched his Economic Freedom Fighters (EFF) with as much populist rhetoric, insults and threats as when he was at the height of his powers as ANC Youth League leader.

And then my Arab Spring theory was also blown out of the water. Egypt held elections, had a new president and stability was returning. But in June 2013 mass protests again rocked the nation, demanding the firing of President Mohamed Morsi. On 3 July the military staged a coup with much popular support and replaced the elected government.

So having had an Arab Spring uprising that resulted in a democracy is no guarantee of stability. It had not been enough of a spring, ordinary Egyptians felt, and so they returned to the streets demanding a real one. Or perhaps we should call this phenomenon the Arab Spring Aftermath.

And this is what the title of this book is about: are we facing a spring of hope, growth and cohesion, or an Arab Spring Aftermath with popular uprisings, economic ruin and instability?

Or are all the rumours of spring false – there will be no mass uprising, but also no new dawn, just a muddling along, treading water?

Let's try to find out.

PART I

How did we get here?

1

Multiply wounded,
multiply traumatised

'I would stop talking about the past, if it weren't so present.'
     ~ Central African Republic politician Barthélemy Boganda, 1910–1959

Only an arrogant fool (and I know a few) can be confident that his or her analysis of what is happening in our country and what it will lead to is correct.

I am confident in stating only one thing as fact, and I think this should be understood before we examine the state of our nation twenty years on. We South Africans – the political parties, government, business, civil society – have hugely underestimated the real impact and legacy of colonialism and apartheid.

It's as simple as this: if we had succeeded in overcoming our bitter past during the last two decades, we would most definitely not be facing the problems threatening our future right now.

I will investigate in the chapters that follow what the ANC government has done to dismantle that legacy since 1994. But without even considering its successes and failures, the evidence relating to the mentality and attitudes of the different racial and ethnic groups, unemployment, inequality, education, health, policing, crime and xenophobia suggests that most of us didn't fully appreciate the lasting harm the decades before 1994 had inflicted.

Most of us, including the ANC, have also overestimated how quickly the former liberation movement would be able to adapt from running a resistance movement, mostly from outside the borders, to managing a modern democracy and economy.

My problem with the present crop of ANC leaders is that they use apartheid as an *excuse* for bad governance rather than as a considered *explanation* for persistent problematic trends.

We saw this in the reaction to senior cabinet minister Trevor Manuel's remarks to the government leadership summit in April 2013 when he said:

'We should no longer say it's apartheid's fault. We should get up every morning and recognise that we have responsibility. There's no Botha regime looking over our shoulder, we are responsible ourselves.' Completely ignoring the context of his remarks, elements in COSATU and the SACP attacked him as a reactionary and a maverick.

President Zuma seemed to join them when he said shortly afterwards that it was a 'mistake, to say the least' to say that the government should stop blaming apartheid.

In a lengthy critique of Manuel's statement, SACP deputy general secretary Jeremy Cronin took a swipe at the economic policies Manuel had championed, but made the distinction between using the past as excuse rather than explanation.

He wrote in *Umsebenzi Online*: 'We have to take active and collective responsibility for transforming our country, but in order to do so we also need to understand the continued, systemic impact of a colonial, semi-colonial and apartheid past upon the present.' It is hard to disagree with that.

All of us, but especially white South Africans, should re-examine the legacies of generations of minority domination and apartheid on our people – on whites too – if we want to understand our society properly.

I have often contemplated what went wrong in our society that would explain the humiliating treatment given to helpless patients by nurses in state hospitals we read about so often; the teachers at township schools who neglect their work and go on strike at the drop of a hat; the policemen who abuse and rape and torture. Ditto the rape of babies, the scourge of child abuse, the hate-filled attacks on citizens of other African states, the extreme violence accompanying many criminal acts, the depressing sense of entitlement among so many, and the massive problems of drug abuse and gangsterism.

How should we understand the phenomenon of the *izikhothane*, the township youngsters from poor homes who have 'dissing' contests, showing off the most expensive designer clothes and shoes before destroying them to say, 'Check it out, I have more where that came from' (see box on pages 9–10)?

In fact, how should we understand the irrational paranoia of so many whites, some of them intelligent, even sophisticated, who still believe that black South Africans can't wait to rape or kill them and are waging genocide against white farmers, despite all the information that disproves these fears?

The terror of violent oppression during the last decade of apartheid, including attacks on ANC camps in neighbouring states, the Border War culture and the violent nature of the resistance to apartheid played no small role. The 'ungovernability' campaigns of the 1980s (remember the more than five hundred necklacings?) and the military campaign of Umkhonto we Sizwe (MK), as well as the conditions in MK camps in Angola and elsewhere, have surely left many deep scars.

Those who lick

A group of about fifty Soweto youngsters are gathered in a circle, all dressed in designer jeans, T-shirts and shoes. They brag about their expensive clothes with labels such as Armani, Rossi Moda and Murac-chini, taking jibes at each other.

A young man enters the circle. He empties a bucket of KFC chicken pieces on the ground and stomps on them with his R2 000 Carvela loafers. He sprays lighter fluid over the food and sets it alight. Then he takes his Carvelas off and burns them too. He performs his 'gloating dance' and is greeted with wild cheers. Some of the smiles show shiny gold teeth.

On another day in a park in Thokoza, a teenage girl takes off her Prada T-shirt, throws it in the middle of a circle of youngsters and burns it. Another teenager pours the contents of a bottle of Johnnie Walker Blue whisky over the fire. Not to be outdone, his friend throws down his smartphone and jumps on it. The group laughs, dances and shouts.

This is the world of the *izikhothane*, 'those who lick'.

They're not rich kids. Many are the children of domestic, shop or factory workers struggling to make ends meet. Some of the teenagers do loose jobs on weekends, some resort to petty crime, others black-mail their parents into giving them money.

Some call it a desperate quest for individualism, others say it is a search for self-value or an attempt to escape the squalid uniformity of the townships. '*Izikhothane* will borrow Armani's name and Diesel's reputation, until they can make one of their own,' says writer Lindo-kuhle Nkosi.

Lebo Motshegoa, who does research into the black consumer market, says it's about extreme waste. The youngsters' message is 'I have more where this comes from'.

Clinical psychologist Simphiwe Sinkoyi was quoted as saying the *izikhothane* have paid no thought to the psychology behind what they're doing. 'It's tempting to think of *izikhothane* as some kind of nihilistic reaction to a rampantly consumerist culture, a negation of the power that "stuff" has over us. But really it comes off as an exaggerated homage to consumerism, the desperate quest for individualism that ties its success to brand names and price tags.

'It is a search for self-value, not notoriety. When all the romanticism has been sucked out of the ghetto, when history's lessons have stripped you of what should be inherent self-respect, dignity is inferred.'

A sixteen-year-old Grade 9 pupil called Kefilwe was quoted in a newspaper report saying: '*Izikhothane* is a big thing. If you're not part of it, you're nothing. We have to spend in order to impress. I'm famous, many people know me.' Her friend Thandi said it was a 'celebration of life'.

It is a big thing. In 2012 fourteen-year-old Kamohelo Tsimane of Tlhatlhogang Primary School in Soweto hanged himself after his father told him he could not afford to buy his son a pair of Carvela shoes for R1 200.

But this kind of seemingly senseless, destructive behaviour is not restricted to young people from the townships. Kenny Kunene is a prominent member of Julius Malema's Economic Freedom Fighters. He is also known as the 'sushi king' after publicly eating sushi off the naked bodies of young women. He once poured the contents of a bottle of expensive French champagne over the exhaust of a high-revving Harley-Davidson to also show he 'had more where this comes from'.

Malema defended Kunene at a press conference in Braamfontein in August 2013, saying his behaviour can be ascribed to a 'damaged mentality' inflicted upon him by apartheid when he was a child.

Malema, brought up by a single domestic-worker mother, could have referred to himself. While still leader of the ANC Youth League, he paraded around in super-expensive clothes, wore a Breitling watch worth R250 000 and a R4 000 Louis Vuitton man bag, and drove several cars, each worth more than R600 000.

It's all seriously messed up, isn't it?

Of course, all societies have their social ills, criminal tendencies and fringe groups. Not everything that is going wrong in our society can be blamed on apartheid. Present and past political, religious, cultural and community leadership certainly also contributed to some of our present negative tendencies.

But after I read about the experiences of Nicaraguan psychologist Martha Cabrera, I became convinced that we should consider that South Africa is also a 'multiply wounded, multiply traumatised, multiply mourning' country, as she called Nicaragua, with serious implications for our social fabric, development and sense of hope. Her work really tallied with my experiences with victims and survivors during my close association with our own Truth and Reconciliation process.

Nicaragua had been plagued by crisis upon crisis for decades with bloody civil wars, dictatorships, economic hardship and natural disasters. Among these events are an earthquake in 1972; the war in the 1970s to overthrow the dictatorship of Anastasio Somoza Debayle; the Contra War of the 1980s; the devastation of Hurricane Mitch in 1998.

Cabrera and her team launched an 'affective and spiritual reconstruction' campaign in Nicaragua in 1997. Workshops, training and counselling were given in virtually every community in the country.

But then Cabrera paused and wondered why the results of all their work were so poor. 'Why, despite so much training, were people not responding to the seriousness of the problems? Why aren't they mobilising and making demands?' she wrote in an article in Nicaragua's *Envío* magazine in 2002.

The answer dawned on her while they were working on the emotional recovery of the survivors of Hurricane Mitch. People did want to talk about their immediate losses, but had an even greater need to talk about traumas they had never talked about before. They wanted to talk about their suffering after the earthquake, their oppression by dictators, the bloody civil wars, the exodus of so many to exile in Honduras and elsewhere, rape, domestic violence, poverty and health problems.

Cabrera and her team created spaces in which people could talk about all their painful experiences and traumas – the 'inventory of wounds', as she calls them.

'We worked a whole year after Mitch with those affected by the hurricane and found an enormous amount of losses, of personal and community wounds that had not been processed or even brought into the open, and thus had not been surmounted, which was the worst part,' she says.

'For a variety of reasons, including the quick succession of dramatic and traumatic events in Nicaragua, people had been unable to work through their experiences. When we asked people to reflect on the impact of what they had suffered and how they had dealt with it, the first thing we discovered was that they never had enough time to process it.'

Cabrera says when a person does not or cannot work through a trauma right away, 'its social consequences, the most frequent of which are *apathy, isolation and aggressiveness,* are only revealed over time' (my italics). She says accumulated pain leads to a diminished capacity to communicate, to be flexible and tolerant, and to accept change.

Cabrera's conclusions are supported by Caitlin Fouratt, a fieldworker studying Nicaraguan migrants in Costa Rica and their families back home, writing in the American Anthropological Association's online journal *Anthropology News* in July 2013. Referring to the series of traumas in Nicaragua, she writes: 'The people of Nicaragua have experienced these wounds as widespread unemployment, skyrocketing levels of crime, violence and domestic abuse.'

Anything sound familiar to you?

Think of the enormous dispossession of land and its ramifications, culminating in the 1913 Natives Land Act. Think of the devastating consequences to families and communities of the migrant labour system (which still continues – we'll talk about Marikana later). Think of the trauma of forced removals; the humiliation of pass laws; the psychological damage inflicted by treating generations of black South Africans as humans of lesser worth and capability; Bantu education; the 'Whites Only' signs on public amenities; police brutality; the torture and killing of anti-apartheid activists; and the ceiling put on black development by job reservation.

I have no doubt that it would be fair to say South Africa is also a 'multiply wounded, multiply traumatised' country. A lot of our fellow citizens present similar symptoms to those of traumatised Nicaraguans: anger, apathy, aggression, violence, lack of direction and ambition, domestic abuse, and so on.

The moment of liberation in 1994 with former prisoner Nelson Mandela at the helm must have brought some sense of justice to most black South Africans.

But Mandela did not have the inclination or luxury of indulging black South Africans in their enjoyment of a successful revolution. There could be no triumphant march to the Union Buildings by armed MK soldiers; no exuberant psychological release for the former oppressed; no Nuremberg-type war-crime trials to still the need for justice.

Mandela had to guard our stability and make the transition smooth and peaceful, which meant he had to concentrate on reassuring the white minority and the business community, on 'nation building' and on presenting us as a stable, progressive democracy to the world – a world that was expecting the worst. He even flew to that island of Afrikaner exclusivity, the whites-only town of Orania, to have tea with the widow of one of the most hated apartheid prime ministers (who was head of government when Mandela was sent to jail), Hendrik Verwoerd.

The new government even had to include the last apartheid president, F.W. de Klerk, and some of his ministers in the new cabinet. The heads of the new police service, defence force and Reserve Bank also came from the old order.

Not much symbolism to satisfy a revolutionary thirst or even a magical moment to make you feel your suffering was worthwhile, was there?

What is more, Mandela and his de facto prime minister, Thabo Mbeki, had little choice but to keep the economy structurally intact.

So once the festivities were over, most people's lives returned to what they had been before liberation. Most of the poor were still poor. Most black South Africans still lived in townships, squatter camps or neglected rural areas. Most of their children still went to bad township schools. Few had the prospects of a good job and a good life. Millions moved from traditional areas (the former Bantustans) to the cities after 1994, where most of them still live in misery and struggle to cope with the change to life in the city.

Most whites were still materially comfortable and some still super rich. Most of them still lived in neat suburbs and drove good cars. Most of their children went to excellent schools and good universities. The Afrikaners' language started thriving more than any other indigenous language. Whites still occupied most of the land.

The Founding Manifesto of the EFF, issued on 25 July 2013, puts it like this: 'Those who fought the gallant wars of resistance did so to resist forced dispossession of land, wealth, livestock and heritage, which they cherished and inherited from forebears. More than 350 years later, the war of resistance has not been won, and the battles that were fought represent almost nothing, because twenty years after the formal political freedom, the black people of South Africa still live in absolute poverty, are landless, their children have no productive future, they are mistreated and they are looked down upon in a sea of wealth … The conditions of the people are generally deplorable and show no evidence of a liberated people.'

Hyperbole, perhaps, and easy to poke holes in, especially as the EFF is headed by the most infamous tenderpreneur, Julius Malema, and counts crass playboy and celebrity Kenny Kunene as one of its members.

But my guess is that the vast majority of black South Africans would support every word of the above excerpt.

The very next day, on 26 July 2013, ANC member of Parliament and leader of the Young Communist League of South Africa, Buti Manamela, said in his Political Report to the Second National Council of the League: 'As we walk towards twenty years since the democratic breakthrough in 1994, myth making at the expense of the youth has become a national pastime. Everyone will have us believe that those born when Madiba was released are the Born Free generation. Born Frees who supposedly have no memory or inkling of apartheid colonialism.

'Let me debunk this myth for the ahistorical nonsense that it is. The concept is ideologically fraudulent and is littered with inconsistencies. It essentially suggests that the struggle ended in 1994 whereas we know that the struggle continues.

'Just ask the millions who still don't have jobs, who still live in apartheid's spatial planning spending the bulk of their meagre wages on transport and food, who can't get loans to pilot start-ups, no matter how good their ideas, just ask the young graduates who still struggle to get into the corporate world never mind climb the ladder. For all of us who battle every day to make a living – it is *aluta continua.*

'We will only be born free if the hospitals we are born in have facilities of the same but better quality; if the crèches and pre-schools we go to have the same but better quality menu of education, quality teachers and quality nutrition; if the schools we get to attend have libraries, computer labs and science labs; if we all have equal chances of graduating at Grade 12 with better quality skills and equal access to further and higher education and training; if we have equal opportunities for work and employment and our qualifications are of a better quality; if we are all born into families who can bequeath inheritances of land and pensions or life covers.

'The truth is we are not all at the same starting line. Those who fail to see how the past inequalities fester in the present and will, unless addressed, explode in the future, are wilfully blind. Put differently, they don't want to see.

'The Born Frees will exist if we live under socialism and we have fully achieved the transition to communism, then we will be regarded as, for the first time, free.

'If it is demanded of us to forego our parents' memory and their visible scars of apartheid, is it not time we also ask those who demand from us to forget that they too forego their inheritances which were in most cases ill-gotten gains from a system that sought to deliberately advance them through disadvantaging others. It is cynical to denounce apartheid as an evil past whilst they enjoy the benefits they accrued under the same system without an iota of guilt and a sense of collective responsibility for what Verwoerd, Botha and De Klerk committed in their name!'

Again, easy to dismiss as rhetoric, but in my view a good reflection of the thinking of most politically active black youngsters. Manamela is one of the crown princes of the ANC and regarded as one of the upcoming intellectuals in the Tripartite Alliance – he even has his own talk show on Power FM. He is also a member of the Politburo of the SACP, Zuma's staunchest ally.

So now, twenty years after liberation, not having dealt properly with our past, the symptoms of our multiple wounds and traumas still manifest.

A small number of people (about two thousand) were given the opportunity to deal with their pain and trauma when they appeared before the Truth and Reconciliation Commission (TRC). I was in charge of the television coverage of the TRC and met many of these people before and after they gave their testimony. Most of them felt huge relief, even closure, because they felt they were being heard and respected for the first time. I suspect many with similar experiences who did not appear before the TRC but who witnessed the process also felt some relief.

But the TRC dealt only with victims, relatives of victims or survivors of gross human-rights violations (severe assault, torture, kidnapping and murder) between 1960 and 1994. Because of the nature and political environment of the TRC and its narrow focus, it could not deal with the broader psychological trauma of apartheid.

The potential healing impact of the TRC process was further undermined by the Afrikaner and broader white establishment's negative reaction to it. The damage done by the denialist and hostile appearances of National Party (NP) politicians and police and defence-force generals before the TRC is, in my considered opinion, grossly underestimated by most. Former defence minister Magnus Malan's and law and order minister Adriaan Vlok's denials of all knowledge of wrongdoing by soldiers and policemen in the turbulent 1980s were particularly insulting.

The Afrikaans newspapers took a decision not to accept the TRC's invitation to testify. They had a lot to answer for: decades of almost blind support for the NP and for apartheid and, more seriously, violating all journalistic ethics by pushing the propaganda of the police and the military without question.

Historian Hermann Giliomee told a meeting of Democratic Alliance functionaries on 15 May 2013 that the board of Naspers (the owners of most Afrikaans newspapers and magazines) had been undecided on whether or not they should turn down the TRC invitation to participate. Then a director 'with many decades of experience in courts and human foibles', Jeff Malherbe, swayed them with these words: 'Never bat on your opponents' pitch.'

I find this astonishing. Cynical, arrogant and short-sighted. It wasn't the ANC's TRC; it was a commission of the people of South Africa, a compromise to avoid going the Nuremberg route. (The ANC wanted the TRC's final report to be suppressed, remember?)

Or were the majority of the nation Malherbe and Co.'s 'opponents'? Under the circumstances, especially with its generous amnesty provisions, the TRC was the very best the Afrikaner establishment could have hoped for. There simply wasn't any possibility of not doing anything about the past, pretending it never happened. It was a special opportunity for all of us to look each other in the eye and deal with our history, so we could walk towards a new society less burdened by the injustices that had been perpetrated.

And the TRC was headed by a fair-minded, generous and brave man of great integrity, Archbishop Desmond Tutu, not by some wild political commissar from MK.

(I have to mention that a number of young Afrikaans journalists did distance themselves from their bosses' decision. I was proud of them.)

There was someone who could have made a huge difference, using this unique, once-off moment in history to talk to black South Africans from the heart on behalf of Afrikaners and whites past and present: Frederik Willem de Klerk. Not only about fifty years of apartheid, but about 350 years of colonialism in South Africa – like me and most Afrikaners, he counted among his ancestors the first Dutch settlers that arrived at the Cape from 1652 onwards, the French Huguenots that started arriving in 1671, and German and other European settlers that arrived in the decades after that. The free elections of 1994 not only marked the end of apartheid; they signified the end of white domination of the subcontinent that started when the Dutch East India Company arrived on 6 April 1652 and established a refreshment station at the Cape of Good Hope.

F.W. de Klerk was more than the last apartheid president and leader of the biggest white political party. His family history was the history of Afrikaner nationalism: his great-grandfather was a senator in the Union parliament after 1910; his one grandfather was a founding member of the NP in 1914, the other a member of the Free State Provincial Council; his uncle, J.G. Strijdom, the 'Lion of the North', was prime minister between 1954 and 1958; his father, Jan, was president of the senate and cabinet minister under three prime ministers; his brother Willem was one of the most influential Afrikaans intellectuals of his time.

When De Klerk appeared before the TRC in May 1997, I sat in the hall with great expectation. I sensed that Black South Africa was waiting for, almost willing, White South Africa to seize the moment. I wanted De Klerk to speak on my behalf, even though he once publicly declared with much venom that I was his enemy; and despite the fact that I have spent most of my adult life fighting apartheid, I needed him to talk on behalf of my ancestors, my family, my children and my ethnic community.

I sensed that this could be a magical moment that could unlock the forgiveness and generosity of millions who had been on apartheid's receiving end over generations. I also sensed that if De Klerk spoke from the heart and with a full realisation of the historical significance of the moment, it could have a profound effect on white South Africans, setting the tone for their engagement with the rest of society in years to come. If he knew ordinary white South Africans as he was supposed to after a lifetime in white politics, he would have realised then, three years after 1994, that most of them had little understanding of what apartheid had meant to its victims and, because of the seamlessness of the transition, thought it was business as usual, just with black faces instead of white ones in power. He should have realised that this was a dangerous state of affairs – he was, after all, a Nobel Peace Prize recipient.

He chose his words well as he started apologising to 'the millions of South Africans who had suffered the wrenching disruption of being arbitrarily deprived of their homes, businesses and land because of forced removals; who over the years had suffered the shame of being arrested for pass law offences; who over the decades – and indeed centuries – suffered the indignities and humiliation of racial discrimination; who were prevented from exercising their full democratic rights in the land of their birth; who were unable to achieve their full potential because of job reservation; and who received inadequate social, medical and education services'.

He mentioned the right things, but his speech was devoid of any emotion, of any sense of momentousness. They were the carefully considered words of a clever politician and lawyer.

It was just too clinical an apology, for something *others* had done, even though they had 'meant well' when they started apartheid, as he pointed out. My heart started sinking. Still, Tutu reacted at first by calling it 'a handsome apology'.

But then the denials started. De Klerk said he and his government didn't know about and never sanctioned any dirty tricks, torture or assassination. The torturers and killers in the police death squad at Vlakplaas, the shady Civil Cooperation Bureau and Directorate Covert Collection of the South African Defence Force (SADF), and the murderous security police units were 'a rogue minority' who had acted outside of their orders. He only learnt about them during the TRC process.

As prominent ANC leader Mathews Phosa remarked at the time: 'De Klerk sat in Pretoria and knew everything that was going on in the ANC's Quatro Camp north of Luanda, but nothing of Vlakplaas twenty kilometres away from him.'

Tutu was in tears. 'How can he just say he didn't know? When these people were killed, I went and told him about it. It makes me sad. I'm really sorry for him.'

Tutu then added to his statement that it was a 'handsome' apology: 'He spoiled it all when he qualified the apology virtually out of existence.'

Leon Wessels, who was a member of the cabinet of the last two apartheid governments, said when he appeared before the TRC: 'I do not believe the political defence of "I did not know" is available to me because in many respects I believe I did not want to know. I had my suspicions of things that had caused discomfort in official circles, but because I did not have the facts to substantiate my suspicions or I had lacked the courage to shout from the rooftops, I have to confess that I only whispered in the corridors.' Wessels later became a highly respected member of the South African Human Rights Commission.

The moment was wasted and it would never present itself again. The TRC provided the timing, political atmosphere, context and stage for white South Africans to finally acknowledge the generations of injustice and all its intended and unintended consequences, and to ask for the understanding, forgiveness and acceptance of black and brown South Africans.

I did not want De Klerk to apologise for being here in Africa. I sometimes get the impression that some of my black compatriots want us to do that. The colonisation of southern Africa, as with the Americas, Australia and the rest of Africa, was probably historically inevitable. Our colonial history took a different route, though. Almost all the European settlers in the rest of Africa went back to the 'motherland' after their colonies became independent. Afrikaners did not have a motherland, being so diverse and mixed, with even some slave and Khoi blood. And unlike the Americas and Australia, South African whites remained a small minority. Afrikaners and many English-speaking white South Africans became Africans themselves and regarded themselves as indigenous with no other home.

We should also not fall into the easy trap of applying today's sensibilities and political sensitivities to the people who came many generations before us.

But I do think it would be appropriate for us Africans with pale skins to get a proper understanding of what our early ancestors' arrival and treatment of the people they found here meant, and then to acknowledge the disruptive, disempowering and traumatic impact it had on local peoples and their spirituality and development. We should admit that apartheid and continuing white privilege flowed from the colonial era.

It's complicated, of course. With all my understanding of the devastation to local communities caused by my Voortrekker ancestors, I am still proud of being an ancestor of Paul Kruger, president of the Transvaal Boer Republic, and of my grandfathers (and other heroes like Koos de la Rey and Christiaan de Wet) who fought against the British Empire during the South African War of 1899–1902. They were 'freedom fighters of a special kind' (to paraphrase the old term 'colonialists of a special kind' that Thabo Mbeki was so fond of) fighting what they saw was an anti-colonialist war.

I wish more of my black compatriots could understand that a little better.

The day after it was announced that Nelson Mandela was 'critically ill', I posted a famous old Afrikaans poem on Facebook, making it applicable to Mandela. It was Jan F.E. Celliers's moving poem in honour of General Christiaan de Wet: *Stil, broers, daar gaan 'n man verby* (Be still, brothers, this is a man passing by). I was attacked in vicious and obscene language for associating a Boer general with Madiba.

Apartheid itself is closer to the bone, because most whites alive in South Africa today lived through that era, or their parents did. The vast majority of white voters supported apartheid when it became the formal state ideology after 1948, at least until P.W. Botha's last election in May 1987.

One can still try to understand why the white leaders wanted blacks to be excluded from direct political participation when the two Boer republics and the two British colonies became a Union in 1910 – the British also wanted it, and the wounds of the war were still fresh.

But that act triggered resistance by black intellectuals and leaders, for the first time across language and regional divides, and led to the founding of the forerunner of the ANC. These dignified leaders clearly articulated to Britain and the new Union leaders that there was something fundamentally wrong with excluding black people from political participation in the land of their birth.

The Natives Land Act of 1913 went further and excluded blacks from most of the land in the country – their country. Whatever your trauma or dream for your own people, this was an evil, selfish act of historic proportions. And it prepared the ground for full-blown apartheid: rigid influx control via passbooks, Bantu education, job reservation, forced racial classification, a ban on sex across racial divides. South Africa was turned into a 'white' country with the black majority shunted into Bantustans and coloured and Indian South Africans living in limbo in their own separate townships and suburbs.

So when De Klerk and others say the initiators of apartheid 'meant well' but it turned bad, I cannot but reject that with contempt. How do you 'mean well' yet restrict the black majority to 13 per cent of the land and treat proud fathers and mothers like children?

De Klerk angered many South Africans when he told CNN's Christiane Amanpour in May 2012 that, as a young politician, he believed 'that the problems of South Africa could be justly resolved by recognising the right of all South Africa's constituent peoples to self-determination through Nation States situated mainly in the areas of the country that they originally occupied'. (This quote comes from a statement he issued on 16 May 2012 in which he tried to contextualise his remarks to Amanpour.)

It was never 'separate development'; it was always subjugation and selfishness. It was always a violent doctrine, because the majority that was supposed to 'develop separately' rejected and resisted it. I cannot shake the suspicion that the real disappointment among those who promoted apartheid, and eventually tried to reform it, was that it didn't work. It didn't work because whites wanted to be wealthy and grow the economy, and they could not do it without black labour. It didn't work because black and brown South Africans refused to be oppressed and humiliated forever.

There were many chances for the leaders of white South Africa after 1948 to come to their senses and introduce measures that would correct the wrongs and lead to democracy and equal rights. Think of the pleas by that mild-mannered man of peace Chief Albert Luthuli in the 1950s. As president of the ANC he declared that the struggle in South Africa was not so much about the ANC coming to power, but about the recognition and human dignity of black citizens. Think of the letters and requests for talks with the government by the young Mandela and Walter Sisulu in the same decade. The aftermath of the Sharpeville massacre of 1960 must have made the NP government think of alternative solutions. But they consistently responded with violence, bannings and the jailing of leaders and activists.

Even during the heated political climate of 1960, the ANC was still remarkably pragmatic and prepared to compromise. Mandela, by then already the commander-in-chief of the fledgling MK, demonstrated this when he spoke to the court during the Treason Trial in August 1960. He said the ANC would even have been prepared to accept a government offer of a limited franchise for black South Africans as a starting point.

'In my view,' he told the court, 'that would be a victory, my Lords; we would have taken a significant step towards the attainment of universal adult suffrage for Africans, and we would then for five years, say, suspend civil disobedience, we won't have any stay-at-homes, and we will then devote the intervening period for the purpose of educating the country, the Europeans, to see that these changes can be brought about and that it would bring about better racial understanding, better racial harmony.'

Justice Simon Bekker asked Mandela, 'As a matter of fact, isn't your freedom a direct threat to the Europeans?' Mandela responded: 'No, it is not a direct threat to the Europeans. We are not anti-white, we are against white supremacy and in struggling against white supremacy we have the support of some sections of the European population ... It is quite clear that the Congress has consistently preached a policy of race harmony and we have condemned racialism no matter by whom it is professed.'

Four years later, during the Rivonia Trial, he spoke again with these famous words: 'I have fought against white domination, and I have fought against black domination. I have cherished the ideal of a democratic and free society in which all persons live together in harmony and with equal opportunities.' He added: 'It is an ideal which I hope to live for and to achieve. But if needs be, it is an ideal for which I'm prepared to die.'

When the NP government's representatives eventually did talk to Mandela in jail twenty-four years later, they found him the same reasonable, pragmatic and democratic man. He could have applied the same reconciliatory, unifying magic and brave leadership that we witnessed after 1990 a good ten, fifteen years earlier if it hadn't been for the triumphalist and pig-headed clinging to white *baasskap* by the NP and its supporters in business and the Afrikaans churches.

After they banned the ANC and most of its leaders went into exile, where they could find a sympathetic ear only from the Soviet Union, the Afrikaner nationalists had a new excuse not to budge: the black political leaders would turn South Africa into a godless, communist state under the heel of Moscow.

The revolt of the youth of 1976 was the next clear wake-up call that the 'natives' didn't much like 'separate development', but the NP government responded with more repression. Then came the formation of the UDF in 1983, a true non-racial movement with prominent Christian leaders such as Allan Boesak, Desmond Tutu and Frank Chikane as part of the leadership. The government of P.W. Botha responded with more repression and by trying to co-opt the coloured and Indian communities into the white political system, but insisted the black majority had to rule themselves in the 'homelands'.

Two years later, as internal resistance was growing and international isolation was increasing, Botha had another chance. His cabinet and caucus were ready for a major jump to start unravelling apartheid and initiate moves that would lead to democracy. In fact, some of his ministers promised the world that it was going to happen. But on 15 August 1985 Botha delivered his famous Rubicon speech in which he rejected the new ideas and wagged his finger at the world.

Most of the torture and killing of political activists by state agents happened between 1985 and 1989. If the NP had started the process of negotiations five years earlier, it would have saved many lives and a lot of trauma. Roelf Meyer, a cabinet minister under Botha and De Klerk and the NP government's chief negotiator with the ANC after 1990, has told me his greatest regret was that his party didn't release Mandela in 1985 and start negotiating a peaceful settlement.

Some Afrikaans writers and commentators are making a living out of rubbishing the notion of whites needing to acknowledge the wrongs of the past and to show contrition. Their message is proving very popular among ordinary folk. They point out the achievements of the white regimes of the last decades before liberation and revel in documenting the chequered history of the ANC in exile and its communist allies.

These revisionists are indirectly aided and abetted by those who continue to compare apartheid with Nazism and genocide, simplistically playing the 'crime against humanity' game. It is too easy to dismiss these arguments as invalid, and they simply shift the focus from the real debate.

These are difficult waters to navigate.

South Africa today has indeed benefited from the presence of people of mostly European origin, although balancing these benefits with the negatives is a whole other question.

They brought technologies with them that didn't exist in Africa at the time. Many of them were industrious and innovative. They helped to build an impressive infrastructure that is one of democratic South Africa's greatest assets.

They are part of the reason South Africa was the only sub-Saharan African country able to host international events such as the 2010 FIFA World Cup successfully. They should get a lot of the credit for making South Africa's economy the strongest and most sophisticated on the continent.

I have no doubt that apartheid was inherently evil, but I honestly cannot state that all white people were evil. It's not that simple. I'm not referring only to those white people who stood up against slavery, colonialism and apartheid; I'm talking about ordinary people, even people who voted for the NP all their lives.

My father was one such person. He supported apartheid and the NP virtually until 1990, but he was, I can assure you, a thoroughly decent human being. At his funeral I looked upon his brothers, cousins and friends, the same people who excommunicated and defamed me as a traitor and a communist for opposing apartheid, and told them: 'You say you loved this man, but let me tell you, it was his sense of justice and human decency that made me into what you hated.'

It's all very complex, contradictory and schizophrenic.

But however much whites contributed to development in this country and however decent many of them may have been, the stark reality remains that they and their ancestors inflicted immeasurable psychological and developmental damage on generations of black people and that we are still feeling the effects of this in 2013.

I don't think white South Africans who had no active, direct role in apartheid should grovel or be paralysed with guilt. But we should acknowledge the hurt and damage it caused, and the direct and indirect ways we benefited from white domination; we should acknowledge that the legacy of apartheid still affects our communities; we should communicate that to the people who were so hurt and damaged; and we should take responsibility for our past and that of our ancestors.

That also means we should be more careful with our utterances and interactions, and actively assist the process of undoing the damage caused by those who came before us. It means all responsible white South Africans have the duty to fight racism among their own ranks.

The bottom line is that black, brown and Indian South Africans were deeply humiliated on a daily basis for many generations. One can put all the lipstick one wants on apartheid, but no one can ever deny the deep humiliation it brought.

We Afrikaners still talk about the injustices of the South African War of 1899–1902, about the inhumane concentration camps, the scorched-earth policies and the after-effects of the war. Some right-wing Afrikaners still prefer to call themselves 'Boere' instead of Afrikaners and still wave the flags of the old Boer republics.

That war ended more than a century ago. How can anyone expect black South Africans to forget and not talk about the injustices and humiliation that ended little more than twenty years ago?

I thought it was crucial to start off with this backstory, because everything we look at in today's South Africa was influenced by this history and these experiences and attitudes.

2

The Mandela factor

An ailing Nelson Mandela spent more than two months in hospital in mid-2013.

Despite a prevailing bout of national depression, 18 July 2013, the day the old man turned ninety-five, was probably the most positive, sharing Mandela Day yet, possibly because of a suspicion that it would be the last one while he was alive.

It would be inappropriate not to consider Mandela's role in our national affairs and his legacy if one is taking a broad look at the state of the nation.

During the many interviews with local and foreign media during the days we thought were going to be his last, the first points I came up with were these: Mandela brought an integrity to the highest office in the country that we had not seen before or after. He brought out the best in the nation he was leading. And he demonstrated to us and the world what real leadership looks like.

One of Thabo Mbeki's closest advisors told me in 2002 that Mbeki's biggest problem was that he was Mandela's successor; Mandela served as president for only the first five years after the liberation election. He basked in the sun of the 'South African miracle' and never had to face the difficult realities of running the government of a state faced with the terrible after-effects of apartheid.

He was right. While Mandela was president, he left the day-to-day running of the country to Mbeki and instead focused his time and energies on Project Rainbow Nation and on being an international symbol of anti-racism, hope and reconciliation.

When Mbeki took over in 1999, the national emphasis had to shift quite urgently from reconciliation to reparation and empowerment of the frustrated black majority. This was an unpleasant surprise to the white minority and the white-dominated business community, made worse by Mbeki's aversion to engagement, his lack of charisma, and his own racial and historical demons.

Mbeki started talking about 'colonialists of a special kind' and of the 'two South Africas – one white and rich, the other black and poor'. It gave whites the jitters and encouraged frustrated and impatient black citizens to believe that the pendulum was about to swing back, but this wasn't happening quickly or visibly enough – and that was in no way entirely his fault.

So South Africans from all sides started turning on Mbeki, while Mandela remained the hero. This annoyed Mbeki no end.

In hindsight, many of the problems that manifested in the post-Mandela era, such as the mismanagement of the rampant AIDS pandemic, the forming of a small black elite under the policy of black economic empowerment (instead of spreading the jam a bit further) and the neglect of the official Reconstruction and Development Programme (RDP), had their roots in Mandela's presidency.

Mandela was president when South Africa bought sophisticated submarines, jet fighters and corvettes for around R65 billion. Most of these are mothballed today. Many senior ANC politicians and hangers-on received substantial bribes from the arms companies, a scandal that is still eating at our political system like a cancer.

I suspect historians will one day conclude that the most negative part of Mandela's legacy was that his reconciliation project lulled white South Africans into a false belief that the past had been dealt with and that life could go on as before, without significant sacrifices. This wasn't what he said or stood for, but I do think it was so perceived. I have seen many whites quoting Mandela as having said something like 'Let's forget the past and move on', but I have never been able to trace such a quote and I doubt very much that he said it – and if he did, it would have been in a specific context.

In 2013 this perception weighs heavily on our fraught political interactions.

But Mandela's achievement wasn't his running of the country between 1994 and 1999. We have to look at the period 1950–1994 to assess his contribution to South Africa and the world.

Mandela clearly believed early on in his political career, before he went to jail for twenty-seven years, that he was destined to be the one to lead his nation to freedom.

Formal apartheid was only fourteen years old when he was arrested and jailed in August 1962.

It was clear from interviews with him that Mandela understood then that his calling was not only to have the discriminatory race laws scrapped. He was to be the leader who would close the final chapter on the colonisation of Africa, which, in South Africa's case, started with the arrival of the first Europeans in 1652.

He knew very well he was facing at least a life sentence when he was found guilty of sabotage and terrorism in 1964, yet he addressed the court with remarkable confidence and clarity of purpose in a speech that reverberated around the world.

Mandela gained his international reputation as a virtual saint after he facilitated the improbable transition from apartheid and white rule to an open democracy in 1994. But his role in reinvigorating and modernising, in fact radicalising, the ANC from the 1950s onwards also deserves mention. With his old friend and later fellow inmate Walter Sisulu, he turned an almost dormant party into a national liberation movement that eventually forced the last apartheid government to settle with the black majority.

Mandela was thus also a revolutionary in the proper, old-school sense of the word.

His role did not stop when he went to jail in 1962. He turned the jail on Robben Island off Cape Town into a disciplined political 'university' where most future ANC leaders were educated. Perhaps that was one of the factors that distinguished the ANC from other liberation movements in Africa.

In prison he remained an inspiration and role model to thousands of ANC cadres in exile and at home.

The prison walls couldn't hide his quiet strength and determination, his charisma and extraordinary dignity, and he became not only the most famous prisoner in the world, but the inspiration for a powerful international anti-apartheid movement.

His interaction with the white prison warders, most of them Afrikaners, tells us a lot about Mandela. No black political prisoner before or after him stood up to their abuse and disrespect like he did. I have heard the story from fellow prisoners of how he confronted a rude warder face to face. It wasn't about arrogance; it was about self-belief and inherent dignity.

At the same time, Mandela made an effort to learn Afrikaans and treated the decent prison employees with dignity, taking an interest in their families and personal lives. Some of them, like Christo Brandt and James Gregory, came to idolise him. According to all accounts, during the last fifteen years or so of his incarceration he was treated with virtual veneration by most in the prison service, almost as if they knew he was going to be their president one day.

The first NP politician who met Mandela was minister of justice Kobie Coetsee, who visited him in hospital in 1985 when he was undergoing a prostate operation. Mandela greeted him with courtesy, but as an equal, and

Coetsee was very impressed with this man in one of his jails. Coetsee ordered the intelligence services to put together a dossier on Mandela's past, his thinking and his personality, and the result was almost glowing.

This encounter led to P.W. Botha asking the head of the National Intelligence Service, Niel Barnard, to form a small committee to engage Mandela in talks in great secrecy. The first meeting between Barnard and Mandela took place in Pollsmoor Prison on 28 April 1988, one of forty-six meetings between them over the following eighteen months.

Barnard told me about this first encounter: 'Mr Mandela walked in, wearing gumboots and a blue prison uniform. His clothes did nothing whatsoever to diminish his dignity and obvious stature; it stared us in the face.' The two men could hardly have been more different: Barnard the staunch Calvinist, Afrikaner nationalist and secretive apartheid technocrat; Mandela the genial, charismatic African revolutionary. And yet they formed a bond of trust, even a friendship that lasted until well after Mandela retired from politics. (Barnard never talks about 'Mandela' or 'Madiba'; he always refers to 'Mr Mandela' or, with fondness, 'the Old Man'.)

I interviewed both Barnard and Mandela at length about this period. Barnard was just about the only man the borderline-paranoid Botha really trusted never to sell him out or be soft on the enemies of his government. Mandela sensed this; he knew that only Botha, Coetsee and a handful of selected senior prison and intelligence officials knew about the talks. He realised that the only way to convince Botha and his State Security Council that his release and full negotiations with the ANC would be in their own interest would be through Barnard. Barnard knew that Mandela would be the key figure if there was to be any kind of settlement with the black majority. Trust between the two was essential.

'I knew early on that I was talking to the man who would probably be my future president,' said Barnard. 'I never treated him like a prisoner. We never abused the fact that he was in our jail. We never tried to drive a wedge between him and his colleagues in jail or the ANC in exile. I knew we had to get him out of the prison environment after twenty-five years in jail and to get him to know what was going on in the country and the ways of life outside of jail.'

The result was that when Mandela was released on 11 February 1990, he already had a relationship with his future interlocutors and their worst fears of making a deal with the liberation movement had largely been dealt with.

Tea with Madiba

Mandela played a role in my life over a very long time. I went to study law at Stellenbosch University at the insistence of my father – he said I could one day be as great a lawyer as Percy Yutar, the prosecutor who years earlier presented the state's case at the Rivonia Trial that saw Mandela go to jail.

I remember reading a book on the trial to figure out why Yutar was such a hero. It painted Mandela and his co-accused as dangerous communist terrorists and I felt a sense of relief that these enemies of my people were now on Robben Island.

But I also remember wondering as a platteland teenager why Mandela was prepared to die for a cause that my society at the time saw as treasonous and un-Christian. Could it just be that my father and the leaders of Afrikanerdom were misrepresenting his cause? My father was angry when I asked him.

I was reminded of this when, as a cub reporter in Soweto on 16 June 1976, I was faced with black teenagers challenging the police to shoot them. I knew then that there was something I wasn't getting.

In 1984 I interviewed a South West Africa People's Organisation (SWAPO) leader, Andimba Toivo ya Toivo, who had just been released from Robben Island, where he had served many years with Mandela. He wanted to talk about Namibia; I wanted to interrogate him about Mandela.

By this time I had had a different exposure as a journalist to what apartheid really meant. After my conversation with Toivo ya Toivo I knew that my country's prospects for peace and freedom were tied in with the fate of Mandela.

Late in 1988 I wrote Mandela an open letter in the newspaper I was then editing, *Vrye Weekblad* – I knew he was a subscriber in jail. I asked him to liberate Afrikaners also when he did come out of jail, to help establish a proper democracy in South Africa.

A few days after his release in February 1990, Mandela phoned me to invite me to his home in Soweto. When I arrived, he came out to my car with an outstretched hand and greeted me in Afrikaans. He poured me tea (prison tea: too milky and too sweet) and explained that he wanted to apologise for not responding to my open letter, but the prison authorities wouldn't allow him to send it to me.

Mandela also apologised for his 'Xhosa accent' when speaking Afrikaans and told me about his vision of a united, free and fair – and non-racial – South Africa.

By this time I had interviewed most political leaders in South Africa, as well as a wide range of African and Western prime ministers, presidents and cabinet ministers. This man was very, very different. He had an aura of moral authority about him; he had a clear vision; he had no doubt about his calling to deliver freedom and dignity to the last country in the world where white people ruled over black people. But he wasn't all politician; he was a proper mensch.

The most remarkable thing about that first meeting I had with him wasn't that he bothered to make personal contact with an ordinary journalist like me. The most remarkable thing was that over the years that followed he stuck to the vision that he outlined to me then.

I interviewed Mandela several times as president and after he retired, and had two private meetings with him. He was fundamentally the same person I met in February 1990.

Three years ago, the London-based publishers of the Rough Guide books commissioned me to write *The Rough Guide to Nelson Mandela*, a book that was published in 2011. I spent two years researching his life before, during and after Robben Island. Last year I made an hour-long documentary on his life for the Afrikaans television channel kykNET.

During this deep research I came across many of Mandela's weaknesses and mistakes, all of which I documented in the book: his womanising and infidelities, his vanity, his short temper, his stubbornness.

He cheated on his first wife, Evelyn Mase (he divorced her shortly before he married Winnie Madikizela in 1958), and had love affairs with a political colleague, Lilian Ngoyi, and with a popular singer and actress, Dolly Rathebe. He divorced Winnie in 1998 and married Graça Machel, widow of the former president of Mozambique, Samora Machel. His old friend and ANC comrade Amina Cachalia recently revealed in her autobiography that Mandela had flirted with her and 'declared his love for me in no uncertain terms' months after his wedding to Graça.

Mandela's cabinet ministers loved to tell stories of his quick temper. He sharply rebuked colleagues who were not punctual or spoke incoherently at cabinet meetings. He hated to be interrupted – I had personal experience of that during some of the live television interviews I did with him.

Rather than seeing a hero with feet of clay, it reaffirmed my view of what a special human being he was. He wasn't a saint sent by some higher being after all; he was an African and South African of flesh and blood. But he was a man with a vision and a mission – and the personality and intellect to match – and he spent five decades fighting to make them a reality.

The magic of Madiba was in part about his charisma and his human touch, respect for his sacrifice over twenty-seven years, and his extraordinary generosity and capacity to forgive.

But it is his leadership example that sets him apart from other politicians and that will be remembered for generations to come, here and abroad. When older South Africans look at the leadership of the Zuma administration, they judge it harshly by the standards set by Mandela.

He was a strong and driven leader when he helped the ANC Youth League re-energise the ANC in the 1940s and as National Volunteer-in-Chief of the 1952 Defiance Campaign; when he and his co-accused faced the death penalty in the 1960s; and when he was jailed on Robben Island and turned the prison into a political university.

But true great leadership involves taking great risks, risks that could destroy you. When Mandela started talking to agents of the apartheid government and even met with P.W. Botha, he did not fully consult or inform his colleagues in jail or in exile. He knew full well that they would be suspicious and critical, but he also knew that it was the risk he as leader had to take: consultations with and mandates from the ANC, the internal resistance and the UDF would most likely have destroyed his chances of making progress at that sensitive stage. In fact, when his contact with the regime did become known, elements in MK, the SACP and the UDF indeed reacted with anger and demands that he stop all contact.

His other considerable risk was that the government would betray his trust, use the contact to weaken and divide the ANC, and the whole initiative would explode in his face, destroying his reputation and his future as a leader.

Mandela took those risks. He believed in his cause and in his ability to use the force of his personality to get both sides of the divide to work together.

And in the period between 1990 and 1994, he sold his vision of a shared, democratic and stable South Africa to the militants in his own movement, to the NP and its government, and to white society in general. It was his good fortune that he found someone like F.W. de Klerk as a process partner in this unlikely transition.

There can't be many other examples of a political leader who fought and outmanoeuvred his opponents and then became their beloved father figure. That was what Madiba achieved with Afrikaners; and that was what undermined the potential for new resentments, racism, fear and right-wing violence.

People sometimes forget how active and dangerous right-wing movements like the Afrikaner Weerstandsbeweging (AWB) and other smaller groups were right into the 1990s.

In 1993 the former head of the defence force and hero of the 'Bush War', General Constand Viljoen, had mobilised tens of thousands of trained men across the country, even some serving SADF units, to be on standby for a military intervention when the country 'was handed over to the ANC'.

Ironically, it was the uninvited participation of the AWB in Viljoen's 'protection of Bophuthatswana' that forced the general to retreat and take part in the elections. But Mandela and some of his lieutenants had met with Viljoen in secret several times before to reassure him, and this played an even bigger role in the disbandment of the reactionary force.

After 1994 the right wing was virtually dead, apart from a small splinter group or two. There wasn't going to be a race war after all.

Mandela's further seduction of Afrikaners through the use of the 1995 Rugby World Cup and symbolic gestures such as having tea with Hendrik Verwoerd's widow Betsie are well documented, among others, in John Carlin's book that Clint Eastwood turned into the film *Invictus*. The outpouring of love and adoration for Mandela on Mandela Day 2013 came as much from Afrikaners as anyone else.

Mandela was the quintessential counter-intuitive leader.

South African author and public intellectual Professor Njabulo Ndebele analyses this Mandela quality in an insightful piece on leadership in Africa and the world. He tells the story of Mandela's secret 1993 meeting with Viljoen and two fellow generals involved in military mobilisation. Mandela told them that if they went to war, the ANC would not have the resources to stand up to them on the battlefield. But, he said, the generals and their followers could not win either, because of the overwhelming number of black people and because the international community would side with said black people. The generals had to agree and face the fact of their 'mutual dependency'.

Ndebele then suggests that 'Nelson Mandela's supreme gift to us is to expose us to the notion of counter-intuitive leadership and its immense possibilities. The characteristic feature of this type of leadership is in the ability of a leader to read a situation whose most observable logic points to a most likely outcome, but then to detect in that very likely outcome not a solution but a compounding of the problem. This assessment then calls for the prescription of an unexpected outcome, which initially may look strikingly improbable. Somehow, it is in the apparent improbability of the unlikely outcome that we can derive principles for its sustainability. A leader then has to sell the unexpected because he has to overcome intuitive doubts and suspicions that will have been expected. In this act of salesmanship is the content that crucially counts.'

It can be argued that it was within Mandela's grasp to enforce a different kind of settlement with the white government of South Africa and then proceed to punish whites for their role in his and his people's suffering, and in doing so satisfy the desire for retaliation most black South Africans, and black people everywhere, felt. Instead he risked the wrath of his own party's radicals and many of the former oppressed, and embarked on a remarkable charm offensive that not only disarmed white intransigents and ensured the end of right-wing militancy, but ensured stability and economic continuity. And he sold his risky endeavour to the nationalists, the communists, the workerists and the Black Consciousness disciples in his party and his country, young and old, through the force of his own personality and his indisputable moral authority.

Perhaps there is recognition in the world that if leaders elsewhere had shown more counter-intuitive vision, risk-taking and leadership like Mandela did, the Middle East would not still be a powder keg, the genocide in Rwanda and the Balkan states (which took place as Mandela assumed office in 1994) would have been prevented, and the wars in Afghanistan and Iraq would not have taken place. During his presidency and in the years after 1999, Mandela was the closest the world had to a global leader.

His stature as an international icon and statesman has everything to do with the fact that he brought peace and democracy to the last state where white people oppressed and ruled over black people.

Apartheid was declared a crime against humanity by the United Nations. It was an assault on the sense of decency and fairness of most people in the world and an unspoken-of prick on the consciences of white-skinned people everywhere, many struggling with their own demons of racial prejudice.

Mandela and his comrades not only defeated apartheid and restored black pride; they did it without driving the whites into the sea or killing them. In Mandela's own words, the oppressed not only liberated themselves, they liberated their oppressors.

South Africa, with its bitter history of Dutch and British colonialism and then ninety years of white minority domination, was seen as a pilot project for all humanity.

Mandela's words and actions held the promise of salvation for all those who quietly felt like oppressors or wondered about their own racial prejudice – and for those who needed psychological liberation.

Looking back, it sometimes appears as if at the end of the twentieth century the world so needed a figure like Mandela that when he surfaced, he was built up into something no human being could ever be.

'Mandela will remain a great icon,' former British prime minister Tony Blair said in a tribute recently. 'The fact that a black man is the most respected figure in the world is also part of what he has brought about. The fall of apartheid was not only important for South Africa and for the world, but it also symbolised the last bastion of all that terrible bullshit you used to get about genetics. When apartheid fell, it was as if racism all round the world was suddenly put in the past. It's not that racism doesn't exist today, but it isn't countenanced as part of respectable society. I think he will be seen as a symbol of equality between the races in a multicultural world where people are respected irrespective of the colour of their skin.'

There can be no denying that Mandela's stature as international icon was partly built on his twenty-seven years in jail. Politicians, leaders and ordinary people everywhere ask themselves how they would have survived such an experience, and they marvel at the way it seemed to have deepened Mandela's resolve to bring about not only freedom, but a peaceful transition from apartheid to democracy; how it seemed to have strengthened his humanity and his capacity to embrace his enemies and turn them into friends and allies. Surviving such a long period of detention and emerging from it a whole human being gave Mandela a lot of licence to be bold and adventurous – how does one challenge such a person's magnanimity, how can anyone ever accuse him of being 'a sell-out' or 'soft' on his former enemies? How could senior Western leaders actually take him on when he publicly criticised them or argued the case of his old friends who were regarded as enemies of the West?

The fact that Mandela was from Africa also contributed. In the eyes of much of the rest of the world, Africa is a dark, dangerous place where civil war, disease, poverty and corruption are rife – the continent of Idi Amin, Mobutu Sese Seko, Charles Taylor and Robert Mugabe. The view is of a place with more failed states than successful democracies; of constant ethnic and tribal conflict; of chaos, illiteracy and superstition.

From this stark landscape emerged a man of rare integrity and moral authority, a sophisticated political philosopher who overwhelmed the world with his humanity, tolerance, capacity to forgive and ability to unite people.

Within a decade of his release from twenty-seven years in prison, Mandela was regarded as the greatest world leader of the modern era. In the minds of millions of people, he was rated higher than Mahatma Gandhi, Winston Churchill and Theodore Roosevelt; he was somewhere between Che Guevara and Mother Teresa, Karl Marx and the Dalai Lama. His image was on more T-shirts than Michael Jackson's and on more fridge magnets than diet mantras. Presidents, prime ministers, billionaire industrialists, rock and sports stars clamoured to meet and have a picture taken with him like with no one else before.

To Africans, African-Americans and black people living elsewhere in the world, Mandela became a supreme symbol of reassurance of their inner worth as human beings. His emergence as a revered statesman and humanitarian was an overdue antidote to the constant message they'd been getting from society and the media since the days of slavery; that black equals inferior.

African-Americans particularly took Mandela on as a sort of messiah. Many prominent black Americans made the pilgrimage to South Africa and many more gathered to meet him when he visited the US: people like Oprah Winfrey, Harry Belafonte, Jesse Jackson, Morgan Freeman, Randall Robinson, Walter Fauntroy, Danny Glover and Maya Angelou.

Actress Alfre Woodard says when Mandela walked free in 1990, he was 'no longer our cause, our battle cry, our inspiration, our mythical brother/father. He became our Madiba. And we could touch him and know him and know our own potential, our own strength and possibility.'

In Africa itself, Mandela became a huge inspiration that the continent could be reborn as a democratic, peaceful and prosperous place. The way he had overcome tribalism, the scourge of so much of Africa, and found a balance between taking pride in roots and tradition and embracing modernisation and globalisation reinvigorated many African democrats.

President Ellen Johnson-Sirleaf of Liberia, in her Nelson Mandela Annual Lecture in Johannesburg in July 2008, said that when Mandela became president of South Africa, dreams were born. 'Africans dreamed of the end of the exploitation of the past. They dreamed of having dignified economic opportunities to provide for their families. They dreamed of sending their children to decent schools. They dreamed of an end to gender disparities. They dreamed of competent governments that were accountable to the people. They dreamed of national reconciliation and national unity. And they dreamed of living in peace and security with their neighbours.'

Many people outside South Africa make the same mistake as many white South Africans: they think Nelson Mandela is an exception, an aberration. Mandela is not like other black people, they say. They elevate him to an unusual phenomenon because of a reluctance to admit that Africa could produce someone so exemplary.

This misconception lies at the heart of the paranoia among right-wing South Africans, recently repeated in some foreign media, that when Mandela dies, black people will drop the pretence of the last twenty years and start murdering whites.

Mandela is a special, gifted man, but he has himself said many times, as has his old friend Walter Sisulu and others, that he is purely and simply a product of African and South African society, history and spirituality.

His character, leadership style, vision and sense of morality were shaped by his childhood in Qunu; his early years at the household of the Thembu regent Jongintaba Dalindyebo; his experiences as a student at the Fort Hare and Witwatersrand universities; his interaction with young ANC revolutionaries such as Sisulu, Anton Lembede and Oliver Tambo; his friendships with people like Yusuf Cachalia, Bram Fischer, Ahmed Kathrada and George Bizos; his twenty-seven years in jail – even by his contact over years with Afrikaans-speaking prison wardens.

A century from now historians will still write about Mandela's spectacular role in bringing freedom, stability and democracy to South Africa. They will still remind their students that he became an international icon as a man of great integrity with an enormous capacity to forgive, to heal and to bridge seemingly impossible divides.

But they probably won't record that he wasn't the first remarkably wise and inspirational leader to emerge from this land. King Moshoeshoe (1787–1870) springs to mind. Unlike his more aggressive contemporaries such as King Shaka and Chief Mzilikazi, he avoided war, gathered together people from many clans and language groups to form a new inclusive nation, and stabilised central South Africa at a time of great turmoil and bloodshed. Pure Mandela.

Moshoeshoe was the protégé of Mohlomi (1720–1850), an extraordinary sage who taught a revolutionary philosophy of non-violence, participatory democracy and egalitarianism. And we can add many others to the list, like the Xhosa theologian and militarist Makhanda, Adam Kok of the Griqua, Sekhukhune of the Pedi, Kgama of the Tswana and Sobhuza of the Swazi.

But there were later leadership figures of great stature that also belong in the same class as Mandela: people such as Albert Luthuli, Walter Sisulu, Oliver Tambo and Desmond Tutu – some would also include Jan Smuts and Robert Sobukwe. Like Mandela, they were reflections of the best of South African history, culture and spirituality.

No nation will ever be blessed with two or more Mandela-type leaders in succession. The present leadership of the ruling party does not, to put it diplomatically, reflect the best of our society.

But there is a little bit of Mandela in most of us South Africans. He wasn't a freak or a saint sent by some supernatural power. We are the products of the same history and society that produced a Nelson Mandela.

Above all, Mandela brought out the best in all his fellow citizens of all creeds, colours and classes. He gave South Africans a glimpse of what they could be as a nation. He will remind them of that long after his passing.

To me, Mandela is living proof that good can prevail over evil, that there actually is something like a shared humanity.

We'd better believe in that in years to come.

3

A silver lining

South Africans are like a bipolar patient with Tourette's syndrome.

We are mostly depressed about the state of our country and curse one another endlessly. And then we have glorious moments of joy, hope and togetherness, like when we host the Soccer World Cup, celebrate Mandela Day, or when a sports star or team does well on the world stage. Afterwards we descend rapidly into depression and insults once again.

White and black South Africans compete in bad-mouthing the state of the nation from opposite ends (if you'll forgive the terrible generalisation). We only agree that there's far too much corruption, but we don't always agree on who is to blame.

Thousands of white South Africans have left the country in the last twenty years, some simply to further their careers, but most because they fear for their and their children's future in a black-governed South Africa. I suspect many more would love to leave, but don't have the money or the education to emigrate. Too many of those who left bad-mouth the country from abroad. We should be happy to be rid of them.

A favourite pastime among many whites, including some public commentators, is to measure how far South Africa has progressed on the failed-state barometer. An old chestnut that gets hauled out often is we're well on our way to becoming 'another Zimbabwe', or we're just another banana republic.

On the extreme right we have a few Afrikaans celebrities and pseudo-intellectuals who scare themselves into a state of apoplexy by manufacturing statistics about a 'low-level genocide' against Afrikaners and about the inherent incompetence of black people trying to run a modern economy.

The dominant middle-class black discourse is that full liberation has not been achieved. My impression is that most blame the 'white establishment' for this. Only some, mostly those outside the ANC, apportion some blame to the governments since 1994, but then mostly because they haven't acted more decisively against white domination of the economy and the professions.

I sometimes find myself looking a bit cynically at members of the new black elite raging against 'white hegemony' and I can't help but wonder if the real source of the anger can't be found in a personal insecurity or a nasty memory of the apartheid era. But of course, one cannot state that because someone is wealthy and empowered he or she can't still feel strongly about the inequality of others.

Senior civil servant and writer Sandile Memela wrote in an opinion piece in *City Press* on 19 July 2012: 'When you listen or read carefully to the discourse of prominent and leading black people, one is hard-pressed to find voices that – despite their class, education and income, for instance – match their success without making reference to or justifying it against apartheid ... Far too many successful black men, in particular, and women choose to hold on to the heritage of colonialism and apartheid instead of focusing on the gains of the past eighteen years of democracy and freedom.'

I'm often tempted to say that those of us South Africans who don't have a sense of entitlement have a sense of victimhood. But that would take generalisation too far. There are a large number of South Africans that I've come across or read or listened to who suffer from neither affliction.

Perhaps what lies behind our malaise is the cheap populism we have seen growing in our society in recent years among angry citizens of all hues. The further one goes to the periphery of society, the worse it becomes.

The white racists are the worst, but they don't have much of a voice other than the internet. Julius Malema remains the champion of hate-filled speak and many of his EFF lieutenants and sycophants follow in his footsteps.

The internet has to get some of the blame for the amount of bigotry and negativity we broadcast into the universe. Facebook, Twitter, the comments sections of online newspapers and news services, and hundreds of hate-filled websites are where South Africans express their crudest emotions, rendering many of these virtual places worthless as forums for public dialogue. I wonder sometimes if there isn't more hatred and intolerance on the internet in South Africa than elsewhere, but some of my foreign friends assure me it is as bad in the United States and places like Russia.

It is safe to say South Africans don't rate highly on the happiness index in 2013.

An old Afrikaans expression comes to mind: *Jy kla met 'n witbrood onder die arm* (You're complaining with a white loaf under your arm). It comes from the days of the Great Depression, the 'poor white' era, when white bread was a luxury only the rich could afford.

I think on a person-to-person level we have progressed spectacularly in the way we get along and respect one another. I have seen this on the factory floor, on many farms, in mixed neighbourhoods, in management, in sport and in new friendships being built.

It is when we operate in groups that we start attacking and defending from our racial trenches. Politicians cynically playing the race card are a major source of discord.

It sometimes takes a keen observer from abroad to acknowledge our real achievements as a nation. It also helps to leave the country for a few weeks or months and then to come back and look at our society with fresh eyes, especially if one has been to other polarised or post-conflict countries.

This happened to me after an extended visit to some of the Balkan states recently. I visited, among others, Mostar, Tuzla and Srebrenica in Bosnia-Herzegovina, where the tension (and residential and social apartheid) between Serbs, Croats and Muslims (nowadays referred to as Bosniaks) is still palpable; Vranje, Bujanovac, Novi Sad and Belgrade in Serbia, where I found the aggressive ethnic chauvinism of many Serbs very disturbing; and Prishtina and Mitrovica in Kosovo, where even a casual observer gets confronted with the dark hostility between Serbs and Albanians. Remember, these countries were formerly part of Yugoslavia, which broke up after the wars of the early 1990s, when South Africa was engaged in negotiations for a new constitution.

I came home, looked around my own society and felt a lot more positive about our gains since 1994.

So, before we analyse all the problems and challenges facing South Africa, let's do a quick count of our blessings.

I really think we don't appreciate our Constitution enough or the role it has played in preventing us from going off the rails. It is a magnificent document and beautifully crafted. It guarantees our freedoms and basic rights and is the blueprint of how we ought to behave as a nation. It is guarded over by a still credible Constitutional Court.

One of the judges on that court, Edwin Cameron, made a special speech at the Sunday Times Literary Awards on 29 June 2013. 'The Constitution is not just a document of high aspiration and idealism,' he said. 'It is a practicable, workable charter. And it has proved itself modestly but practically effective as a basis for the democratic exercise of power in our half-broken, half-fixed country.'

He said the separation of powers in the Constitution has proved practically effective, with the legislature, executive and judiciary settling into a 'sometimes tense but reasonably effective' working relationship.

'In a time of structural disintegration, social fraying and predatory looting, the Constitution is proving itself a viable framework for the practical play of power needed to vest our future beyond our current problems,' Cameron said.

It is to the credit of the ANC that they have never tried to change the essence of the Constitution and that all its senior leaders still hold it up as our national guiding principle.

We are as free as any nation in the world to say what we want, do what we want, go where we want and associate with whom we want. The only restrictions to these freedoms are extreme poverty and patriarchy.

I know this is not the common view, but in my experience of other countries, South Africa is still one of the most open societies in the world.

Our media are diverse and freer from legal restriction than in most societies. And when those in power tried to restrict that freedom, civil society organisations fought them – and won.

We have two terrestrial broadcasters, a satellite broadcaster that beams all over the continent, and dozens of radio stations. Talk radio is vibrant and popular, giving a voice to anyone with a phone and a point of view.

We have dozens of newspapers and magazines covering the whole political spectrum and virtually all sectors of the society, apart from the very poor. Our book-publishing industry is among the very best outside the wealthy democracies.

The rule of law still reigns supreme. If someone wrongs you, if government or someone else limits your freedoms, you can go to court – and you can trust that you will get a fair hearing. If you don't have enough money to pay for legal representation, you can approach the Legal Aid Board or one of several non-governmental organisations (NGOs) working in the field.

Our faith communities are still strong and there is an almost complete absence of religious intolerance.

Our Independent Electoral Commission is headed and staffed by efficient men and women of integrity. We have not had one election since 1994 whose integrity has been questioned. That is a big thing: look at the impact of contested election results to the north of us and elsewhere in the world.

Our top five universities are also the top five on the continent, and new universities and training colleges are being established.

Our sports teams punch far above their weight. Our national rugby and cricket teams have for years been ranked in the top three in the world, and our golf and swimming achievements are extraordinary when compared with other nations with much bigger populations and a lot more money.

What about our little banana republic's economy? Well, it is still the biggest on the continent and we are by far the biggest investor in other African countries.

Our economy is 63 per cent bigger now than in 1990, according to analyst J.P. Landman, and per capita incomes are 27 per cent higher than in 1993. Yes, 63 per cent and 27 per cent, in just two decades. The nominal value of tax revenue grew by 491 per cent, from R114 billion to R674 billion, between 1994/1995 and 2010/2011. Yes, 491 per cent.

South Africa's fiscal management since 1994 has been exemplary, and analysts worldwide have called it that. Treasury, the South African Revenue Service and the Auditor-General are strong, credible institutions. Not one of our financial institutions experienced the problems those in Western countries did during the global financial crisis of 2007 onwards.

South Africa's debt to gross domestic product (GDP) ratio is 32 per cent, compared to 100 per cent in the US, 200 per cent in Japan and 90 per cent in the UK.

South Africa ranked seventh out of forty-five countries in the 2012 Big Mac Index. The price of a McDonald's Big Mac is 42 per cent less in South Africa than in the US, while in Switzerland and Norway it is 62 per cent more.

The World Economic Forum's 2012/2013 Global Competitive Index makes for interesting reading – South Africa's overall ranking is 52 out of 144 countries. We're the best or among the best with the first nine criteria, but among the worst when it comes to education, labour regulations and productivity:

Auditing standards: 1; securities exchange regulation: 1; legal rights: 1; efficacy of corporate boards: 1; soundness of banks: 2; financial services availability: 2; minority shareholder protection: 2; competition policy: 6; strength of investor protection: 10; air transport quality: 15; legal system (challenging): 16; legal system (settling disputes): 17; favouritism in official decisions: 110; burden of government regulation: 123; primary education quality: 133; life expectancy (HIV and TB): 133; pay and productivity: 134; business costs of crime: 134; higher education quality: 140; flexibility of wage setting: 140; hiring and firing practices: 143; quality maths and science education: 143; labour/employer cooperation: 144.

Correcting a huge blunder

If you mention the name Thabo Mbeki outside South Africa, more often than not the response will be, 'Oh, that AIDS-denialist guy?'

One of the greatest achievements of Zuma's administration was to turn the Mbeki administration's policies on HIV and AIDS around completely and to make treatment available to most HIV-positive people in the country.

Mbeki has been accused by researchers at Harvard University and by local activists of causing the deaths of 365 000 people by denying access to antiretroviral drugs and failing to roll out treatment to help prevent the transmission of HIV from mother to child.

About six million people in South Africa were living with HIV in 2012.

'A virus cannot cause a syndrome,' Mbeki claimed, although he and his biographers have spent much energy after his dismissal as president to deny that he was a denialist. He was fully supported by his minister of health, Manto Tshabalala-Msimang, who advised people to eat garlic and beetroot to increase their immunity.

The attitude changed dramatically when Zuma took over as president in May 2009. Access to state-sponsored treatment and care increased dramatically. Today South Africa administers the biggest public antiretroviral treatment programme in the world. More than two million people with HIV can now look forward to a much longer life.

By 2012, the HIV infection rate and the number of deaths due to AIDS started dropping.

Why would the powerful nations Brazil, Russia, India and China invite us to become part of BRICS if we were a faltering state and couldn't add value to their grouping? Former ambassador to Thailand and opposition politician Douglas Gibson calls our BRICS membership a significant achievement and says: 'Many South African observers are tepid at best and scathing at worst about the "S" in BRICS. I believe they are wrong and I reject the inferiority complex that talks us down ... We need now to make the most of the political and economic possibilities it offers.'

There is a widely held view that black South Africans as a group are as poor today as they were in 1990 and little is being done for them. The facts contradict this. According to the South African Institute of Race Relations (SAIRR), the proportion of South Africans living on less than two dollars a day has declined from 12 per cent in 1994 and a peak of 17 per cent in 2002 to just 5 per cent in 2012. This is the opposite of the general worldwide trend.

Living standards measures (LSMs) are a tool to categorise people according to their living standards, with LSM1 the lowest and LSM10 the highest category. Between 2001 and 2011, adults falling under LSM1 fell from 11 per cent to 1 per cent, while those under LSM10 increased from 5 per cent to 6 per cent. In 2001 the greatest proportion of adults, 14.3 per cent, were classified as being in LSM3. In 2011 this figure dropped to 6.1 per cent and the greatest proportion of adults, 22.4 per cent, were grouped in LSM6. The picture is one of a significant increase in living standards, with a general migration from LSM1–3 to LSM4–7.

Moneyweb reported on 8 May 2013 that in 2004, 1.6 million black people were part of the middle class comprising 5 million people. In 2012 this had skyrocketed to 4.2 million, a 240 per cent growth in the middle-class segment.

According to a 2013 research report by the University of Cape Town (UCT) Unilever Institute, the average personal disposable income of the black middle class stands at R8 191, with household income at R22 634. The black middle class's disposable household income grew by 35 per cent since 2004, with white disposable income growing by 10 per cent. The black middle class have a spending power of R400 billion compared to the white middle class's R380 billion. There is still huge inequality, but good progress has been made.

Bonded home ownership is an important indicator of the middle class. According to the SAIRR's 2013 *South Africa Survey*, there were 363 000 black African homeowners paying bonds on their properties – significant if one remembers that black people were not allowed to own property under apartheid. The figure for whites is 386 000.

In an article published by the Carnegie Endowment for International Peace, Uri Dadush and Shimelse Ali suggest the number of cars in developing countries is also indicative of the size of the middle class. Using this car index, they calculate that about nineteen million South Africans qualify as middle class. There are about ten million registered vehicles in South Africa. In July 2013, 58 140 new vehicles were sold, 40 274 of them passenger cars and 15 047 bakkies, light commercial vehicles and minibuses.

Talking about cars: we South Africans have expensive tastes. Almost

22 per cent of cars sold in 2010 were classified as 'luxury' – compare that with 2.8 per cent in China and Mexico and 9.6 per cent in the US. The land of 'luxury German sedans' stands at 26.6 per cent.

According to New World Wealth's list of African millionaires (assets of more than $1 million), South Africa had 48 800 millionaires in 2012, 9 per cent more than in 2010. There were 594 multimillionaires (people with assets of more than $30 million, excluding their primary residence). Johannesburg had 23 400 millionaires, Cape Town 9 000, Durban 2 700 and Pretoria 2 500. The city outside South Africa with the most millionaires is Lagos, with 9 800.

'Service delivery' is the new buzzword in South Africa, referring to the provision of housing, water, electricity and toilets to the townships, squatter camps and rural areas. Service-delivery protests have become an almost daily occurrence over the last few years.

And yet the government has built 3.5 million sub-economic or RDP houses since 1994, not something any government anywhere (apart from China, perhaps) has achieved in recent years.

When Zuma told the South African Local Government Association late in 2012 that 'no country could have produced the delivery we produced in the last eighteen years', he was met with derision.

And who came to his defence? Frans Cronjé, deputy CEO of the SAIRR, not exactly a left-wing organisation: 'The ANC may be accused of many things, and it can be debated whether State delivery is the best development model for the country to follow, but the data we have published is unambiguous that the ANC and the government it leads deserves considerably more credit for improving the living standards of poor and black South Africans than it has received.' The protests are more a function of raised expectations than a failure to deliver, he added.

These are the figures for the period 1996 to 2010 he refers to:

The number of households living in formal houses increased from 5.8 million to 11 million, or by 89.9 per cent. Over the same period, the proportion of all households living in a formal house increased from 64 to 76 per cent.

The number of households with access to electricity increased from 5.2 million to 11.9 million, or by 127.9 per cent. The proportion of all households with access to electricity increased from 58 to 83 per cent.

The number of households with access to piped water increased from 7.2 million to 12.7 million, or by 76.6 per cent. The proportion with access to piped water increased from 80 to 89 per cent.

The most effective weapon against extreme poverty in South Africa is the system of social grants. Towards the end of 2013, a little over 16 million people were receiving grants from the state, costing around R113 billion, or more or less 3.4 per cent of GDP. In 1998 only 2.5 million people received grants. Most grants are old-age pensions and child-support transfers.

Those in favour of a rigid free-market system point out that more people receive grants from the state than have jobs and that it is too heavy a burden on the small tax base. This is a very short-sighted view. Apart from the obvious humanitarian issue of looking after our most vulnerable citizens, the social grants have brought a stability that we would otherwise not have. As the National Development Plan points out, 'poverty would be deeper and social unrest more widespread if these programmes did not exist'.

Treasury expects that the annual growth in the number of beneficiaries will drop to below 3 per cent and that GDP growth will be more than 3 per cent over the next three years, which means the burden on the state coffers will be contained. The South African Social Security Agency has already introduced new systems that will reduce the cost of delivering the payments by half, to about R16 per payment.

Sanlam economist Jac Laubscher was quoted in the *Financial Mail* on 24 July 2013 as saying current social-grant spending equals 10 per cent of government spending. An overspending of 10 per cent on grants would require that general expenditure be cut back by only 1 per cent, or that taxes be raised slightly.

Unemployment is unlikely to decrease and growth is likely to be slow in the short term, which means welfare benefits will remain the most important strategy to prevent the scourge of poverty from increasing.

But there is a lot more to South Africa than welfare grants, poverty and unemployment.

What other 'failing state' or 'banana republic' has the extensive, sophisticated infrastructure South Africa has? Three of the most efficient and attractive airports in the world, all new – Cape Town, O.R. Tambo and King Shaka (voted best, second-best and third-best airports in Africa by the World Airports Awards in 2012) – plus good regional airports in Bloemfontein, George, Upington, Port Elizabeth, East London and Nelspruit. The ultra-modern Gautrain. Cape Town's MyCiti bus rapid-transit system. A national road system that is being upgraded all the time. Five modern harbours. And many new office blocks, shopping centres and housing estates being built every year.

It would be easy to say one should look at Sandton, Waterkloof or

Constantia, but it is more meaningful to advise a sceptic to go to Soweto, South Africa's most famous black township.

I spent a few days in Soweto covering the 1994 election campaign. It was as drab and depressing as when I worked there in the 1980s.

In 2009 I attended the semi-final of the Super 14 rugby tournament at Orlando Stadium. I was bowled over by the friendliness and relaxed atmosphere then, as white Blue Bulls supporters swamped the place and were welcomed by Soweto residents, but I didn't walk the streets and talk to the people. In 2011 and 2012 I spent quite a few days there working on two documentaries. I was blown away.

I stayed at the Soweto Hotel on Freedom Square in Kliptown and had the opportunity to walk and drive around and engage with residents. I even bumped into a few Soweto-based celebrities while having lunch at the impressive Maponya Mall.

Soweto is a proud, warm-hearted, relaxed place today. There is still a lot of poverty in pockets, but for the most part it is a clean, orderly and functional African city. I was struck by the friendliness, openness and willingness to engage of the people I met. I felt safer on the streets of Soweto than I feel in the inner cities of Johannesburg or Durban. I phoned my family from there and said, 'You know, we could live very happily in Soweto.'

I recalled the history of the 'South Western Townships', as the apartheid government called the series of squalid townships in the early 1960s. This city came into being as a dumping yard for black migrant workers from the early nineteenth century onwards and, after 1948, for black people who had been forcibly removed from places like Sophiatown. For much of its history, the apartheid government tried to force people from different language groups to live separately.

The people of Soweto have stubbornly overcome the cruelty of the past; they have buried the ugliness of the birth of their city under an unstoppable love of life and good-neighbourliness. They have built a proud city on the racism of the past. There can't be any sweeter way of avenging the hatred and brutality of the D.F. Malans, J.G. Strijdoms, Hendrik Verwoerds and John Vorsters.

After 1994 some successful middle-class people moved to the formerly white suburbs of Johannesburg and Sandton, but I know some of them who soon regretted it and moved back. The leafy white suburbs simply didn't have the soul, the warm heart of Soweto.

I wish the leaders of our other cities would take a few days off and visit

Soweto, not as VIPs, but as ordinary citizens. Mamelodi, KwaMashu, Cato Manor, New Brighton, Kwazakhele, Khayelitsha, Nyanga and Langa can also one day become proud cities in their own right instead of depressing 'dormitory towns' where people are forced to stay and from where they commute to work. Soweto is a jewel in the crown of the new South Africa. Go visit, and be proud.

On any given day you will encounter hundreds of tourists in Soweto, visiting Nelson Mandela's old home, the Hector Pieterson Museum and Freedom Square, where the Freedom Charter was signed in 1955, and having lunch at one of the fine eating places. They simply love it.

Despite the bad press we've been getting outside the continent, tourists from all over are coming to South Africa in increasing numbers. More than 7.5 million tourists arrived in South Africa between January and October 2012, 11 per cent more than the year before. A lot of people come again and again.

Living in the Cape as I do, I cannot avoid reminding you pessimists that we make some of the best wines in the world in one of the most scenic places on the planet.

Okay. Enough of playing Pollyanna. I thought this chapter would perk you up a bit and prepare you for reading on, because the rest of this book is not about such good news.

4

What did we expect?

My first direct contact with the exiled ANC happened on 8 January 1985, in Lusaka, when I attended the annual ANC international press conference on the occasion of their birthday. I shook hands with the legendary O.R. Tambo and with the movement's information head, Thabo Mbeki, and had quite a few drinks with the media man, Tom Sebina.

I was by then a committed supporter of the internal resistance, the United Democratic Front, but as a journalist I refrained from any active participation. To me and most other UDF supporters not near the inner circle, the ANC was a different organisation, not even a mother body, more like an admired uncle we didn't know that well.

That 1985 meeting was unremarkable to me because the speeches were very propagandistic, and, as a young Afrikaner from the Free State platteland, I had had my fill of propaganda and fiery nationalist talk. Mbeki was the one exception: he stood out as the one man there who didn't talk in clichés and didn't act as if he was expecting the Boere to grab him any minute.

Still, I found it interesting to watch and listen to the men (and one or two women, if I remember correctly) regarded by my family, my society and the government as nasty, violent, communist terrorists. They were all very ordinary people, I thought, and quite boring and predictable too, not much different from the leaders of Namibia's SWAPO, Mozambique's FRELIMO and Angola's MPLA that I had met before. The only known ANC members that I had interacted with before then were Christmas Tinto, a gentle old-timer who was a Robben Island veteran and a UDF leader in the Western Cape, and Albertina Sisulu, wife of Walter and one of the most special human beings I had ever met.

I returned to Zambia in January the following year, but my first experience of interacting freely with the ANC leaders came in 1987, when the ANC celebrated its seventy-fifth anniversary at a big bash in Lusaka's Mulungushi Hall. I also visited an ANC farm north of Lusaka where the locals showed me a fattened pig named P.W. Botha and where we were served a grey mush that turned out to be scrambled eggs. Being a farm boy, I advised them that their chickens needed some green leaves to eat and should be allowed to run free to catch insects, which would make the yolks more yellow. The local foreman, impressed with my knowledge, asked my advice about their miserably small maize plants. I promised to send him more advanced cultivar seeds from home. I never found out if he got my parcel.

Again, the one senior ANC leader that stood out as articulate and more than just a professional revolutionary type was Mbeki. He seemed to understand the conditions and attitudes back home a lot better than the others I spoke to, and had a well-informed opinion on world affairs. Most of the others were still talking about a military victory over the apartheid regime.

In July 1987 I joined Van Zyl Slabbert's 'Dakar Safari', the trip to Senegal by sixty mostly white Afrikaans-speakers to meet with a delegation of the ANC to discuss the future and the chances of a negotiated settlement. It was the Van and Thabo Show – two clever, resourceful men with enough gravitas and standing to make such an event significant. I had serious conversations with ANC delegates such as Mac Maharaj, Pallo Jordan, Kader Asmal and Barbara Masekela. I found them all reasonable and balanced politicians, and I found myself in agreement with most of what they said and believed.

From Dakar we went on a trip to Ghana and Burkina Faso. In Accra, the Ghanaian government organised a public meeting between us South Africans and several hundred local intellectuals, students and politicians. It started off very aggressively and awkwardly when several speakers questioned the ANC's wisdom to talk to whites, and said some nasty things about us. Mbeki's reaction was strong and, I thought, brave: the struggle wasn't against whites, but against apartheid. The whites in the delegation took risks going to the meeting and he welcomed their move. Here in Accra we were one delegation, he said.

I knew by then that Tambo was not well, but I had no idea what Mandela's state of health and mind was in jail. I wrote reports and analysis of the historic encounter that were published in the then *Sunday Star*, saying, among other things, that Mbeki was the kind of leader who could lead South Africa after apartheid and that the white minority didn't have to fear him.

This came back to bite me. When I criticised Mbeki fourteen years later when he was president, I was reminded that I was an Mbeki 'groupie'. In fact, Mbeki's biographer Mark Gevisser went a lot further in *Thabo Mbeki: The Dream Deferred*. I was one of Mbeki's 'conquests' at Dakar and now I was acting like a jilted lover. Mbeki was the Don Juan seducing naive little whiteys for his own purposes and they all fell for it, not only me but also people such as Van Zyl Slabbert.

Mbeki told Gevisser it was always uppermost in his mind during the pre-negotiations period to reassure whites that the ANC wasn't going to break South Africa apart 'or start slaughtering you and all that'. When he became president and moved on from Mandela's position of reconciliation, he said, some whites began saying, 'Now this is a departure from the national reconciliation of Mandela. What is this talk of transformation? This is now a different Mbeki. He never said these things to us!'

I'm sure Mbeki did his best to bullshit some whites he came into contact with, and succeeded often, especially with the writers and artists who also visited the ANC in exile. But to suggest people like Slabbert and myself fell for it is pure megalomania, and a very naive or dishonest analysis on Gevisser's part.

Mbeki was a disappointment as president. But I never once criticised him for his commitment to 'transformation' – in fact, my strongest criticism of his leadership in my columns between 1999 and 2007 was that he kept the structure of the apartheid economy intact; that he had a weak commitment to genuine redistribution and development; that he managed a system where a few dozen politically connected people got stinking rich very quickly while the poor remained poor; and that he welcomed it when big corporations listed overseas. I took him to task in August 2000 for delivering a glowing tribute to Anglo American supremo Harry Oppenheimer without even mentioning the role his empire had played in the evil system of migrant labour. I criticised Mbeki because of his absurd and deadly AIDS denialism; his lack of communication with ordinary people; his secretive and conspiratorial style of leadership; and his hypersensitivity to criticism.

Perhaps what he and Gevisser saw as my criticism of 'transformation' was the point that I made several times during that time in my writing: that Mbeki was unnecessarily divisive and did not suppress his clear inner resentment of white South Africans as a group. I did not want him to be a mini-Mandela; I wrote several times that it was good that he sensed that the time for constant reassuring of whites was over and that his job was to effect real change and social justice. But he was the president of all South Africans and he would have been more successful doing that if he had just been a little more magnanimous and less rancorous. You don't take people with you into a new, transformed society if you accuse and insult them all the time.

It suited Mbeki's tendency of caricaturing all whites as pampered, selfish people with little regard for the needs and frustrations of the black majority to paint people like Slabbert and me as naive individuals who could be bamboozled with cheap reassurances but who had no real understanding of what a properly transformed society should look like. He sold his cheap shot of us being 'useful idiots' to a star-struck Gevisser. Van Zyl Slabbert a naive, useful idiot? Come on.

Was I wrong about Mbeki being a pair of safe hands for the presidency of the country? I still regard him as a decent man with abundant grey matter – he was possibly more intelligent than any other politician in recent times (sophisticated philosophical arguments were what drew Mbeki and Slabbert together in a good friendship in the 1980s and early 1990s, until Mbeki's insecurities destroyed it). Looking back, he was a much better president than Zuma (if we put the AIDS denialism aside for a moment). His job was almost impossible, stepping into the shoes of Saint Mandela and all, and inheriting a country with an angry and impatient majority. I admired the way he walked on the world stage on our behalf. And I liked and vocally supported his African Renaissance initiative.

I think I was wrong about Mbeki in one respect. I did not fully comprehend the power of the military men, the raw black nationalists and the Stalinists in the ANC. Mbeki was never one of them. He was an intellectual, a diplomat. He only really had to deal with these elements and control them after he became president. It made him paranoid. He was outside of his comfort zone. He couldn't play the brutal power game well enough.

I had also misread the discomfort with which Mbeki apparently lived inside his own African skin. I always got the impression that he would be more at home as a professor at his alma mater, the University of Sussex, than dealing with Africa's depressing problems of underdevelopment and poverty. Yet he was the poet of 'I am an African' fame. This dichotomy must explain some of his attitudes and actions.

My bottom line is that Mbeki the ANC's super diplomat, charmer and negotiator didn't exactly translate into Mbeki the brilliant president. And yet, his presidency was inevitable: he was just too bright to not reach the top; he was Tambo's protégé; he did more for the cause of the ANC in its last years of exile than the MK generals combined.

But Gevisser and Mbeki are not the only ones reminding me of what I said and wrote before 1994. To this day, whenever I criticise the ANC or government, people (read: right-wing whites) regularly bombard me with statements like: 'Well, what did you expect? You were the one who attacked and embarrassed

P.W. Botha and his police and military. You wanted an ANC government. We told you it was going to be a disaster, now live with it. What did you think they were going to do when they got into power?'

Actually, let me try to answer that last question without even getting into an argument about the evils of apartheid that had to be stopped. When I was 'hero-worshipping' Mandela and 'talking up' Mbeki; when I was 'soft on the liberation movement' and 'hard on the Botha and De Klerk regimes'; when I was pushing, as a newspaper editor and commentator, for a swift transition to democracy, what kind of South Africa did I envisage two decades later?

Let me start off with this statement: even knowing what I know now in 2013 would not have changed my belief that the ANC had to get into power as soon as possible. I would still have voted for the ANC in 1994 and 1999. I would still have supported the letter and spirit of the Interim Constitution and the 1996 Final Constitution.

If I try to get back into my mindset in the 1980s and early 1990s, I must say I expected South Africa to be a much more unstable place during the two decades after liberation. I expected more ethnic conflict after 1994. I certainly didn't think South Africans of different races and backgrounds would get along so well on a personal level so quickly. At the same time, I didn't expect the ANC to ditch the old ideal of non-racialism so quickly and completely re-racialise the country. Non-racialism was, after all, embedded in the Freedom Charter, practised by the UDF and entrenched in the Constitution.

I was pleasantly surprised at the disciplined, professional way in which the macroeconomy and the Treasury were managed. I didn't think the integration of the military forces of the old SADF, MK and the Azanian People's Liberation Army (APLA) would be nearly as smooth as it was. Back then, I thought that the ANC would be tempted to keep a strong military as a close partner, such as Robert Mugabe had done. I was also surprised at the way thousands of former guerrilla fighters were simply abandoned by the ANC and government to go and make a living on their own without much help.

I thought then that the first part of the Constitution that would be under threat from the ANC would be the sanctioned freedom of the media. This threat only really materialised after Zuma became president in 2008. I thought the ANC would, while they still had a two-thirds majority in Parliament, try to fiddle with elements in the Constitution clearly not supported by the majority of South Africans: namely, clauses related to the death penalty, abortion and homosexuality. They didn't.

I knew back then that we would inevitably be in for a period of weak management of state departments, especially at provincial and local government level. The civil service couldn't stay as it was, stocked with mostly conservative Afrikaners. But only a handful of black South Africans had proper experience as bureaucrats, mostly in the Bantustans, so the first ANC governments simply had to employ thousands of inexperienced people in the civil service. The sunset clause agreed to during the negotiations had many negative effects, but a positive one was that there was at least some gradual transition in management positions.

I still think Mbeki was in too much of a hurry to get rid of white skills and experience when he took over, rather than manage a proper handover of skills and knowledge. But I didn't think the problem of useless, unproductive civil servants would still be so huge after twenty years.

Allow me to interrupt myself and take you back to our Dakar Safari of 1987. The whole group of us, those from inside and those in exile, went to Ouagadougou as guests of the government of Burkina Faso. We met and spent time with the extraordinary president, Thomas Sankara. Let me tell you a bit about him.

Sankara was only thirty-three years old when he seized power in a military coup in 1983. He changed the name of the country from Upper Volta to Burkina Faso, Land of the Upright Men.

In just a few years, Sankara established himself as a kind of African Che Guevara. He built hundreds of schools and jacked up the education system; he launched agrarian reform and self-sufficiency programmes; he protected women's rights and even banned polygamy. His theme was that the Burkinabé should decolonise their own minds.

He lived frugally. We met him in his modest official residence with old (and cheap-looking) furniture. I remember his kitchen had a green melamine-and-chrome table and chairs. He drove around in an oldish Peugeot. He waged war on corruption. We attended one of his 'people's revolutionary tribunals', where civil servants were tried for theft and fraud involving as little as ten dollars. We drove past government buildings one morning and saw the civil servants outside doing organised exercises – they were too fat and didn't serve the people well enough, he said. Sadly, Sankara was assassinated three months after we met him during a coup staged by his old friend Blaise Compaoré.

Now I didn't expect the ANC to exactly copy Sankara when they took over in 1994. Our history was different and we have a far more modern economy and a lot more wealth than Burkina Faso; our demographic make-up is vastly different.

But I remember looking at Mbeki and his comrades during our meeting with Sankara and thinking: Surely these guys have a similar commitment to the genuine liberation of our people? Surely they will be equally committed to education, skills training, public service and clean government? Surely they will be more like Sankara than like Mobutu Sese Seko and his ilk?

Ouch. I couldn't have been more wrong.

The absolute worst was the way the ANC neglected the education of the black youth (the Model C and private schools are in fine enough shape) through bad management, bad policy decisions and corruption, and by being too cowardly to confront a trade union. It is the worst sin that the ANC has committed in its more than one hundred years of existence. It has resulted in the most serious threat to our long-term stability and development. It is unforgivable. It is the one thing I really didn't expect of the ANC.

Rampant corruption is another thing I didn't expect. Some corruption was inevitable and occurs in all countries. But today, corruption is almost part of our political culture, from policemen and prosecutors taking bribes to civil servants stealing money meant for feeding schemes for poor children to tender fraud and top officials, politicians and even senior government leaders getting money for political favours.

In this regard, I should admit to being naive. I did not realise how much corruption there was in the ANC during its time in exile.

I was surprised by the ANC government's appetite for spending state money on luxurious living. If you told me in 1989 that the general secretary of the SACP in 2013 would be driving a limousine worth R1.1 million and living it up in fancy hotels like the Mount Nelson, I would have laughed in your face. If you told me in 1989 that the president of the ANC would have three official state mansions and would then spend more than R200 million of state money on a private villa, I would have suspected you of Afro-pessimism or even racism.

I got a shocking surprise on 13 April 2011, when I saw police kill Ficksburg community activist Andries Tatane in cold blood without him posing any physical threat – and again when those whom we saw doing the killing were not found guilty in court. I was shocked eighteen months later when police-men mowed down thirty-four striking mineworkers at Marikana, and again in February 2013 when policemen dragged Mozambican Mido Macia behind a police van. Police brutality has become a daily fact of life and communities fear the police like they did the apartheid police – not so much the wealthier white communities, mind you, but those communities that were supposed to be most in need of liberation.

The arrogance and insensitivity of the present crop of ANC leaders were demonstrated clearly when the president and his ministers stayed away from the first anniversary event of the Marikana massacre on 16 August 2013. This was my reaction that week:

Callous. Petulant. Scandalous. Proof of the contempt with which our government and ruling alliance regard the citizens of this country if they're not loyal party members.

These were the words that came to mind when I watched the commemoration of the Marikana massacre last Friday and noticed the absence of the South African president, the deputy president of the ANC, the minister of safety and security, the minister of labour, the commissioner of police, the leadership of the biggest trade-union federation and of the former liberation movement.

I was anticipating a public outrage in the media on Saturday and Sunday at this cruel disregard of the victims, their families and the survivors of that history-changing event near Rustenburg a year ago. There was no outrage. It was as if it was simply normal behaviour. Have we all become immune to the insults to our fellow citizens' humanity?

Marikana was the first massacre of civilians by police in the post-apartheid era. It will forever stand as a day drenched in blood next to Sharpeville and Boipatong. Thirty-four mineworkers and four policemen died there. The mineworkers demanded better wages and living conditions.

We saw the almost indiscriminate mowing down of workers on our television screens. We know now that some of the workers were shot in the back by policemen. We saw evidence that some were executed in cold blood away from the main killing field.

We know that most of the dead workers were from elsewhere in the country; 'migrant workers' as we still call that ugly colonialist and apartheid practice of taking workers from their homes and families to work on the mines and in the industries in the cities. We know they were all black.

The media have shown us the desperate circumstances under which those workers lived around the mine: rows and rows of shacks with limited or no water, electricity and sewerage systems.

This was not supposed to happen eighteen years after we cast off the shackles of apartheid and white domination gave way to a liberated nation and an open democracy.

Marikana was the day we as a nation got our final warning to wake up to the realities of the poor and underpaid: if we don't do something drastic, we will see more blood spilled and we will see our stability and development drain like water in the sand.

More than six out of ten voters have voted repeatedly for the ANC since 1994 because they promised the former oppressed freedom, dignity and fairness.

And now these very same leaders show the dead, their families, the wounded and the traumatised of Marikana a thick middle finger by refusing to attend the national commemoration of this tragedy?

Like spoilt children they stayed away just because they didn't organise the event. COSATU and the National Union of Mineworkers, once the undisputed champions of the workers, didn't attend because a rival trade union was now the top dog at Lonmin. The SACP, the so-called vanguard of the class struggle, was absent and shtum. The president and his cabinet ministers found something else to do.

No wonder the nation's rabble-rouser-in-chief, Julius Malema, was treated as a hero by those who did attend.

'The ANC today is all about power, not the people,' a union organiser, Teboho Masiza, told a *New York Times* reporter as he listened to local preachers offer prayers for the dead. 'They are supposed to be here to listen to the problems of the people of South Africa. But they are nowhere to be seen. They only look after themselves.'

Jacob Zuma and his cabinet and fellow ANC leaders knew early enough that new union AMCU [Association of Mineworkers and Construction Union] was going to be the main player at the commemoration. The AMCU president made it clear that government representatives would be welcome and twenty seats were reserved for them on the stage. Zuma's office and representatives of his ministers in charge of mining and police could have negotiated a way in which their attendance would be dignified and safe. The most hated man at the mine, Lonmin CEO Ben Magara, did attend and speak and he was listened to and not attacked.

The now suspended general secretary of COSATU, Zwelinzima Vavi, not only stayed away from the memorial, but staged his own sensational media conference in Johannesburg at the very same time as the Marikana ceremony.

The ANC in North West's statement said it all, even though it was criticised by Luthuli House: the commemoration had been 'organised by an illegitimate team' and therefore the ANC wouldn't attend. They're not our dead, so why should we care, is what I read into it.

That is the Zuma-ANC for you: a party that behaves like it is the state itself. If you're not with them, they'll treat you like the enemy.

So there's your answer: I really expected a much different ANC to govern in 2013.

I didn't for one second think that with the history of apartheid repression and the violent resistance to it we would simply have a smooth change of government in 1994 and become a gentle, caring democracy overnight. I realised that the new government would have to deal with jittery capitalists, insecure minority groups and a neglected black majority with huge expectations. I knew that the apartheid governments were focused mainly on the well-being of whites and that the new government would have to look after all fifty million of us.

Having said that, I didn't expect the ANC of 2013 (actually, the post-Polokwane ANC) to be closer to Mobutu Sese Seko than to Thomas Sankara.

I want to add a caveat to this statement. The ANC of Mandela, Tambo and Sisulu isn't entirely extinct. There are substantial numbers of ANC supporters and many in its leadership structures who are committed democrats and who are as unhappy with the present tendencies in the ANC as I am. They're just not in the dominant faction at the moment and they are far too quiet for my liking.

5

A leopard and its spots

I learnt rather late in life that a true understanding of issues and behaviour patterns demands a good appreciation of history.

I stated in numerous written pieces and speeches over the years that I considered the ANC the most mature liberation movement in Africa. I still believe that, but, in the heat of the struggle against apartheid, I closed my eyes and ears to some unpleasant truths about the ANC in exile between the 1960s and the late 1980s, writing off much of the bad publicity as apartheid propaganda. I suppose I was guilty of not wanting to know, because in my eyes the apartheid system had to be defeated at all costs.

The international anti-apartheid movement, made up mostly of left-leaning democrats and human-rights activists, helped to establish in many minds a picture of the ANC as a progressive, non-racial, non-sexist move-ment fighting for democracy, human rights, human dignity and the genuine liberation of all South Africans.

The reality was different. Perhaps it wouldn't be completely unfair to say that the ANC in exile was primarily focused on the overthrow of apartheid and the gaining of power by the black African majority. And there's the difference.

I was puzzled by some of the tendencies in the ANC after 1994: corruption, cronyism, perpetual power struggles, abuse of power, paranoia, hostility to criticism and free speech, and self-enrichment. These tendencies became more apparent after Jacob Zuma took over the party presidency.

Only after I researched the ANC's years in exile in depth – partly triggered by disturbing revelations to the TRC I was associated with – did I realise that these weaknesses had been part of the culture since the late 1960s. Sadly, I have to add, a culture that allowed bullying, abuse of women, strong-arm tactics, and even torture, murder and execution.

If you are wondering about ANC leaders' blatant abuse of the intelligence services for political purposes, the tolerance of police brutality, the immunity given to some senior leaders guilty of corruption and abuse, the intolerance of dissension, and the custom of calling critics apartheid agents, the answer is that history is repeating itself.

Twenty years on, too many in ANC leadership positions refuse to internalise and face up to the fact that they're no longer a liberation movement but a political party ruling a modern, liberal democracy and a mostly free-market economy. They're still talking the talk of the 'glorious revolution' of the past and of the yet-to-be-fulfilled National Democratic Revolution; of the 'titanic ANC army' (Mbeki's words); of being the only true representative of the people of South Africa, as the world once saw them. They still call their critics counter-revolutionaries. Too many believe they have a God-given right to stay in power, as Zuma's often-repeated statement that the ANC will rule until Jesus returns testifies. Some still perpetuate the myth that the apartheid regime was forced to its knees by MK, and at ANC rallies men in green camouflage still march and leopard-crawl. (As my dear old friend Van Zyl Slabbert once said: 'One thing the "old" and the "new" South Africa have in common is a passion for inventing history.')

ANC members still call one another 'comrade' (even when they're about to stab each other in the back) and struggle songs are constantly being revived. The SACP still behaves as if communism didn't die in virtually every other society in the world, and struts around proclaiming it's still the vanguard of the working class.

Nostalgia is a natural human reaction, but it is also a convenient way of hiding from the stark realities of the world around you. And if you live in the past, you will behave as you did in the past.

Of course, a liberation movement in exile with a military wing and underground structures inside the country can never, almost by definition, be like the Boy Scouts. Resources were often scarce, communication difficult, supply lines long, and the political realities of the host countries and of the donor countries had to be considered at all times. They didn't have the luxury of choosing their friends, but the friends they did get, mostly from the old Soviet Bloc, had a very bad influence on them. In the case of the ANC, there were additional challenges: the might and ruthlessness of the apartheid military, and the constant threat of infiltration by agents of the security police.

It goes without saying that not all ANC, SACP and MK members in exile misbehaved. There are hundreds of genuine heroes that emerged from exile. I have met quite a few of them and I believe all South Africans should honour and thank them. I would say Chris Hani was one such hero.

Exiles behaving badly

Some of the information about gross human-rights abuses in ANC camps came to light through the ANC's own commissions of inquiry – the most revealing being one in late 1991 led by Advocate Louis Skweyiya – and through the ANC's submissions to the TRC and other evidence gained by the TRC. But a 1992 report by Amnesty International and several books, papers and magazine articles have been published since then with much additional information. The latest book is *External Mission: The ANC in Exile*, a meticulously researched and documented (and disturbing) work by Stephen Ellis, a former editor of *Africa Confidential* and nowadays Desmond Tutu Professor in the Faculty of Social Sciences at the Vrije Universiteit Amsterdam. I know Ellis and I accept his credibility and bona fides as a researcher and analyst.

The picture that emerges from all these sources is deeply disturbing: assaults and torture were almost routine and sometimes unspeakably cruel; people were thrown in jail or 'rehabilitation' camps at the slightest provocation and sometimes even without provocation; large numbers of people were executed after being sentenced by tribunals, more often than not on the flimsiest of evidence and without representation. I could not find a reliable figure for those executed, but the ANC itself gave the TRC a list of about nine hundred ANC members who had died in exile. That figure included those shot during mutinies and the small number who had died of natural causes or in traffic accidents.

After the 1976 youth revolt, thousands of youngsters left the country and joined the ANC. Most were sent to MK training camps ill-equipped to deal with so many new recruits, many of whom were impatient to return home quickly as guerrillas. During that time, the most ruthless intelligence service in the world, the East German Ministry for State Security, or Stasi, started training the ANC's Department of Security and Intelligence, also referred to as NAT (apparently for National Security) and later Mbokodo, the stone that crushes. The ANC body was never as effective as Stasi, but certainly became as brutal.

Accounts abound of savage floggings and the arbitrary incarceration of MK members for complaining, mostly about bad food, or smoking dagga, while many commanders were known to have serious drinking problems. The ANC admitted in its later reports that NAT men had become a law unto themselves.

But the worst that could happen to you as an MK soldier was if you were suspected of being an apartheid agent. The paranoia increased after two mutinies, a suspected poisoning of camp inmates (that some insisted was merely food poisoning) and the bombing of an Angolan camp by South African Air Force planes. The accusation was often levelled at people regarded as cocky or too clever, and sometimes it was simply used to get rid of personal enemies. Of course there were apartheid spies among them, but if all the people who had been so accused really worked for Pretoria, MK would have been an empty shell.

The real spies, the suspected spies and others that the leadership thought were problematic cadres were sent to the notorious Quatro camp, also known as Camp 32 and later the Morris Seabelo Rehabilitation Centre. The worst atrocities took place here.

Gabriel Mthembu, known as Sizwe Mkonto, a camp commander who also headed Quatro at some point, told the TRC under cross-examination that some apartheid agents volunteered the information that they worked for the security police, but others came under suspicion because of their behaviour.

This is, according to Mthembu, how flimsy this suspicious behaviour sometimes was: 'They would be people who would unwittingly demonstrate a level of understanding in terms of military equipment that could only be associated with somebody who might have received a very specialised type of training. Some of them, for instance, the precision with which they would manipulate artillery weapons, the calculations involved and what have you, however good they may be in mathematics, you don't really understand some of these things unless after a certain period of time, so there would be an indication one way or another.' (Nobody apparently bothered to inform the TRC that the spies the security police sent to MK camps were never trained artillerymen, but mostly men with no or just a little police training.)

True to their Stasi training, NAT had its own spies among the cadres. 'Then others would make slips, they would slip in terms of their communication,' said Mthembu. 'I must point out that there were also covert structures within the comrades themselves, people who would gather because when we used to sit and chat informally you tended to speak about each other's backgrounds and then people would say certain things not said in their biographies, and then the discrepancy would emerge.'

Mthembu also confirmed that some men who had been harshly disciplined had complained about the leadership. 'They would often speak about other people having a nice time staying in London whilst we were suffering here, suffering from malaria, being killed by landmines, being ambushed by UNITA [National Union for the Total Independence of Angola] and what have you

… So those that went out of their way actually to try and ascribe their difficult conditions to leaders would invariably be suspected also of pursuing certain agendas within the movement itself and some of them were obviously regarded as suspects.'

University of Massachusetts professor Padraig O'Malley, who has interviewed large numbers of South African politicians and recorded South African history over the last few decades, spoke to a KGB-trained MK soldier who had landed up in Quatro. 'Mwezi Twala and nine other black soldiers in the ANC's armed wing, MK, one day decided to ask their superiors what was happening with regard to the vast sums of money the ANC was receiving from European sources,' O'Malley writes. 'They figured that this money was being donated to the cause of the black people and therefore their superiors were accountable for this money. They did a bad thing. For asking a simple question about the financial accountability of the ANC, they were tortured. Of the ten of them, six died from torture. Mwezi and three others lived.'

Twala wrote a little-known book on his experiences, *Mbokodo: Inside MK*. 'Gradually the Mbokodo tried to instil in cadres the belief that the ANC leadership was infallible, and any cadres who refused to voluntarily accept this premise was coerced by threats. [NAT chief] Mzwai Piliso summed up this approach when he said: "If you as much as point a finger at the ANC leadership, we will chop your whole arm off"', wrote Twala.

Another Quatro survivor, Diliza Mthembu, told the TRC he had been subjected to severe torture during his four years in the camp. Among other things, he was given electric shocks, suffocated with gas masks, hit with broomsticks all over his body, hit with a tree branch on the buttocks continuously for a whole day, forced at gunpoint to simulate sex with a tree, forced to chop down a tree full of bees and to climb a tree full of wasps, and forced to undress and lie on the ground among ants. (Diliza Mthembu seemed to have been cleared of suspicions that he was a spy, because after 1994 he was given a senior job in the SANDF.)

Several other former MK members told similar stories to the TRC. One, Ntombentsha Makanda, told the TRC she had been detained in Lusaka in 1980 and in 1985. Her hands were tied behind her back and she was kicked and punched, a dirty towel was put in her mouth, she was whipped with an electric cord and she was sexually abused.

These are just examples of the hundreds upon hundreds of horror stories that emerged from the MK camps and ANC jails in Angola, Zambia and Uganda, mostly during the period 1979 to 1989. There was no way in the world that the senior ANC leadership did not know what was going on – but I found references to only two senior leaders, Chris Hani and Gertrude Shope, who had actively intervened to stop some of the abuse.

In fact, one MK soldier says that when Oliver Tambo visited Pango camp around 1985, he walked past several bloodied men hanging from trees as punishment and said nothing, not even when the national commissar, Andrew Masondo, declared in his presence that those men could end up in shallow graves.

While most senior ANC leaders in Angola and Zambia must have known of at least some of the excesses, there is proof that at least three had first-hand knowledge and that two of these had an active part in it: Joe Modise, head of MK; Andrew Masondo, national commissar; and Mzwai Piliso, head of NAT and in charge of all the Angolan camps. On more than one occasion these three men formed a tribunal that ordered the execution of MK members.

A black priest testified before the TRC that Modise had personally tortured an ANC soldier, beating the soles of his feet with a golf club. The priest said Modise had ordered the summary execution of several exiles accused of being turncoats.

Masondo told the TRC he refused to apologise for the execution of enemy agents because 'we were at war. If it can be proved that they were executed wrongly, I would be stupid not to say I apologise.'

Piliso admitted to the ANC's Motsuenyane Commission that he personally took part in the beatings of cadres because he wanted information 'at any cost'.

In 1992, the Skweyiya Commission concluded: 'We strongly recommend that urgent and immediate attention be given to identifying and dealing with those responsible for the maltreatment of detainees. It is for the ANC itself to ensure that it cleanses its own ranks of those responsible for the acts of brutality described in this report.' Skweyiya supplied the ANC with a list of those implicated who were still, in 1992, working in the ANC's security department.

Skweyiya continued: 'We consider this recommendation to be of the greatest importance, particularly in the light of the role the ANC is likely to play in a future government. No person who is guilty of committing atrocities should ever again be allowed to assume a position of power. Unless the ANC is prepared to take decisive action, the risk of repetition will forever be present.'

So here's the rub. Joe Modise became the first ANC government's minister of defence in 1994. Andrew Masondo was made a general in the SANDF. Mzwai

Piliso became an ANC MP. Quatro camp commander Gabriel Mthembu was given a senior position in national intelligence.

When TRC commissioners asked the ANC how it could justify giving Piliso and Masondo senior positions after 1994, the ANC replied that they had been censured by the leadership and that they were performing well in their new postings. Their actions in exile should be viewed within the broader context of weaknesses and problems afflicting the ANC as a whole, it said. To hound loyal anti-apartheid fighters who made mistakes in the course of the struggle would be to perpetrate a gross injustice, the ANC said. Many other camp commanders and NAT members were also given good jobs in the SANDF, the SAPS, the civil service or parastatals.

Another peculiar thing is that several high-profile ANC leaders who did in fact cooperate with the apartheid regime and were found out were never exposed and expelled by the ANC. Some of them were even given senior jobs in the post-1994 administration and within ANC structures. In *External Mission*, Stephen Ellis writes: 'Quite why the ANC failed to act against proven spies at such a senior level remains a matter of speculation. An ANC cabinet minister confided: "There are people at the top of the organisation who are scared their own links with the enemy might be exposed if anything is done."'

The question of Jacob Zuma's involvement in these atrocities has been raised by many inside and outside the ANC. He was a member of the ANC's political and military council from the mid-1980s and chief of intelligence after 1987. In my book, this means that it would have been impossible for him to have been ignorant of what was going on with NAT and in the camps, but there is no evidence I know of linking him directly to any human-rights violations.

Actually, there is one incident: the killing of Thami Zulu, real name Muziwakhe Ngwenya, in Lusaka in 1989. I got to know his parents, former teachers from Soweto, during their campaign to get to the truth of their son's death through the TRC. Despite many denials and counter-allegations, Zuma has never shaken off suspicion of his involvement in Zulu's death.

Zulu was a rising star in MK and trained in the Soviet Union. In 1983 he was appointed commander of MK's Natal operations, an appointment opposed by Zuma, apparently because Zulu was from Soweto and not KwaZulu-Natal. Zulu's problem was that the South African security police had many spies and agents in Swaziland, from where the guerrillas infiltrated Natal. I know this first-hand through my involvement with the exposés in my former newspaper, *Vrye Weekblad*, of the operations of the SAP's Vlakplaas unit and its commanders Dirk Coetzee and Eugene de Kock.

It was thus inevitable that MK's operations under Zulu did not go well and that several MK guerrillas were caught or ambushed by the police. In mid-1988 the two new top men of the ANC's security apparatus, Jacob Zuma and Joe Nhlanhla, ordered Zulu to report to Lusaka, where they held him for questioning despite Chris Hani's protestations.

Zulu's father went to Lusaka twice to secure his son's freedom and was told by NAT officials that he would be released. When he saw his son in December 1988, he was fit and healthy.

In mid-1989 Zulu was transferred to a NAT building referred to as the White House, from where he succeeded in phoning his father, telling him he was being tortured, and getting a message through to Hani and Joe Modise that he feared for his life.

In November 1989 Zulu was released from NAT detention. People who saw him said he was emaciated and very sick. He died five days later.

An ANC investigation into his death declared that no evidence of wrong-doing against Zulu was found. It was furthermore discovered that he died of poisoning after ingesting an organic pesticide. This was, of course, blamed on the security police, but no one really believed it, considering the circumstances. Thami Zulu was buried a hero.

In his book, Stephen Ellis quotes Chris Hani saying Zulu had been a victim of 'paranoia and hysteria about the ability of the regime to send in agents', while Pallo Jordan later wrote that the ANC had never offered a credible explanation for his death. NAT insisted for years afterwards that Zulu had been an apartheid agent.

Ellis also notes that one of Zulu's associates, Thabo Twala, was beaten to death by NAT members in Lusaka a few weeks after Zulu's death.

Nobody has produced evidence that Jacob Zuma ordered or participated in the torture or poisoning of Thami Zulu. But Zuma has never successfully explained how he, as head of intelligence and one of those who ordered Zulu's detention, had no knowledge of the man's maltreatment and indeed torture, and why he didn't order his release after it became clear he wasn't an apartheid agent. Often, when I see Zuma in public or on television, I think to myself: was this man, my country's president, at least partly responsible for the vicious torture and murder of an innocent and brave man?

Joe Nhlanhla, one of the men held responsible by Zulu's father for his son's death, became deputy minister of justice in 1995 and minister of intelligence in 1999.

Talking of Pallo Jordan: in 1983, while he was working in the ANC's information department, he made a mocking remark about NAT. He was detained in NAT's Lusaka headquarters (called the Green House) for six weeks, denied any water and ordered to write down his autobiography over and over, the way Stasi had taught the men from NAT. It was clear that no one, not even the paranoid security men, suspected him of any wrongdoing. He was simply being taught a lesson for being an intellectual and an independent thinker not liked by communists in high places.

According to ANC insider Oyama Mabandla: 'Pallo was detained on the orders of party member and Mbokodo chieftain Peter Boroko. Pallo was accused of exposing the Mbokodo informant network within the Department of Information and Publicity by mockingly referring to department official Francis Malaya and another man named Ace as Amapolisa [the police] – warning other DIP staffers to be careful of them. On that basis, Pallo was detained and was to spend six weeks in detention.

'I participated in an informal meeting at Green House which discussed Pallo's arrest. During the discussion one Mbokodo officer made a chilling remark which seemed to capture the essence of the entire saga. The comment went thus, "leli intellectual lase Merika lisijwayela kabi": this American-trained intellectual is uppity – and thus in need of straightening out.'

Clearly the present ANC's aversion to free speech and criticism has old roots, as has the anti-intellectualism we've been experiencing since Zuma became president. (Remember his attack on black people 'who become too clever' when he spoke to traditional leaders in November 2012?)

The custom of branding opponents and personal enemies as spies and apartheid agents has also not died out entirely. In 2003 the director of public prosecutions, Bulelani Ngcuka, was investigating claims that Jacob Zuma, then deputy president, had received bribes from a French arms manufacturer. News of the probe leaked to the media, whereupon ANC stalwart, former cabinet minister and Zuma loyalist Mac Maharaj declared that Ngcuka had spied for the apartheid government during the 1980s. He said this was proved in a report given to him by Mo Shaik, an ANC underground operative who worked with Maharaj and Zuma.

President Thabo Mbeki appointed a commission of inquiry under Judge Joos Hefer. When it became clear that there was no substance to the claims and that Shaik would not reveal his sources, Hefer declared he could find no evidence that Ngcuka had ever worked for the apartheid government. (Mo Shaik is the brother of Schabir Shaik, who was sent to jail because of his corrupt dealings with Zuma.)

One of the genuine heroes of the ANC underground and a former political prisoner, Raymond Suttner, asks in his book *The ANC Underground in South Africa*: 'If Ngcuka was a spy, why was the case put in the public domain only when certain individuals faced prosecution or were being investigated, including relatives of Shaik and Maharaj himself?'

Suttner also asks why many ANC cadres who were falsely accused of being agents and were detained and tortured had not been cleared publicly: 'I have conducted an interview with one such person, who was held in Quatro and very badly tortured and later released without explanation. He returned to work for the democratic government after 1994 with some of the individuals who had tortured him.'

I was reminded of the callousness of the ANC's security types when, on 28 March 1993, thousands of angry Inkatha Freedom Party (IFP) supporters armed with traditional weapons marched to Shell House (now called Luthuli House), the ANC's Johannesburg headquarters. The ANC security men opened fire with AK47s and other firearms, killing seventeen protestors. Eleven ANC officials later received amnesty from the TRC, even though the commission found that Shell House was not under attack.

The roots of corruption

There is another facet of the ANC in exile we need to look at if we want to understand the party's weaknesses today: corruption. Central to this story is one of the dominant figures in the ANC and MK between the early 1970s and late 1980s, and a key cabinet minister even well into the 1990s: Joe Modise.

The story goes that Modise was a bit of a high roller during his young days in Sophiatown and had links with the gangs of Alexandra. He joined the ANC in the early 1950s and took part in the protests against the demolition of Sophiatown. He was among the first recruits of MK and, after training in the Soviet Union, rose quickly in the ranks to become MK commander.

Stephen Ellis, former SACP activist and political prisoner Paul Trewhela and others have written extensively about Modise's role in smuggling stolen cars from South Africa to Zambia. As early as 1969 Chris Hani had raised concern about corruption in the ANC's senior ranks, and in 1980 Alfred Nzo, then secretary-general, wrote in a report that the 'evil of car smuggling is threatening our very healthy body in this region'. Modise's activities were apparently known to his old friend Thomas Nkobi, the ANC's treasurer-general, but he never acted against him.

'By the early 1980s,' writes Ellis, 'the contraband routes were said to extend as far as Luanda, with the Angolan branch being under the control of a high-ranking NAT official; smuggling convoys were escorted by regular MK troops.'

In the late 1970s key ANC officials started smuggling Mandrax tablets, a highly lucrative business. By 1980 the corruption and criminal activities became so serious that the ANC working committee appointed a three-person committee to investigate. Joe Modise was one of them, despite the fact that many in the ANC had for years been pointing fingers at him as the prime suspect. There is even an account of how he once sent an MK cadre into South Africa to buy him Johnston & Murphy shoes in Johannesburg. Former ANC activist and MP Andrew Feinstein refers to this in his book *After the Party*: 'He [Modise] was reviled, however, by those who were aware that he sometimes sent guerrillas into South Africa and into great danger to shop for the luxury goods he so coveted.' Modise was arrested in Botswana in March 1980 after he was found in possession of a large amount of cash, diamonds and weapons.

Ellis explains Modise's impunity: 'His control of strategic networks vital to the ANC's leadership, added to his propensity for violence and his skill as a political infighter, allowed Modise to preserve his position inside the movement. Time and again, Tambo defended him against critics in the knowledge that any attempt to remove Modise from the leadership of Umkhonto we Sizwe risked opening up a damaging conflict with ethnic and regional overtones.'

Despite Modise being hugely unpopular with the rank and file, despite many rumours that he had contacts with the Pretoria regime while head of MK, and despite his role in corruption, he became democratic South Africa's first minister of defence in 1994.

And a leopard doesn't change its spots: the biggest scandal of the post-1994 ANC, the arms-procurement scandal, started under Modise's watch and he reportedly pocketed many millions from the deal. It is known that his special advisor until January 1999, Fana Hlongwane, received more than R200 million in commission from British arms company BAE Systems in the decade following the arms deal. In June 1999, after he left politics, Modise became chairman of a company that had benefited from the arms deal, and his many millions of rands in shares were allegedly paid by one of the arms-deal beneficiaries.

And yet, on 22 November 2001, President Thabo Mbeki awarded Modise the Order of the Star of South Africa (Non-Military), Class 1: Grand Cross (Gold). Modise died shortly afterwards. Mbeki called him 'a man of conscience' at his funeral and said he was the 'architect of a future that is good for all our people'. (Of course, he would be correct if his definition of 'our people' meant those in the ANC inner circle.)

The tradition in the ANC not only to protect but to honour and promote those in its leadership guilty of corruption continues to this day and makes a mockery of its lip service to the fight against corruption. Let's put Jacob Zuma's example and the evidence in the case against Schabir Shaik aside for the moment and look at the cases of John Block, Tony Yengeni and Baleka Mbete.

John Block, a former leading member of the ANC Youth League, became the party's provincial chairman in the Northern Cape in 1991. At the time of writing, he faces two separate court cases related to his activities as the province's MEC for finance, economic affairs and tourism. He is charged with corruption, money laundering, fraud and racketeering involving some R100 million in the one case and R42 million in the other. In the first case, the province's MEC for social development, Alvin Beukes, and ANC MP Yolanda Botha will appear with him and, in the second, the controversial Uruguayan businessman Gaston Savoi. Savoi's trial in another corruption case involving tenders in KwaZulu-Natal is still ongoing.

City Press reports that the records of Block's 2003 corruption trial have gone missing. Kimberley regional court president Khandilizwe Nqadala reportedly said after that trial: 'I cannot allow a chairperson of the ANC to go to jail.' Block was simply ordered to pay back the public money he had used irregularly.

Block's assets, worth more than R20 million, were frozen by a High Court order in June 2013 after an application by the Asset Forfeiture Unit.

Block's ANC comrades in the province have stuck by him and in fact treat him like a hero, saying the charges against him are a political conspiracy. He was re-elected as provincial ANC chairman and was reappointed as MEC responsible for the treasury, economic development and tourism in June 2013.

Tony Yengeni, a former MK soldier and later ANC chief whip famous for his designer clothes and collection of fast cars ('the Gucci socialist', a newspaper called him), was convicted in 2004 for accepting a huge discount on an expensive car from one of the bidders in the arms deal. He lied to Parliament about it and took out expensive newspaper advertisements accusing his accusers of a racist witch-hunt. The ANC had earlier used its majority to stop an investigation into his affairs by Parliament's ethics committee.

Yengeni was accompanied to prison by a cheering commando of ANC luminaries that included the Speaker of Parliament. He served only four months of his four-year sentence and was given a hero's welcome when he was released.

The ANC chief whip at the time, Mbulelo Goniwe, famously said: 'Tony Yengeni is us and we are Tony Yengeni.'

Yengeni's former comrade and colleague Andrew Feinstein says: 'The chief whip who had gone to great lengths to stop the arms-deal investigation was a convicted fraudster and a fêted hero ... Like much else, the broader Yengeni allegations – including that he received a million rand from one of the bidders – were never meaningfully investigated by the investigators.'

In November 2007 Yengeni, then still on parole and thus not allowed to drink, was arrested for drunk driving in Cape Town. The case against him was dropped because a senior police officer had statements in the police docket changed and allowed his blood sample to be fiddled with. The officer was found guilty of attempting to defeat the ends of justice. Yengeni walked away. He was again arrested on charges of drunk driving in August 2013.

In 2010 Yengeni had to resign from six directorships because the Companies Act prohibits people convicted of fraud, theft or perjury from serving as company directors. His excuse for not disclosing his conviction was that he believed the law applied only to public companies.

At the ANC's congress in December 2007, Yengeni received more than two thousand votes that put him on the national executive committee. He was appointed head of the ANC's political school where young cadres are trained and remains a very powerful figure in the party.

Baleka Mbete is one of the most powerful women in South Africa (and one of the ANC leaders who joined the cheering cavalcade that accompanied Yengeni to prison). During her years in exile, she worked for the ANC in Lusaka and Dar es Salaam.

Mbete was appointed deputy Speaker of Parliament in 1996. In 1997 it was revealed that she had obtained a driver's licence without taking a driver's test with the help of the MEC for safety and security in Mpumalanga, Steve Mabona. 'I don't have time to stand in queues,' she explained, adding that she had done a rudimentary driving test in Delmas, 'basically just driving around town, stopping at robots and moving through traffic to see if I could control the vehicle'. Mabona sent his official limousine and bodyguards to fetch her from Johannesburg, she said.

It was later pointed out that there were no traffic lights in Delmas at the time. Furthermore, the *Sunday Times* revealed that there was no record of Mbete ever having been tested at the Delmas test centre – the licence, in any case, had been issued at Kabokweni, 350 kilometres away. The newspaper also said that the licence was issued the day before she was supposed to have been tested. It pointed out that Mbete lived in KwaZulu-Natal, worked in Cape Town and had no links with Mpumalanga. The traffic officer who reported the issue of her licence was called a racist counter-revolutionary by Mabona and his privileges were withdrawn.

The premier of Mpumalanga at the time, Mathews Phosa, appointed a commission of inquiry under Magistrate Heinrich Moldenhauer to investigate Mbete's licence issue. He found in May 1997 that her licence was invalid and she would have to return it, but said he could find no evidence of a guilty mind on her part.

Mabona resigned after Moldenhauer found that he had irregularly interfered in anti-corruption investigations, lied to his legislature and misled the commission. The ANC said his resignation 'demonstrates moral courage' and accepted Mbete's apology (not admission of guilt, though) 'without reservations'. The ANC prevented a parliamentary committee to investigate her from being formed and instead adopted a motion of confidence in her in Parliament.

Six weeks after the Moldenhauer findings, the national minister of safety and security at the time, Sydney Mufamadi, told Parliament that it was a contravention of the Road Traffic Act for someone who lived in KwaZulu-Natal and worked in Cape Town to apply for a driver's licence in Mpumalanga.

Recalling the scandal, political journalist and commentator Gareth van Onselen wrote in *Business Day* in September 2013 that 'Mbete carried on her merry way – seemingly the victim of a range of people who, unknown to her, had manipulated the system to get for her an illegal learner and driver's licence'. The scandal, Van Onselen wrote, 'had everything the ANC needed to practise its particular brand of accountability: an admission that some rules had been violated but a complete disregard for any ethical consideration. Technical inappropriateness was made a substitute for ethical misconduct, the former openly acknowledged, the latter fervently denied and certainly never for a moment acted upon. Today, that same attitude still exists, well entrenched and promoted and defended as good governance.'

In the interim, Mbete has been no stranger to scandal. She was one of the parliamentarians who misused subsidised travel privileges in the Travelgate scandal. In 2006 she chartered a jet at a cost of about R500 000 to fly to Liberia for the inauguration of President Ellen Johnson-Sirleaf. She was accompanied by one member of staff. Then president Thabo Mbeki also flew to Liberia in his presidential plane, while foreign minister Nkosazana Dlamini-Zuma used a commercial flight.

The scandals did not affect Mbete's meteoric rise in the ANC. She became Speaker of Parliament in 2004, and even served as deputy president of the country under Kgalema Motlanthe between September 2008 and May 2009. In December 2007 she was voted in as the ANC's national chairperson. Her name has been mentioned as a possible future president of the ANC and thus of South Africa.

On 6 September 2013 the *Mail & Guardian* revealed that the 2010 black economic empowerment transaction involving the gold-mining giant Gold Fields, which bagged Mbete R25 million in shares, was being investigated by US authorities after a report by an American law firm. The allegation was that Mbete was given the shares as a form of bribe associated with the granting of a mining licence for the South Deep mine. She was apparently initially offered only R2 million in shares. At the time of writing, the investigations are still under way and a police spokesperson has said that the Hawks will also look into the matter.

Mbete's extravagant gift provoked an angry reaction from Raymond Suttner in a piece in the *Mail & Guardian* on 27 September 2013:

There is no evidence of any value that Mbete (or for that matter most ANC leaders who go into business or are drawn into similar 'empower-ment' deals) brings to this deal. She brings her name and position, which supposedly signifies access to people who make decisions that benefits Gold Fields in ways that far exceed the share she has been granted.

In this deal, which was supposed to be about empowering the formerly disempowered, there is no condition set by the ruling party that would relate to how the mine should operate; nothing about whether it should provide conditions for the accommodation of the miners that are fit for human habitation, say. There is nothing built into the agreement that would address the needs of surrounding communities – or the afterlife of the mines once they are depleted.

In short, the poorest of the poor are not of any concern. The deal only relates to rewarding the 'players', the people who are in the inner circle of the ANC leadership.

This is just one instance, but it is a most glaring instance that exem-plifies the erosion of any semblance of moral integrity once attached to the ANC. It has nothing to do with the ANC that once pledged to make 'a better life for all'.

… The ANC led a variety of forces because it previously offered a political direction that unified a broad range of people. This was because they believed they saw, through the ANC, a plan that could unfold in a way that benefited the people of South Africa as a whole.

The ANC can no longer offer such direction. Its leaders are too greedy. And they have shut down debate.

I met Suttner twice at clandestine meetings in the late 1980s, while he was on the run from the police, and again after 1994. I can imagine how hard it must have been for an old UDF, SACP and ANC underground stalwart to utter these words about his former comrades.

Three other highly respected ANC veterans I know said similar things about the new ANC leadership: the late Kader Asmal, Jay Naidoo and Ronnie Kasrils. I can only think that they also preferred to turn their heads when signs of the ugly side of the ANC in exile surfaced. Or perhaps they thought the ANC would correct its errant ways once the struggle was over.

Years ago I wrote an angry column about the way in which the ANC was trying to make the Cape Town City Council ungovernable after they lost the city in the local elections. What kind of democrats are you, I asked. The next day, just before midnight, I had a phone call from a senior ANC leader and cabinet minister whom I knew well. He was clearly slightly intoxicated and spoke frankly.

Why were you surprised, he asked me. The comrades behaving in this way have a different understanding of democracy and accountability than those of us who came from the UDF and COSATU. They saw things differently in exile: leaders gave orders that had to be executed without question. Leaders were never wrong. The will of the leadership was the will of the people, my friend said, and I could hear the anger and frustration in his voice. Then again, he stayed right where he was with all the trappings of power and comfort.

If the bad old habits and often Stalinist tendencies of the military and security men were suppressed during the presidencies of Nelson Mandela and Thabo Mbeki, they clearly resurfaced after the former intelligence chief of the ANC in exile became our president.

6

Triple challenges, triple failures

All South Africans sense that something has shifted, that there has been a significant rise in the political temperature. When you press them on when they started noticing this, most say: Marikana.

August 16, 2012, was more than 'the Marikana massacre'. It was 'the Marikana wake-up call'. Like Sharpeville on 21 March 1960, it was a watershed event.

On that day in August, shocked South Africans watched seemingly disorganised, badly trained and aggressive policemen mow down protesting mineworkers on live television. They were mostly black policemen, answering to a black police commissioner and a black ANC minister of police.

Afterwards we learnt that many more workers had been shot and killed away from the cameras, some apparently in cold blood. Thirty-four of them died that day. Black mineworkers, for decades the symbol of apartheid dispossession, violation and cruelty.

We learnt a lot more in the days following. We learnt that many of the workers at Lonmin's Marikana platinum mine had turned their backs on the ANC-aligned National Union of Mineworkers (NUM) and joined the virtually unknown Association of Mineworkers and Construction Union (AMCU). We were told that at least eight people, including miners and policemen, had been brutally murdered in the days before.

We learnt that Shanduka, whose founder and executive chairman, Cyril Ramaphosa, is the deputy president of the ANC and the man who built NUM and COSATU, owns a sizeable chunk of Lonmin. We were told that Ramaphosa had urged the government to deploy the army at Marikana and had called for 'concomitant action' to be taken to end the wildcat strike and the violence it had generated.

We found out that other senior ANC figures also own large chunks of the gold, platinum and coal mines.

We noted the half-hearted, almost cold reaction of the ANC government to the massacre. And we didn't fail to notice that those who still call themselves the vanguard of the struggle and the champions of the working class, the South African Communist Party, had almost nothing to say about the tragedy.

In the aftermath of the massacre, the media showed us that the Marikana miners were living in squalor around the mine. We were reminded that the destructive migrant-labour system is still very much alive, as most of the Marikana workers see the Eastern Cape as their real home.

It was almost as if 27 April 1994 had never happened. The visuals of the miserable shacks, the dead bodies, the moaning wounded, the racing armoured police trucks, the barking rifles and the grieving widows were just too similar to what we had got used to in the 1980s.

But this time, the former liberation movement, the movement of O.R. Tambo, Nelson Mandela and Chris Hani, was running the country, not the apartheid machine of P.W. Botha, Magnus Malan and Louis le Grange.

The AMCU-aligned workers felt it too, and angrily accused Jacob Zuma and his party of selling them out, of being a rapacious elite trampling on the poor and the working classes.

And in the days and weeks afterwards, we started witnessing a surge of pent-up black rage surfacing in the public domain. South Africa was supposed to look a lot different nineteen years after liberation. The country is still one of the most unequal in the world. One in three able-bodied citizens who want to work can't find a job. Millions, most of them black, live undignified lives struggling to feed and clothe their children.

Much of the anger was directed at the ANC that had failed to deliver on their promises over two decades, but the ANC quite successfully diverted this anger in the direction of whites and 'white monopoly capital'.

How did this happen?

How did it happen that the once proud liberation movement didn't deliver on its promise of a better life for all? How did it fail the triple challenge of inequality, unemployment and poverty, as its leaders themselves call it? Or was it simply inevitable?

We have to go back more than twenty years to search for an answer.

The ANC in exile was always more focused on the political than the economic – shades of Kwame Nkrumah's famous 'Seek ye first the political kingdom and all else will follow'. Says Hein Marais in *South Africa Pushed to the Limit*: 'When the ANC was unbanned in 1990, it had no economic policy to speak of, a peculiar situation for an eight-decade-old liberation organisation, despite the efforts internationally on the left to train a cadre of ANC exile economists.' Ben Turok, an ANC veteran who helped write the Freedom Charter, also refers to the 'insufficient preparation of economic policy in exile' in his book *From the Freedom Charter to Polokwane: The Evolution of ANC Economic Policy.*

Yes, the ANC had the Freedom Charter, but that wasn't a set of economic proposals; it was more a political credo and it was forty-five years old in 1990. The communists had their outdated dogmas, but by 1990 orthodox socialism ('standard Marxist-Leninist waffle', as Van Zyl Slabbert once called it) wasn't exactly the flavour of the month, what with the collapse of the Eastern Bloc and Soviet communism at that time.

In September 1989 I was a participant in a conference in Marly-le-Roi in Paris organised by the Institute for Democracy in Africa (IDASA) and the French government. Thabo Mbeki led the ANC delegation from Lusaka, there were several COSATU and UDF leaders such as Trevor Manuel (he had hair then, and I remember him wearing a T-shirt with the words 'Viva No Compromise' on it) and Jay Naidoo, as well as some South African business people, academics and a few journalists. The theme was 'A future economic policy for South Africa'.

I can't remember much of the discussions. I do remember that at a special gathering one evening the French brought out a cask of very old cognac in our honour – spectacular stuff. And then one of the UDF guys called out 'Garçon!' and promptly asked the waiter for Coke to mix with the brandy.

Actually, the story I want to tell happened one evening while the delegates were standing in groups talking about the situation in South Africa – F.W. de Klerk was about to take over as president, but there were no signs then that he was going to unban the ANC five months later. I was standing in a group with mining executive Murray Hofmeyr, Van Zyl Slabbert, *Business Day* editor Ken Owen and a few UDF delegates when Alec Erwin, then national executive officer of the National Union of Metalworkers of South Africa, pointed a finger at Hofmeyr's face and said something like: 'You fat cats have had your day. When we take over, we will nationalise the mines and banks and only the state will own property.' Slabbert wrote later that Ken Owen was shocked and said: 'God save us if these people take over.'

Erwin's outburst was testimony to the underlying sentiment in the broad liberation movement that there would have to be radical structural changes in the economy to meaningfully benefit the black majority, especially the workers and the poor. These would be enforced as soon as they gained political power, was the thinking.

Six months later, Nelson Mandela was a free man and the exiles started returning home. The bravado disappeared like mist before the morning sun.

The ANC's first discussion document on economic policy, issued in 1990, was prepared by the newly formed Department of Economic Policy and based on work done by COSATU. The thinking was that 'growth through redistribution' would be the way to go, where redistribution 'acts as a spur to growth and in which the fruits of growth are redistributed to satisfy basic needs'. The document was savaged by establishment economists and the financial media as socialist and populist.

The thinking changed very quickly and few people mentioned growth through redistribution again.

'Over the next two years,' says Marais, 'the party's economic thinking would increasingly take aboard central precepts of neoliberal dogma. Macroeconomic stability became the watchword, and the virtues of liberalisation and privatisation were soon being sung by party members.'

What happened was an all-out assault by big corporations and financial institutions on ANC thinking. Nedcor and Old Mutual launched a scenario-planning exercise called 'Prospects for a Successful Transition'; Sanlam launched the 'Platform for Investment' scenario; and then came the 'Mont Fleur Scenarios', four weekend meetings of a mix of twenty-five key political, business and civil-society leaders. Top industrialists such as Harry Oppenheimer hosted many private meetings and weekend getaways with key ANC and COSATU leaders. Multimedia presentations, documentaries, books and papers popped up all over the show. Foreign experts were flown in and ANC leaders were flown overseas. The South African Chamber of Business, the South Africa Foundation and others all joined in the seduction and cajoling, showing these comrades from the bush the economic realities of the modern world. Even the World Bank soon launched a charm offensive to build relationships of trust with key ANC figures.

Stellenbosch professor of economics Sampie Terreblanche is blunt in his assessment: 'The whole transition process was orchestrated by the minerals-energy-complex with Harry Oppenheimer and to a lesser extent Anton Rupert. They organised everything. Early in the 1990s there were regular lunches between Mr Mandela and Harry Oppenheimer. These lunches developed into regular meetings at Little Brenthurst, the Oppenheimer estate. When too many people attended these secret meetings, the meetings were shifted to the Development Bank between Johannesburg and Pretoria, normally at night ... And there the ANC was persuaded to forget about their ideas of socialism and large-scale government intervention, etc.'

Among the key ANC figures, those leaders who were going to be influential in determining economic policy were Thabo Mbeki, Trevor Manuel, Tito

Mboweni, Cyril Ramaphosa, Alec Erwin and Lesetja Kganyago. And, of course, Mandela himself.

All these initiatives were aimed at persuading the ANC to abandon their fantasies about redistribution, social restructuring and an interventionist state. Macroeconomic strictness, fiscal discipline, privatisation and trade liberalisation were the way to go. Pay your debt, keep the state small. Build trust. Make it easy to do business and a combination of economic growth and direct foreign investment would deliver jobs and prosperity.

The ANC realised by this time that it had a serious shortage of sharp economists and sent promising candidates for training – for instance, Tito Mboweni, Maria Ramos and Lesetja Kganyago spent time at Goldman Sachs in New York. Mboweni later became governor of the Reserve Bank, and Ramos and Kganyago both served as director-general of the Treasury.

When the ANC entered into a transitional government with the NP during the last stages of the negotiations, they secretly borrowed US$850 million from the International Monetary Fund (IMF) to deal with the country's balance-of-payment problems.

Sampie Terreblanche says the eight NP and eight ANC members of the Transitional Executive Committee who signed the agreement for the loan in November 1993 also signed a document entitled 'Statement on Economic Policy', 'which was pure neoliberal economics'.

The ANC meanwhile formed the Macroeconomic Research Group (MERG) with the involvement of some foreign economists. Its 1993 report, 'Making Democracy Work', proposed a strong interventionist and supervisory role for the state in the economy – as well as a national minimum wage. This report was far more in line with the thinking of the main body of the ANC, COSATU and the SACP.

But, says Marais, the MERG report came too late. 'The left had failed to defend MERG politically and advance its proposals within the ANC. By the time it arrived on the scene, it was seen to threaten the emerging consensus that was being assembled. The report was ignored. The left was outgunned.'

It is hard to tell whether the likes of Mbeki and Manuel were true converts, whether they truly believed that the advice they were getting was the best way forward for the first post-apartheid government, or if they simply believed that it was inevitable – that the alternative would have alienated and angered the West, the World Bank, the IMF and the powerful private sector in South Africa with disastrous consequences for all. Probably a bit of both.

(An old friend of mine, one of the very few real communists left in the universe, remarked to me: 'Thabo and Trevor should have spent fewer long nights drinking expensive whisky with the big-money men and we should have banned them from reading *Business Day* and *Financial Mail*.')

But Mbeki, Manuel and others in the early 'economic cluster' knew, and Nelson Mandela and Walter Sisulu indicated at the time that they also knew, that the big capitalists here and abroad were already jittery about a black liberation movement with a decades-long association with Moscow taking over the biggest and most modern economy in Africa. To insist on redistribution strategies and state intervention in the economy, not even mentioning the nationalisation of mines, banks and industries, would have pushed them over the edge and could have damaged the economy irreparably. The ANC leadership had to keep in mind that such an economic collapse, coupled with the huge expectations of their primary constituency, could have led to major instability and suffering. There was no more Soviet Union to save them.

Mandela explained the implications of globalisation and the integration of capital markets to the ANC's national conference in 1997, saying it had become impossible to decide on national economic policy 'without regard for the likely response of the markets'.

The ANC further reassured business that it was going to pursue conservative and responsible economic policies by appointing business leader Derek Keys as the first finance minister and retaining Chris Stals as governor of the Reserve Bank.

One ANC leader of that era who has now spoken out angrily about the ANC's 'capitulation' is MK hero and former cabinet minister Ronnie Kasrils. In his foreword to the 2013 edition of his book *Armed and Dangerous: From Undercover Struggle to Freedom*, he refers to the period 1991–1996 as the time 'the battle for the soul of the ANC got underway and was lost to corporate power and influence. That was the fatal turning point. I will call it our Faustian moment when we became entrapped – some today crying out that we "sold our people down the river".'

Kasrils says the IMF loan that the ANC took just before the 1994 elections had strings attached that precluded a radical economic agenda. 'We walked into that in the misguided belief that there was no other option. Doubt at that time had come to reign supreme: doubt that there was no other way; doubt that we had to be prudent and cautious since by 1991 our once powerful ally on whom we had relied so much – the Soviet Union, bankrupted by the arms race – buckled, collapsed and disappeared.'

Kasrils doesn't believe that it was necessary or inevitable for the ANC 'to lose nerve, to go belly-up', but they nevertheless 'chickened out'. He says it was by no means certain that the old order had the will or the capability 'to resort to bloody repression of the nightmare scenario envisaged by Mandela's leadership if we had held our nerve and stood up to the corporate blackmail. My belief is that we could have pressed forward without making the concessions we did.'

Kasrils adds: 'Too often both the revolutionary soldier and political activist leave economic affairs to the specialists.'

My own view is that it was indeed inevitable – that the ANC had to embrace a market-related economy with limited state intervention when they took power in 1994. But I'm not so sure that what they did in the years afterwards was wise or inevitable.

In 1993 COSATU decided to push for a 'Reconstruction Accord' that would serve as an election platform in 1994 and would promise proper housing, health, jobs and education. After many meetings between the ANC, COSATU and the SACP, a sixty-page document was agreed upon that would lay a foundation for future government policy and 'provide a framework for mass expectations in civil society'. Most of this document was retained in the Reconstruction and Development white paper accepted by government in 1994. The Reconstruction and Development Programme (RDP) was now government policy with the president's office responsible for implementation. Jay Naidoo, former trade unionist and the driving force behind the project, was appointed minister without portfolio in charge of the RDP office.

Naidoo was energetic and ambitious. He launched several projects to fast-track delivery and created development initiatives. He was pushing to have the national budget restructured to achieve new socio-economic objectives. 'The whole budget must become our RDP fund,' he told Parliament.

But not all his cabinet colleagues shared his enthusiasm or appreciated his intrusion on their turf. A year later, in March 1995, Naidoo was removed from his position and the RDP fund relocated to the finance ministry. Provincial RDP commissions were closed down. This was done, writes Ben Turok, 'because the cabinet was persuaded that the inherited economy was marked by so many distortions, including a large domestic debt, high inflation and interest rates, that its imbalances had to be tackled through macroeconomic reforms which in the short term were incompatible with the objectives of the RDP'.

Turok, who was also in charge of the RDP in Gauteng, says, 'This all amounted to a devastating setback for development across the country.'

In June 1996 the brainchild of a small think tank led by Manuel and Mbeki proposed a new plan for growth and development: the Growth, Employment and Redistribution (GEAR) plan. It was 'jumped' on the rest of the ANC leadership and adopted as government policy before the left could even protest – the SACP even publicly endorsed it in a statement, only to turn around a year later and demand its scrapping.

GEAR predicted 400 000 new jobs every year, an economic growth rate of 6 per cent by 2000 and a boost of exports by an average of 8 per cent per year. Ja, right.

GEAR was pure neoliberal economics and was welcomed as such by the private sector. Fiscal austerity; reducing public-sector debt; countering inflation; liberalising financial controls; reducing tariffs; tax incentives to stimulate new investment; and introducing more flexibility in the labour market. It was about growth, driven by investment.

When COSATU and the SACP refer to 'the class project of 1996', as they often do, they are referring to GEAR.

In 2006 GEAR was replaced by the Accelerated and Shared Growth Initiative for South Africa (ASGISA) with a new focus on public-infrastructure investment and on the stimulation of small and medium enterprises. R850 billion was budgeted for the expansion of infrastructure. Even those on the left agreed that this was a welcome shift, although they would have preferred a paradigm shift to what they saw as a mere adjustment. The term 'development state' was beginning to be bandied about, but never properly defined.

Turok, still an ANC MP, says in his 2008 book:

The irresistible conclusion is that the ANC government has lost a great deal of its earlier focus on the fundamental transformation of an inherited social system. It has given almost total concentration to the first economy and the creation of macroeconomic stability in the hope that this would bring foreign direct investment. However, even the most proactive measures to boost the first economy will not overcome the social legacy of apartheid in terms of unemployment, poverty and inequality. This requires the creation of a developmental state strategy which includes a focus on overcoming dualism and underdevelopment rooted in the urban townships and former homelands by boosting productive capabilities, including a serious review of raising agricultural production aimed at creating sustainable self-generated economic growth and development.

The ANC governments did a lot right after 1994. The finance department, the Treasury and the revenue service were all very well managed and were acknowledged as such internationally. The fiscal discipline exercised in the face of populist protest and pressure from the left was brave and commendable.

But the expected rivers of foreign direct investment flowing into South Africa after 1994 didn't materialise and the growth that South Africa experienced up to 2008 did not translate into creating large numbers of jobs.

Two other developments further undermined the government's efforts to face up to the triple challenge: the flight of capital, legal and illegal, and the worldwide recession of 2008 onwards.

'The cardinal economic legacy of post-apartheid economic policies has been the facilitation of capital flight and divestment, the globalisation of South Africa's largest corporations and corporate unbundling and restructuring,' says Marais.

Marais quotes sources which estimate that illegal capital flight from South Africa ran to about 5.4 per cent of GDP between 1980 and 1993, and almost doubled to 9.2 per cent of GDP between 1994 and 2000.

After GEAR's financial liberalisation, capital flight became legal. Vast wealth, accumulated with South African labour and from South Africa's mineral resources, was transferred out of the country with the consent of the government. This included huge amounts of pension-fund capital. Seven of the country's largest corporations moved their primary listings abroad, including Old Mutual, Liberty, Anglo American, Billiton and South African Breweries. The rationale was that these corporations would recapitalise once based in New York or London and then reinvest in the South African economy.

South Africa could not escape the global recession of 2008/09 and its aftermath. The growth rate was reduced as mining output shrank by a third, the manufacturing sector shrank by a fifth and company failures rose by half. Inevitably, unemployment rose, and poverty and inequality with it.

Poor Jacob Zuma: he became president in 2009, just as the recession was wreaking havoc.

The ANC and the economy

So, here's my take on the ANC's performance in shaping and managing the South African economy since 1994.

The ANC inherited a stunted, skewed and damaged economy in 1994. In the last decade of apartheid, the NP had jumped on the neoliberal bandwagon and embraced the concept of globalisation. The ANC had no choice but to be very wary of white business and international fears and prejudices as they took power. It didn't help that they were ill-prepared to deal with the promises, threats and blackmail when they started engaging with big business and international bodies, interest groups and corporations.

I think Ronnie Kasrils is wrong, and there are many nowadays who argue like he does. If the ANC had just kept faith 'in the ability of our own revolutionary masses to overcome in united action, with correct theory and reliable leadership', he says, moves to 'control the heights of the economy would have placed us in a position to truly turn things around'.

Large-scale nationalisation and state intervention in the economy, and a failure to respect private property rights, would have been catastrophic, also to the poor and the working class – and such plans would have meant a wholly different Constitution, which the NP and its government would never have agreed to; thus the settlement of 1994 would not have happened when it did.

Sorry, Ronnie, I think you have forgotten what South Africa and the world looked like in the early 1990s and I do think you over-romanticise the power of the 'revolutionary masses' to force the immensely powerful white establishment into a crude socialist state. I really don't think Madiba, Thabo, Trevor, Tito, Alec and their team had the option of embracing the free market, even to go the 'neoliberal' way, at least initially.

We can't blame the ANC for trusting the promises of huge foreign investment and the undertakings by the private sector that they would join in rebuilding a new society.

We shouldn't be too hard on the ANC for believing that economic growth was the be-all and end-all to create jobs, and that the prosperity it brought would trickle down to the poor. Most South African and Western economists still believe that. Of course, growth is crucial. But to make a meaningful dent in unemployment and poverty purely through economic growth would mean South Africa would have to grow at 10 per cent or more. We're stuck with 2 to 4 per cent for the foreseeable future.

We should, I think, blame corporate South Africa and business in general for coaxing the ANC into the kind of economy that would suit them, and for then sitting back to suck out every cent of profit they could with little commitment to being a partner to government to develop and broaden the economy and to combat inequality, unemployment and poverty. Mercifully, there are some exceptions.

When we assess the ANC's record of delivery over the last two decades, we should also factor in two aspects that the ANC had little control over and made their job much more difficult: the massive rate of urbanisation and the HIV/AIDS pandemic.

I have read several books and many learned papers on how to deal with inequality and unemployment. The short answer is: it is almost impossible for a government in a democracy to achieve this in any quick or significant way without trampling on rights, creating instability and destroying future economic prospects.

But I do think Nelson Mandela did enough in the first three or four years after liberation to pacify and reassure the white establishment and the international community that the ANC wasn't a bunch of reckless communists. By the time GEAR was implemented, there was much more manoeuvring room for the ANC to move closer to a developmental and redistributive model without causing too much alarm. If Mbeki had used the charm I saw him use so spectacularly before 1994, he could possibly have secured the consensus of most in the business community.

It is my considered view that even if the ANC had no choice but to accept a model of fiscal austerity and liberalisation in 1994, they could have achieved an awful lot more to benefit the poor and unemployed if they had governed more efficiently and cleanly, and if they hadn't defined black economic empowerment (BEE) so narrowly.

The failings of BEE

BEE was born in sin, one could say, as far back as 1993, as an effort by big corporations to demonstrate their loyalty to the new order, and to buy the loyalty of strategically placed individuals as a buffer and as access to the political elite. Typically, chunks of shares were given to select black business people and politicians, funded by debt provided by the corporation and repaid through rising share prices and dividends.

The ANC saw the advantages of the creation of a black bourgeoisie sympathetic to the party, partly because rich comrades would help fund the ANC and benefit the political leadership. But there was also the legitimate feeling that it was high time that black capitalists took their rightful place in the economy and on the Johannesburg Stock Exchange. There was a belief that these men and women's wealth would more readily be trickling down to the masses and would lead to greater black entrepreneurship.

At least R500 billion in BEE deals were done in the last two decades. It was symbolically important that black and white South Africans saw black millionaires (and more than one billionaire) drive their limousines, live in glorious mansions and buy wine farms and villas in Europe just like white millionaires had done for so long.

But BEE was restricted to a small clique of well-connected individuals. Many of them did not grow into innovative entrepreneurs or grow their businesses substantially. They did not really constitute a vibrant, new, economically productive driving force. A few even ransacked their new businesses and left their workers destitute and jobless.

Finance minister Pravin Gordhan declared in 2010: 'BEE policies have not worked and have not made South Africa a fairer or more prosperous country.'

Businessman Moeletsi Mbeki is scathing about BEE in his book *Architects of Poverty: Why African Capitalism Needs Changing*. It 'strikes a fatal blow against black entrepreneurship by creating a small class of unproductive but wealthy black crony capitalists made up of ANC politicians', he says.

Wide condemnation led to a change to broad-based black economic empowerment – BBBEE. It now included measures to stimulate broader black management control, employment equity, preferential procurement and broader empowerment. Now we found that most ministers and deputy ministers in the ANC cabinet and a majority of members of the ANC's national executive committee were directors or shareholders of companies, many of them doing business with government. (Remember, the ANC also has its own 'investment arm', Chancellor House, also doing big business with government ...)

Anthea Jeffery, head of special research at the South African Institute of Race Relations, says BEE and other forms of redistribution help to tether the growth rate to about 3 per cent a year and make it hard to break through that level. BEE, she says, is fatally flawed and cannot be made to work: 'What the poor need most of all are jobs, backed by good schooling, and the growth rate needs to reach 7 per cent to bring increasing prosperity.'

Examining the messy empowerment deal at Gold Fields in 2010 – former bank robber Gayton McKenzie facilitated the deal, and ANC chairperson Baleka Mbete received shares worth R25 million – *Business Day* said in an editorial on 16 September 2013:

We have come to accept that BEE deals are grubby by nature; that they are simply the price that has to be paid to the politically connected elite in order for them to allow businesses to operate. At the core of the problem is a series of laws ostensibly intended to reverse the effects of discrimination against black people during apartheid by promoting affirmative action and the redistribution of wealth. Whether by design or unintended consequence, these have ended up favouring an elite group of politically connected individuals, and the government has strongly resisted attempts to amend them to include the masses of ordinary black South Africans. Appending the words 'broad based' to BEE policies has had little practical effect, especially since recent amendments to the BBBEE Bill continue to emphasise ownership transfers and the criminalisation of 'fronting', rather than initiatives – such as affirmative procurement, skills transfers, mentorships, the funding of start-ups, encouraging entrepreneurs, and ensuring pupils get a good educational grounding – that genuinely empower those who were most disadvantaged by apartheid.

Businessman Itumeleng Mahabane of the consultancy firm Brunswick South Africa says BEE has had significant unintended consequences that place a serious restraint on development and genuine transformation. Current empowerment, he says, is about 'our turn to eat', regardless of the economic costs, 'because we have equated fairness with instant gratification' that can accommodate only so many people and replaces one unfairness with another.

Mahabane is not against the principle of BEE, but says an empowerment system should be designed 'that is not about historical redress through instant gratification, but historical redress through building capacity and broad-based empowerment'.

In July 2012, when another round of debates about BEE was raging, I annoyed many by suggesting there was another example of empowerment in our past that we could look at:

Having lived through most of the apartheid era and the heyday of Afri-kaner nationalism, I can confidently say there is nothing about our former ruling class that I would recommend as an example of how our new ruling class should behave itself.

No, there is one: the way the Afrikaner nationalists approached the upliftment and economic advancement of their own people.

During recent research into the Afrikaner Broederbond, the secret society of Afrikaner men that determined so much of South Africans' lives until the late 1970s, it struck me that borrowing some of its methods could be much more effective than nationalisation, land grabs and threats if the ANC and the government were really serious about the 'triple threat' of poverty, inequality and unemployment, the theme of last week's ANC indaba.

The Broederbond was founded in 1918 with noble ideas. It was a mere sixteen years after the end of the South African War that devastated the Afrikaner community in the Free State and Transvaal. The scorched-earth policies of the British Empire forced large numbers of Afrikaners to the cities, where they were completely out of their depth. They were badly educated and had few skills apart from being good farmers. There was, in the language of the time, an *armblanke* (poor white) problem.

Professor Pieter de Lange, Broederbond chairman after 1983, says the Broederbond's main aim during the early years was 'to make the Afrikaner a modern urban being while remaining an Afrikaner'. Together with the National Party and other Afrikaner institutions, it did a remarkable job.

The programme to empower Afrikaners started early in the previous century with the establishment, with very little capital, of Nasionale Pers (which then published *Die Burger* and *Huisgenoot*), the winemakers' cooperative KWV, Volkskas bank and the insurance companies Santam and Sanlam. Agricultural cooperatives were formed all over the country to assist farmers.

Sanlam and the Broederbond organised the First Economic People's Congress in 1938 where *volkskapitalisme* was born: a concept that determined that free enterprise was more than a way to enrich individuals, it had to help Afrikaners escape 'economic servitude'.

The Reddingsdaadbond was born from the congress. It was a movement to mobilise Afrikaner money and establish Afrikaner businesses (almost a national *stokvel*). It was said at the time that if every Afrikaner family contributed only 25 cents, mighty financial power would be unleashed. A Broederbond document of 1969 stated that the Reddingsdaadbond 'brought a message of strength to a nation which had almost become disheartened in its struggle against poverty. To a nation that regarded a position of economic subservience as almost natural, it presented the ideal of an Afrikanerdom which would not only be employee, but also employer, not only a foreigner in the economic life of his fatherland, but also the owner of material power, which rightfully belonged to him.' (Does the language sound familiar?)

The financial institution Federale Volksbeleggings (FVB) that invested Afrikaners' savings also grew out of the Volkskongres. By the end of World War Two, FVB had substantial investments in fisheries, wool, steel, chemicals and agricultural implements. From FVB came Federale Mynbou, the first Afrikaner participation in mining, which eventually morphed into General Mining. FVB gave the young entrepreneur Anton Rupert his first capital loan to start the Rembrandt Group, which is today an international conglomerate.

According to historian Hermann Giliomee, the Afrikaner share in the private sector grew from 1 per cent to 18 per cent in mining between 1938 and 1975, 3 per cent to 15 per cent in manufacturing, and 8 per cent to 16 per cent in trade. From there it grew exponentially.

The Broederbond and the National Party practised their own form of cadre deployment and affirmative action with the placement of their own men in strategic positions and providing sheltered employment to lesser-skilled Afrikaners with state corporations such as the Railways, Iscor and Evkom (now Eskom).

Cadre deployment and affirmative action, yes, but with one big difference: in those days a heavy emphasis was placed on good education and training, and workshops to increase skills. The Helpmekaarfonds helped many thousands of Afrikaans students through university and teachers' training colleges with grants and study loans at almost zero interest.

There is no need to state that circumstances were vastly different then compared to today and that the narrow ethnic nationalism practised by the Broederbond and the National Party would be very undesirable in today's democratic South Africa.

But surely there is a lesson in the commitment, hard work and clever strategising rather than just rhetoric and blaming the colonial heritage that brought such amazing results?

Surely there is something to be learnt from the dedication to the benefit of the many rather than the enrichment of the few?

Surely the example of placing an emphasis on education and training is worth emulating?

Perhaps it is time for a new form of people's capitalism.

To governance, corruption, bad decisions and vanity projects

If the ANC leadership had decided to make the best of what they had inherited, our society would look very different today. Instead they bought billions of rands worth of military hardware, allowed corruption to take root, ran an ineffectual bureaucracy and education system, and spent millions on vanity projects such as Nkandla.

I could spend the next twenty pages documenting how extraordinarily inefficient South Africa's bloated civil service is, but I won't – most South Africans experience it every day. It is true of national government, but provincial governments are worse (think Eastern Cape and Limpopo, but not Western Cape), while most local governments are unmitigated disasters (excluding Cape Town and, to a lesser extent, Johannesburg). There has been on average at least one service-delivery protest every single day in the last four years.

There are about 1.4 million employees in the public service, just over 400 000 employed by national government and over 900 000 employed by the nine provincial governments. In 2012 they cost about R380 billion.

Of every R100 generated by the economy, about R12 goes to paying civil servants. According to figures supplied by Treasury in 2012, civil servants were paid 11.5 per cent of the country's GDP. Economist Mike Schussler believes this figure is closer to 14 per cent if state-owned entities are factored in. This makes South Africa's civil service the most expensive in the world. Compare this figure to Russia's 3.7 per cent, Brazil's 4.6 per cent and Nigeria's 4 per cent.

Finance minister Pravin Gordhan admitted in 2012 that the growth in government wages had outstripped all other categories of state spending in the previous four years.

Imagine what our country would look like if all of these 1.4 million well-paid bureaucrats did an honest day's work.

Continuity is a huge problem in the civil service. A 2013 analysis by the *Sunday Times* of the thirty-three national government departments found that 114 different directors-general have served in either permanent or acting capacities in President Zuma's first fifty-two months in office. Some clashed with their ministers and left; some were fired because of poor performance, others because of corruption or mismanagement. Directors-general are the administrative heads of departments responsible for implementing policy and overseeing financial management.

But there is hope. Her name is Lindiwe Sisulu of the esteemed Sisulu dynasty: her father, Walter, stands right alongside Mandela as one of the greatest heroes in our history, and right next to him stands his wife Albertina, the only woman deserving of the title Mother of the Nation. Lindiwe's brother Max is Speaker of Parliament.

Sisulu was appointed minister of public service and administration in 2012. She has vowed to whip the civil service into shape and she's talking tough with a Public Service Charter that she's determined to implement. She's already launched a review of all national and provincial departments, as well as an assessment of the state's capacity to implement the National Development Plan.

In March 2013, when Auditor-General Terence Nombembe announced that more than R60 billion in irregular expenditure by departments was unaccounted for, Sisulu declared that the entire public service 'may need to go back to school'. She said government was busy with the establishment of a school of governance where public servants would be trained.

If anyone can take on the powerful trade unions in the public service it is Sisulu. And the ANC is beginning to realise that if they still want to be in power after 2019, they will have to govern far more efficiently, so Sisulu is guaranteed much political support when the going gets tough.

The rampant corruption among politicians and bureaucrats is probably a tougher nut to crack. Corruption has infested the body of the ANC like an aggressive cancer and it starts right at the top. Despite almost daily lip service to the fight against corruption, senior politicians suspected of (and even caught) being corrupt are kept in their positions. Business people say it is almost impossible to do business with government without bribing someone.

One of South Africa's foremost public intellectuals, Njabulo Ndebele, has made this stark warning: 'South Africa may currently be moving through a dangerous transitional phase from the ad hoc practice of corruption to its steady institutionalisation through law and regulation. It is a phase that, once crossed, will be difficult to reverse.'

I don't see this process being stopped by government or the ruling party. But civil action groups, such as Corruption Watch, and investigative journalism, as well as the bravery and independence of Public Protector Thuli Madonsela, can still make a difference.

Nobody has, as far as I'm aware, done a thorough audit on exactly how much public money has been wasted, mismanaged or stolen since 1994, but it is believed to be several hundred billion rand.

When people such as Desmond Tutu and Sampie Terreblanche proposed a wealth tax to build a development fund of a few billion to spend on job creation and restoring dignity to the poor, I wholeheartedly and publicly supported it. I still think it is a good idea in principle. But I can't help wonder how much of that fund will be mismanaged, wasted or stolen.

And that, in the end, is the crux of the problem: even if one agreed that the state should play a bigger role in the economy, the state doesn't have the capacity, discipline, skills and productivity to manage it properly.

Stop building, start fixing

The ANC has had many plans for development and dealing with inequality, unemployment and poverty: the RDP, GEAR, ASGISA, the New Growth Path and the Industrial Policy Plan. Pages and pages of good intentions. If the one plan doesn't deliver the goods, tweak it and propose another.

And then came the NDP, formally accepted by the ANC's national congress in Mangaung in December 2012 as the party's official vision and blueprint for development until 2030. Zuma seems to see the NDP as the legacy for which he will be remembered.

The NDP is the work of the National Planning Commission (NPC) appointed by Zuma in May 2010. The NPC is an advisory body consisting of twenty-six people drawn largely from outside government, chosen for their expertise in key areas, and driven by chairperson Trevor Manuel and deputy chairperson Cyril Ramaphosa. Their five-hundred-page report was handed to Parliament in August 2012.

Many South Africans sat up and took note when the NPC published its frank 'Diagnostic Report', identifying a failure to implement policies and an absence of broad partnerships as the main reasons for slow progress. It identified nine primary challenges: too few people work; the quality of school education for black people is poor; infrastructure is poorly located, inadequate and under-maintained; spatial divides hobble inclusive development; the economy is unsustainably resource-intensive; the public health system cannot meet demand or sustain quality; public services are uneven and often of poor quality; corruption levels are high; and South Africa remains a divided society. Few can argue with this diagnosis.

The NDP proposes policies and projects to deal with all these challenges, and how these should be implemented in stages over the coming years; sometimes in detail, often just formulating the vision. It is part plan, part discussion document. I found it an inspiring, honest, realistic and formidable document.

The ice cubes in the Johnnie Walker Blue at Mangaung had barely melted when first some unions in COSATU and then the SACP rejected critical parts of the NDP, especially those dealing with the economy and labour. Irvin Jim of NUMSA called it a 'cut and paste' of Democratic Alliance policies.

This dance will continue. A lot will depend on what happens over coming months inside the deeply divided COSATU and on how strong Zuma's standing will be after the 2014 election – and Cyril Ramaphosa's, because he is a strong driver of the NDP. Trevor Manuel's already shaky political standing in the ANC and the role he will play after May 2014 could also have an impact.

The NDP will need to be popularised and sold to the nation as a national vision and guideline that gives hope that there is a new urgency and clarity to put South Africa back on the road to prosperity.

I agree with academic and columnist Steven Friedman when he says it is safe to assume that 'just about everyone who praises or denounces it, who demands its implementation or insists it be resisted, has never read it'. He says:

> So why is everyone so keen to accept or reject the document they have not read? Because they believe they know all they need to know about the NPC – the name of its chairman. The fact that Trevor Manuel chairs it – and, at least until recently, that Cyril Ramaphosa is its vice-chairman – heartens pro-business interests because they see Manuel and Ramaphosa as politicians who take business and middle-class interests seriously. The left of the alliance opposed the NPC for precisely that reason, which is also why some in the Congress of South African Trade Unions insist the NDP is a Democratic Alliance–inspired plot against the people. The truth about Manuel and Ramaphosa is far more complicated. But, more to the point, so is the truth about the NPC and NDP. There can be no more obvious example of what can go wrong if we turn politics and policy purely into a battle between individuals than the fact that a major policy document is being boosted and condemned by people who don't know what it says.

I agree. I blame Zuma's weak leadership for the fact that the NDP is still seen as a Manuel/Ramaphosa plan by so many, rather than an ANC and national blueprint for the future. Zuma has allowed the NDP to become a political football instead of a unifying, inspiring call to reconsider our future development.

In his book *Zumanomics: The Road from Mangaung to 2030*, economist Raymond Parsons says the successful implementation of the NDP must rest on sound political foundations. 'While ultimately most citizens can benefit from the NDP, without strong political constituencies supporting it, the inclusive outcomes will be difficult to achieve. It must not become a casualty of the vagaries of "low" politics,' he says. 'It needs inclusivity in its implementation not only to generate continued support but also to keep narrow vested interests at bay. People will support what they helped to create. Leadership here is all about smart change management. The political management of the NDP process and the demonstration of its positive outcomes over time are thus of great importance.'

Business writer and academic Pierre Heistein alerted me to a story that I think is highly relevant.

India built the massive Middle Vaitarna Dam at great cost in 2011 to supply a struggling Mumbai with 455 million litres of water a day. But studies showed that if the city had fixed the leaks in its old underground pipelines, it would have saved in excess of 600 million litres a day. They didn't need a new dam; they needed to fix the pipes.

We should consider all reasonable proposals for a new economic order that would deal with our inequality. But our best bet is not ambitious new projects or repeated policy overhauls. We should first fix our leaking pipes and taps before we build a new dam.

We should make the state, the economy and the nation work more efficiently, live more frugally, and fix our education and skills-training systems and our divided cities.

The NDP is a good owner's manual to help us do this.

'History will judge government leaders and MPs harshly if they fail to implement the NDP,' Trevor Manuel told Parliament in June 2013.

7

Jacob the survivor

Polokwane, 12 December 2007. A shell-shocked Thabo Mbeki walks over zombie-like, with a frozen half-smile, to gingerly hug the man who has just defeated him for the presidency of the ANC.

It was the day politics in South Africa changed.

Mbeki will be remembered as the intellectual president who championed the African Renaissance. History will remember Jacob Gedleyihlekisa Zuma as the president who fought to stay out of jail.

Neither Dan Brown nor John Grisham could have written a narrative as gripping and intricate – and, at times, bizarre – as the story of the rise (and fall?) of Jacob Zuma: betrayal, intrigue, endless conspiracies, sordid sex, phone tapping, shady foreign friends and suspicious financial transactions.

In this thriller, the main protagonist's middle name means 'the one who smiles in your face while causing you harm' – writer Fred Khumalo's translation of Gedleyihlekisa. Zuma himself says his middle name is a shortened form of the Zulu phrase '*ngeke ngithule umuntu engigedla engihlekisa*', which, according to him, means 'when people conspire or gang up against you'. So victim, rather than perpetrator.

(Mbeki's middle name, Mvuyelwa, means 'he for whom the people sing' ...)

If you don't understand how and why Zuma became president of South Africa, or how he's succeeded in still calling Mahlamba Ndlopfu his official residence instead of Pretoria Central Prison, you won't understand much of government's decisions and appointments over the last seven years.

The drama started a few years before 2007.

The rise and rise of Jacob Zuma

It was at Mbeki's insistence that Zuma became his deputy when he took over the presidency of the country from Nelson Mandela in June 1999. The two had known each other for a very long time, and during the negotiations between 1990 and 1994 they often operated as a team.

The two couldn't have been more different. Mbeki was a well-educated, urbane intellectual and former ANC diplomat. Zuma was an uneducated Zulu traditionalist and polygamist, and former ANC security chief. Mbeki was reserved and aloof. Zuma was warm and charming, and a brilliant dancer.

There were other strong candidates for deputy president, such as the Mpumalanga premier, accomplished lawyer, poet and former MK leader Mathews Phosa, who did indicate his ambitions at the time. But Mbeki chose Zuma, the deputy president of the ANC since December 1997, and Phosa has been an Mbeki enemy ever since.

Zuma was a popular man in the ANC and a clever party strategist, but no one, not even Zuma himself, ever thought that he had what it took to be president. Clearly Mbeki agreed: what better sidekick than a man who could never have presidential ambitions and thus could never become a threat?

Zuma's ethnicity also must have been a consideration – the deputy president had to be a Zulu-speaker. According to Mbeki's biographer Mark Gevisser, in *Thabo Mbeki: The Dream Deferred*, Mbeki had first offered the deputy presidency to IFP leader Mangosuthu Buthelezi. '[I]t would have enabled Mbeki to bypass Zuma,' says Gevisser, 'whom Mbeki had already concluded, according to his confidants, was not presidential material.' Buthelezi declined the offer and Mbeki later vehemently denied that he had made it.

If Mbeki did appoint Zuma the Zulu traditionalist as his deputy in the interests of the ANC, it worked. In 1997 the IFP was still ruling KwaZulu-Natal, but it has since become the ANC's strongest province. If he had not appointed Zuma, already his deputy in the ANC, it could have angered many Zulu-speakers in the province. One of the few positive achievements Zuma will be remembered for is the way he helped to bring peace to KwaZulu-Natal.

It was not long before Mbeki's paranoia started surfacing and he began to see powerful enemies wanting to overthrow him in every corner. In 2001 his minister of police and close friend, Steve Tshwete, announced on television that he was investigating a coup plot against Mbeki, with Cyril Ramaphosa, Tokyo Sexwale and Mathews Phosa the alleged chief conspirators. Mbeki then confronted Zuma and accused him of also being party to the plot.

The upshot of this meeting was that, on 3 April 2001, Zuma, who had never been publicly accused of being part of the fake conspiracy or of having higher ambitions, issued a public statement completely out of the blue, stating that he had never been involved in any plot against Mbeki and that he had no ambitions to be president.

Also at that time, Mbeki publicly humiliated Winnie Madikizela-Mandela for telling people he was having an affair with businesswoman Wendy Luhabe, wife of Gauteng premier Mbhazima Shilowa. Winnie wrote a furious letter to Zuma repeating this and other accusations that Mbeki was sleeping with prominent comrades. The letter was leaked to the media, either by Winnie or Zuma.

On Sunday 8 April 2001, I took part in an SABC radio show on current affairs called *The Editors*. I raised Zuma's unexpected and unexplained statement and said it could only indicate a huge falling-out between Mbeki and his deputy. I also mentioned Winnie's letter to Zuma, saying that Mbeki's womanising was becoming an issue in the ANC and that the movement was becoming increasingly divided. I added that I wasn't saying it was scandalous, but that it was now in the public domain and we should talk about it. (Over my decades in journalism, I have consistently opposed newspapers digging into the private lives, especially sex lives, of politicians. In my view, it should become news only if it has an impact on the politician's ability to execute his/her functions.)

Two days later, the *Citizen* ran a big headline above its main story: 'President's a womaniser, says Max'. The ANC issued a statement that I had 'declared war' on the ANC, while the Youth League wanted me to be charged with high treason. The more I tried to explain that I was referring to Winnie's allegations already published in the media, the more I was attacked as a racist and a counter-revolutionary. Poor Van Zyl Slabbert, then chairman of the *Citizen*'s owner, Caxton, even had to publicly apologise for the paper's treatment of the story. I thought it was a bit spineless of him because he knew the background, and I told him so.

The size of the cracks in the ANC and the first undeniable indications that Mbeki and Zuma were at each other's throats became public in 2003. The founding head of the National Prosecuting Authority (NPA; previously called the Office of the Attorney-General), Bulelani Ngcuka, was a bright young lawyer and much liked by Mbeki. He made it known that there was a *prima facie* case of corruption against Zuma, but said that he wasn't going to prosecute.

Two Zuma loyalists, Mac Maharaj and Mo Shaik, then accused Ngcuka of being an apartheid spy. A special commission under Judge Joos Hefer found no evidence to support the allegations. The ground was prepared for a bitter battle, and Maharaj and Shaik became key players in defending Zuma.

In October 2004 Durban businessman Schabir Shaik was charged with fraud and corruption in the Durban High Court. Schabir is the brother of Mo, one of Zuma's operatives when he was intelligence chief of the ANC in exile. His other brother, Chippy, was chief of acquisitions for the SANDF during the massive arms deal. Schabir acted as Zuma's financial advisor.

The court heard how Schabir Shaik paid many of Zuma's private bills and wrote off what were supposed to be personal loans. In exchange, Zuma had to help him with his business dealings that included a French arms dealer.

Judge Hilary Squires found Shaik had a corrupt relationship with Zuma and declared him guilty of fraud and corruption in 2005. He was sentenced to fifteen years in prison, which was confirmed by the Supreme Court of Appeal in 2006.

But a corrupt relationship has to involve at least two people, argued most South Africans after the verdict. What about the other partner in the relationship?

Shortly after the judgment, on 14 June 2005, Mbeki rose to speak in Parliament. The media and the country were abuzz. Was he going to defend Zuma? Could he do what had never been done before and fire him? Here is what he said:

Both the deputy president and I are acutely sensitive to the responsibilities we bear as prescribed by our Constitution. We understand very well that we should at all times act in a manner that seeks to 'uphold, defend and respect the Constitution', as required by the same Constitution. As I have already indicated, this includes, among other things, the need to 'respect the constitutional status, institutions, powers and functions of government in the other spheres', to quote the Constitution once again.

We have had no precedent to guide us as we considered our response to the judgment by Justice Squires. We have therefore had to make our own original determination on this matter guided by what we believe is in the best interest of the honourable deputy president, the government, our young democratic system, and our country.

I am fully conscious of the fact that the accused in the Schabir Shaik case have given notice of their intention to lodge an appeal. I am equally aware that a superior court may overturn the judgment handed down by Justice Squires.

However, as president of the Republic I have come to the conclusion that the circumstances dictate that in the interest of the honourable deputy president, the government, our young democratic system, and our country, it would be best to release the honourable Jacob Zuma from his responsibilities as deputy president of the Republic and member of the cabinet. Necessarily, we will continue to monitor and respond to all developments in relation to this and other relevant legal processes.

The deed was done. Mbeki, who could never even summon the courage to shuffle his own cabinet, had fired the deputy president. Zuma's own actions had handed Mbeki the dagger he had wanted for so long to plunge into Zuma's political heart. No more threats from the grinning Zulu, Mbeki must have thought.

Actually, the *coup de grâce* would be to charge Zuma with corruption and fraud, using the same evidence that had landed Shaik in jail – evidence now accepted by the High Court. You mess with Mvuyelwa, he for whom the people sing, you pay.

The investigators and the prosecutors did their job diligently. The specialised investigating unit, the Scorpions, raided Zuma's home and office, and those of his lawyer, Michael Hulley. Zuma and Hulley challenged the legality of the raids in court, but lost.

After the Shaik case, the prosecutors ascertained that he had actually paid Zuma a lot more than first thought – 783 payments totalling more than R4 million, in fact. The payments had continued after Shaik's corruption trial started, and even after he had been convicted. Charges of money laundering and racketeering were added to Zuma's charge sheet. The case against Zuma was stronger than the case against Shaik, prosecutors said privately. If convicted, he would get at the very least fifteen years in jail. They were ready to go to court and a date for August 2008 was set.

In the interim, Zuma found himself back in court – this time not as an applicant, but rather the accused in a criminal case. He was accused of raping the young daughter of an old struggle comrade. She was HIV-positive, and he knew it. The scenes outside court were among the most disgraceful South Africa had ever seen. Hordes of supporters, including members of the ANC Youth League, protested his prosecution, even taunting the complainant and calling her a whore.

Zuma's defence was that it was consensual sex – actually, it was his manly duty to satisfy her. He took a shower afterwards to make sure he wasn't infected with HIV. He was found not guilty of rape, but the judge had a few harsh words about his conduct. Zuma later apologised to the ANC and to the nation. It wasn't the last time he had to apologise for his sexual indiscretions.

The young woman left the country shortly afterwards. One of the senior politicians whom she went to after the incident at Zuma's home, and who knew her father well, still believes she was speaking the truth.

Zuma's supporters in the ANC Youth League, COSATU and KwaZulu-Natal were getting louder and more aggressive, and T-shirts with the words

'100% Zulu boy' became very popular. The ANC was now publicly divided into an Mbeki camp and a Zuma camp.

Matters were coming to a head in the run-up to the ANC's elective conference in Polokwane scheduled for December 2007. Anti-Zuma elements in the ANC and a strong ANC constituency in the Eastern Cape wanted Mbeki to stand for a third term as president of the ANC. Some of Mbeki's sycophants, such as Essop Pahad, Geraldine Fraser-Moleketi and Andile Nkuhlu, told him it was a sure thing, and he publicly declared his candidacy. He couldn't be president of South Africa for a third term, but he could be ANC president and control Zuma from Luthuli House.

This galvanised all his old enemies. The SACP, COSATU and the Youth League were unhappy with the economic policies, such as GEAR, that Mbeki had espoused and, perhaps more importantly, were bitter that they had been excluded from the inner circle of power in government. He hardly talked to them during his years in power. He was arrogant and out of touch with the people, they said.

But there were others not part of these formations who also wanted Mbeki out; leaders such as Mathews Phosa and Tokyo Sexwale, whom Mbeki had alienated, and those who were close to Zuma and hoped to get closer to the fire if he became president.

Together, all these elements formed what was called at the time the 'coalition of the wounded', those who thought it was 'their time to eat'. They wanted to get rid of Mbeki at all costs, and the readily available battering ram to push him off the throne was an angry and humiliated Zuma. Just under the surface was a feeling that Zuma, because of who he was, because of his obvious limitations and because of the way he was going to get into power, would be much more easily manipulated than Mbeki. Some may even have thought that his legal troubles probably meant he wouldn't be president for long, and then their chance would come.

And then came Polokwane

Nothing like the Polokwane conference had ever happened in the hundred years of the ANC's existence. As Mandy Rossouw, senior political journalist and author of *Mangaung: Kings and Kingmakers* (she also co-authored a book on Julius Malema with me, but, sadly, passed away in March 2013), remarked: 'As journalists, we were about to witness the spectacle of a lifetime. A national ANC conference spun out of control, right in front of the nation, courtesy of SABC's rolling coverage. Delegates openly sang opposing struggle songs, inserting where appropriate the name of their leader of choice. It became almost impossible to make a speech, with Fikile Mbalula, now sports minister but then Zuma's cheerleader-in-chief, interrupting speakers by singing Zuma's anthem "Umshini Wam" into the microphone from his seat in the back of the hall.'

I watched the proceedings on television and I couldn't believe my eyes and ears. I have seen some rough stuff at political meetings in my time, but the way young (and even old) thugs disrespected and publicly humiliated dignified leaders such as Mbeki and Mosiuoa Lekota was completely unexpected. The noise was deafening, with hundreds making the rolling-arms soccer substitution sign. Zuma just sat there with a slight grin.

The Zuma crowd refused to accept the standard method of electronic voting and insisted it be done manually, supposedly out of fear that someone would cheat.

Mbeki, protégé of O.R. Tambo, son of ANC stalwart Govan, for almost three decades the brightest son of the liberation movement, was humiliated in the crassest possible way. He was replaced by a man who was supposed to be answering serious criminal charges, a man of highly questionable ethics, ill-equipped in almost every respect to lead a modern economy and democracy.

Looking back now, Polokwane 2007 signalled the moment when cheap populist politics, the culture of insults and threats, started flourishing in South Africa; when the sluice gates of corruption were opened wide. It gave birth to the phenomenon of Julius Sello (Pedi for 'wail') Malema, which would dominate the public discourse for the next five years.

Zuma was touted as a 'progressive' and Polokwane as a significant step to the left by the ANC. There is nothing progressive about Zuma. He is an arch-conservative, anti-intellectual, homophobic, patriarchal traditionalist and nationalist. The ANC did not move one iota to the left after Polokwane. In fact, with the Protection of State Information Bill (the Secrecy Bill) it tried to severely limit freedom of expression and curtail the media's role in exposing state abuse. And it is trying to further entrench the power of traditional chiefs. Zuma's ANC has shown a tendency to undermine the judiciary and to question the Constitution's supremacy.

But at least Mbeki was still president of the country after Polokwane. He still had sixteen months left in his last term as president. Or so he thought.

The new management in Luthuli House couldn't wait that long. They wanted the levers of power and privilege in their hands and they wanted it immediately. And there was the matter of Zuma's court case looming – he had to be made president at all costs before his case came to court. The few sane voices advising caution, such as Kgalema Motlanthe, were drowned out in the frenzy.

Zuma's legal team was using what is called a 'Stalingrad strategy' by challenging every move the state made and appealing every ruling going against them to the highest court.

On 12 September 2008, Zuma struck gold in the High Court. In one of the most bizarre and discredited decisions in a long time in South Africa, Judge Chris Nicholson declared that there was undue political interference in Zuma's prosecution and that it should be stopped. Zuma's spokesman, Zizi Kodwa, called Nicholson 'that beautiful judge'.

The Zuma camp moved quickly. Ten days later, the national executive committee – sans Mbeki – met at Esselen Park east of Johannesburg. It lasted for hours as the last Mbeki supporters tried to caution against rash behaviour but were once again drowned out by the Zuma commando, now armed with the Nicholson judgment, which, they said, proved that Mbeki was behind the charges against Zuma.

That same night, ANC secretary-general Gwede Mantashe and ANC deputy president Kgalema Motlanthe set off for Mahlamba Ndlopfu, Mbeki's official residence in Pretoria, to tell him he was being 'recalled'. Remarkably, the director-general in the presidency, Frank Chikane, decided that Mbeki shouldn't be woken up and asked the ANC emissaries to come back at 9 a.m. the following morning.

Chikane, who was absolutely outraged by the ANC's decision and actually wrote a book about it that became a bestseller, *Eight Days in September: The Removal of Thabo Mbeki*, says that when Mbeki came down from his quarters after eight the next morning, he was cool and collected but walked more slowly than usual. 'The closest to an expression of emotions was when he repeated his belief that no true cadre of the movement [the ANC] could make a decision of that nature given the circumstances and issues involved … For him this meant that something had gone radically wrong in the ANC and it was a cause for great concern. It was out of character and a manifestation of the first fruit of the Polokwane Project.'

Motlanthe and Mantashe saw Mbeki at 9 a.m. that Saturday morning. Mbeki acted with great dignity and accepted the decision, only asking the two about a 'constitutional way to leave office without leaving a vacuum'.

But the Zuma gang had smelt blood. They ordered him to immediately cease to perform all functions as president – he was due to speak at the UN a few days later – and to announce his resignation on television the next day.

This was all clearly in violation of the Constitution. The president is elected by Parliament and cannot be 'recalled' by a political party, and stopping a sitting president from executing his responsibilities is even worse. Chikane says: 'This act brought us close to a coup d'état. The act of stopping the president from exercising his constitutional responsibilities and mandate was tantamount to "an illegal change of government" – in this case, the president. As long as a president is in office, no one can stop him or her from executing his constitutional responsibilities and duties.'

There was a dangerous blurring between party and state, Chikane says – a blurring we have seen a lot more of in the years since.

Mbeki did as he was told and announced his resignation in a live television broadcast. 'I have been a loyal member of the African National Congress for fifty-two years,' he said. 'I remain a member of the ANC and therefore respect its decisions. It is for this reason that I have taken the decision to resign as president of the Republic, following the decision of the national executive committee of the ANC.'

Mbeki also rejected the judgment made by Judge Nicholson that he had interfered with Zuma's prosecution. He said it in a characteristically Mbeki way: 'In this context it is most unfortunate that gratuitous suggestions have been made seeking to impugn the integrity of those of us who have been privileged to serve in our country's national executive.'

Motlanthe was sworn in as president of South Africa the next day, 25 September 2008, and immediately asked all those cabinet ministers who had resigned in sympathy with Mbeki to take up their posts once more.

The wild men and women in the ANC rejoiced at Mbeki's humiliation. Some of the more decent ones in the leadership tried to put a positive spin on the outrageous 'recall': it showed that democracy was alive in the ANC and it was an opportunity for a new start. They were wrong on both counts.

On 22 April 2009, the ANC went into the general election with Zuma's face on their posters. The breakaway Congress of the People, or COPE, under the leadership of Mosiuoa Lekota and Mbhazima Shilowa, got 7.8 per cent of the vote, quite something considering the short time they had to organise. The ANC got 65.9 per cent, just 3.8 per cent less than in the 2004 election, thanks to masses of IFP supporters defecting to the ANC, which now offered them a traditional Zulu president.

Those who wanted to vote for the ANC did not have to worry about its leader being under a cloud of suspicion of having committed fraud, corruption, money laundering and racketeering. Because, just three weeks before the election, the acting director of public prosecutions, Mokotedi Mpshe, announced that the charges against Zuma were finally being dropped. (Mpshe was made an acting judge shortly afterwards and later became a land court judge, a move many interpreted as a reward for dropping the charges.)

Mpshe said it was 'the most difficult decision I ever made in my life' to drop the charges.

Four years later, the *Mail & Guardian*'s investigative team of Stefaans Brümmer and Sam Sole revealed that what Mpshe did not tell South Africans at the time was that he was the one who had decided to make a decision on the prosecution only after Polokwane, against the advice of his prosecutors. He did this after consulting with then justice minister Brigitte Mabandla.

He should have made the decision after the Supreme Court of Appeal ruled in favour of the NPA on disputed search warrants and evidence from Mauritius, which cleared the last hurdle to the prosecution, on 8 November 2007, five weeks before Polokwane. The team of prosecutors told Mpshe that it was 'inadvisable for the prosecution to dabble in matters of politics, even with the best possible intentions'. To deliberately withhold from the public the fact that a decision had been taken to prosecute until after Polokwane 'is in conflict with the constitutional duties of the team and the NPA'. The team was convinced at the time that Mpshe was going to follow their advice and announce that the prosecution was going to go ahead.

The reason Mpshe gave for his controversial decision was in line with the Nicholson judgment: there was political interference. But the Supreme Court of Appeal had comprehensively rejected and overturned the Nicholson judgment just weeks after it had been made.

Mpshe found new ammunition: tape recordings of telephone conversations between the former head of the Scorpions, Advocate Leonard McCarthy, and the then head of the NPA, Bulelani Ngcuka. They were apparently discussing the timing of the prosecution. The tapes were given to Mpshe by Zuma's lawyer, Mike Hulley, as part of an argument why the prosecution should be dropped.

The tapes were allegedly made by the SAPS's crime intelligence unit, headed by one of Zuma's chief henchmen, Richard Mdluli. Brümmer and Sole revealed back in February 2009 that crime intelligence was monitoring McCarthy's conversations after, I was told, getting the necessary permissions, but under false pretences. Crime intelligence launched a secret campaign against the Scorpions, widely regarded as enemies of Zuma and supporters of Mbeki, in 2003, ostensibly because of suspicions of drug deals. No evidence of drug dealing came to light, but McCarthy was taped discussing the Zuma case – allegedly talking about the timing and when would be politically opportune.

It seems to me that even if the tapes were legally made, it would have been highly irregular, even illegal, for Mdluli or the intelligence services to supply Zuma's lawyer with copies.

The tapes were then played to two NPA representatives. They were concerned that the tapes had been made illegally and approached the National Intelligence Agency (NIA). The NIA, also staffed by Zuma loyalists, revealed that it was also monitoring McCarthy's phone calls and emails because of an earlier report by one of McCarthy's agents that the Angolan government was secretly supporting Zuma's candidacy for president.

In August 2013 the *Mail & Guardian* published excerpts of internal NPA correspondence regarding the Zuma prosecution, after they were made aware of the spy tapes. It is a devastating indictment of Mpshe's decision and makes it abundantly clear, at least in my opinion, that it was purely political and not legal.

The team of investigators and prosecutors tasked with the Zuma case held many discussions on the implications of the tapes and the suggestion by Hulley that there was a conspiracy to prevent Zuma from becoming president. They even asked two of the country's top advocates, Wim Trengove and Andrew Breitenbach, for their advice.

'Advocate Trengove advised in essence that the Mpshe decision to prosecute lay at the heart of the fairness of the trial,' one excerpt read. 'If this remained defensible in that it was unaffected by the alleged political machinations of advocate McCarthy and those with whom he was alleged to have been conspiring, and based on evidence that is also untainted, then the decision to prosecute should remain. Even if advocate Mpshe may have been unwittingly influenced to some degree by advocate McCarthy, as long as he is still satisfied that the decision was the correct one on the merits, he advised against acceding to the representations.' Trengove's view was supported by Breitenbach.

The team told Mpshe that they had gone back to their notes, memoranda and diaries concerning the events of November and December 2007. 'Having done so, we are satisfied that the position is quite clear. All the members of the Bumiputera team [as the team of investigators and prosecutors tasked with the Zuma case was called] and all the NPA management to whom our recommendations were presented were unanimous that Mr Zuma should be charged.'

The team said in a memo that to accede to Hulley's representations would 'forever leave the impression that the NPA has become a pawn of the political establishment and cause irrevocable damage to public confidence in the system of justice'.

In short, what the prosecutors were saying was that even if others such as McCarthy were guilty of political meddling, it had no effect on the prosecutors' recommendation to prosecute Zuma and had no impact on the integrity of the evidence against him.

The astonishing fact is that Mpshe not only disregarded all the recommendations from his colleagues and the legal advice of two of South Africa's top legal minds, he hardly consulted them before he announced his decision not to prosecute. 'In our view, the legal motivation for the decision is questionable and may be vulnerable on review,' the team said in a memo on 14 April 2009. 'We are still of the view that the ultimate test should be whether the abuse in question would prevent the accused from having a fair trial, a question which was not even addressed.'

Bulelani Ngcuka, who was supposed to be in conversation with McCarthy on the spy tapes, released an angry statement after Mpshe's decision. He had not been given access to the tapes or the notes made by the two NPA officials who had listened to them. That was unfair and against natural justice, he said. He was 'dismayed and disappointed' by the assertions made by Mpshe and categorically denied that he had ever 'been party to any conspiracy to frustrate the political ambition of Mr Zuma to ascend to the highest office in the land'.

In 2012 the Democratic Alliance then went to court to demand access to the spy tapes and Hulley's oral representation to Mpshe in order to ascertain whether his decision was a legal one. The Supreme Court of Appeal determined that the NPA needed to file a so-called reduced record, which would include all material related to its decision to drop the corruption charges against Zuma, but exclude his personal representations made to the NPA.

The NPA wasn't forthcoming and in 2013 the DA went back to court. This time Judge Rammaka Mathopo ordered the NPA to hand over copies of the tapes within five days. Two weeks later, Mathopo granted Zuma leave to appeal, because the parties to the case had different versions of what the Supreme Court of Appeal's order meant. At the time of writing, the appeal had not been heard.

The bottom line: if the Supreme Court of Appeal finally decides that the NPA should divulge the reasons for Mpshe's decision to drop charges against Zuma, the chances are probably very good that Zuma will be charged. Zuma's

Stalingrad strategies to challenge, oppose and appeal every move by the prosecutors have to run out of steam at some point.

If it's true that the criminal case against Zuma is as strong, or stronger, than the one against Schabir Shaik, Zuma could be heading for jail before his next term is over.

Imagine the repercussions of a sitting president going to prison, especially a populist one like Zuma.

Will the ANC leadership really allow Zuma to begin his second term in office after the May 2014 elections if it seems likely that he is going to go to jail?

Is a more likely scenario not that they will keep him on as president of the party, but find a reason (age, health, family) to propose a new candidate for the presidency of the country?

If Shaik was sent home on so-called medical parole after just two years, which he mostly served in the prison's hospital, Zuma would be unlikely to actually spend much time in a prison cell.

Another possibility, of course, is that he is pardoned by the new president ...

The Zuma prosecuting team was right: the impression now is that the NPA has become a 'pawn of the political establishment' and that irrevocable damage has been inflicted on public confidence in the judiciary. No judiciary where the prosecuting authority is dysfunctional or politically manipulated can, in the long run, be fully trusted. And this is where we are in South Africa right now. This is a grave matter.

'The NPA is now run by a cabal not unlike a nouveau broederbond in the criminal justice system. It is all about personal loyalties and protecting incumbent networks,' *City Press* legal reporter Charl du Plessis wrote on 30 September 2013. And at the centre of it all is Gedleyihlekisa, the man who smiles as he is harming you.

The rot set in long before the Mpshe decision. His predecessor, Vusi Pikoli, was fired because he insisted on prosecuting the then commissioner of police, Jackie Selebi, which ended up in a jail sentence.

But since Zuma took over as president, the NPA has gone from crisis to crisis. There is no doubt in my mind that most of these crises have a direct connection with Zuma's resolve to stay out of court.

After Pikoli, Zuma appointed Advocate Menzi Simelane as director of the NPA, but this was reversed in 2011 because the Constitutional Court declared that Zuma's decision to appoint Simelane was 'irrational'. Simelane's evidence to a commission of inquiry (he was director-general of justice then) led by former Speaker Frene Ginwala into Pikoli's fitness to head the NPA was found to be 'contradictory and, on its face, indicative of Mr Simelane's dishonesty and raised serious questions about Mr Simelane's conscientiousness, integrity and credibility'. (Pikoli was cleared by Ginwala and his reputation is intact.)

Zuma then appointed Advocate Nomgcobo Jiba as acting head of the NPA. He couldn't make her appointment permanent, because he knew it would not stand up to scrutiny. Jiba was involved in the highly irregular arrest of top Scorpions investigator Gerrie Nel, the man responsible for the prosecution of Selebi. It was part of the police's efforts to undermine and discredit the Scorpions, an operation called 'Destroy Lucifer', because the Scorpions were regarded as pro-Mbeki and anti-Zuma. (The war the police waged against the Scorpions on behalf of the Zuma camp was a scandal in itself.) Jiba and the specialised commercial crimes unit head, Lawrence Mrwebi, were suspended by the NPA, but reinstated, apparently on the orders of Simelane. Jiba's colleagues in the NPA saw her as a Zuma favourite and pointed out that Zuma had expunged her husband's criminal record in 2010. Jiba was instrumental in blocking the DA's efforts to have the spy tapes released.

In the Simelane case, the Constitutional Court emphasised that the president was obliged to use objective criteria to determine whether a candidate for director of the NPA was fit and proper, and not merely rely on his subjective perspective. Jiba was clearly not fit and proper.

When the pressure mounted on Zuma to make an appointment, he picked Pinetown magistrate Stanley Gumede. But when it became known that Gumede had been formally charged with misconduct by the Magistrate's Commission, the appointment wasn't made.

The *Sunday Times* quoted an unnamed government official on 7 July 2013 as saying: 'The president has in excess of 700 corruption charges hanging over him and has to make sure that whoever he appoints will not reinstate the charges.'

Eventually the Council for the Advancement of the South African Constitution (CASAC) forced Zuma's hand with an urgent application to the Constitutional Court. The post of director of public prosecutions had not been filled for eighteen months, they said. Zuma then appointed a little-known lawyer, Mxolisi Nxasana, in September 2013. He is a University of Zululand graduate and was admitted as an attorney in 1997.

Always in the background in most of these shenanigans was Richard Mdluli. Unlike the other Zuma insiders and henchmen, he was never in the struggle. In fact, he was a senior member of the apartheid regime's hated and feared security police, his last posting being at Thokoza outside of Johannesburg, where he, according to Mandy Rossouw, 'is said to have run his own fiefdom'.

Mdluli was appointed head of crime intelligence in 2009, despite the protestations of then acting police commissioner Tim Williams, who described it as irregular and politically motivated. Mdluli's meteoric rise from being an apartheid tool to a top cop under the ANC was, it is rumoured, achieved through sensitive information he had collected on some very senior people in the new regime. A shrewd man, he proved his loyalty and indispensability to Zuma by reporting the goings-on of Zuma's enemies in the ANC to him. He wrote a report (although he denied being behind it), known as the Ground Coverage Report, which revealed among other things that cabinet ministers Tokyo Sexwale and Fikile Mbalula, police commissioner Bheki Cele and others had met secretly in Estcourt to plot against Zuma to make sure he wasn't re-elected at the 2012 ANC conference in Mangaung.

As head of crime intelligence, Mdluli was also in charge of the VIP Protection Unit. This, and the fact that he was in charge of phone tapping and the monitoring of emails, made Mdluli one of the most powerful men in South Africa – even bodyguards of ministers and other important figures had to tell him about the movements of the people they were guarding. A letter by Mdluli in which he promised to help Zuma become president also came to light.

(Julius Malema once remarked that if you're a cabinet minister and your phone rang, you first had to say hello to Mdluli.)

In 1999 Mdluli was accused of the murder of Oupa Ramogibe, the husband of Mdluli's lover. He was arrested on charges of murder in March 2011, but the NPA instead referred the matter to an inquest, which did not link him to the killing. But it did give some of his colleagues the courage to come forward with evidence that he allegedly abused his unit's covert slush fund. He was arrested on fraud and corruption charges in October 2011. Senior NPA prosecutor Glynnis Breytenbach took charge of the investigation.

But her colleague Mrwebi, another Zuma sycophant, would have none of it. Shortly before Zuma appointed him head of the specialised commercial crimes unit, Mdluli's lawyers asked Mrwebi to withdraw the charges. He ordered a full report from Breytenbach, who urged him not to drop the charges as the representations from Mdluli's lawyers did not amount to more than a wild conspiracy theory.

Mrwebi ignored her and withdrew the charges. He went one step further: he advised Jiba to suspend and charge Breytenbach because of the way she was handling another case. Breytenbach threatened to take Jiba, as acting director, on review if she did not reinstate the charges against Mdluli. Jiba's reaction was to suspend Breytenbach in April 2013.

Breytenbach's disciplinary hearing drew a lot of media attention and was a fascinating legal drama. She was represented by Wim Trengove, SC, and was cleared of the fifteen charges brought against her. When she went back to work, she was told that she had been transferred to another office and that more charges were being laid against her. She was even accused of working for the Israeli secret service, the Mossad.

Furthermore, the police dropped disciplinary charges against Mdluli after a meeting between a top general and the minister of police, Nathi Mthethwa.

Mrwebi has not had an exemplary career himself. He was implicated in an irregular payment of R150 000 to a non-existent police informer and was again in hot water when a document he wrote landed in the hands of Jackie Selebi's lawyers.

Rights group Freedom Under Law asked the North Gauteng High Court in September 2013 to order the reinstatement of the charges against Mdluli. Justice John Murphy did just that, declaring that the decision by Mrwebi to withdraw the corruption charges against Mdluli was 'illegal, irrational, based on irrelevant considerations and material errors of law'. Strong language.

It was reported that the acting head of crime intelligence, Chris Ngcobo, had abandoned his post after being undermined by a pro-Mdluli faction and that the commissioner of police was about to reappoint Mdluli. The Freedom Under Law application had at least temporarily put a stop to those plans.

The Mdluli case has been called 'almost a dry run' for the DA's bid to have the courts review the decision to withdraw corruption charges against Zuma. If Justice Murphy's decision is upheld, legal experts believe, the corruption and fraud charges against Zuma will probably be reinstated. The principle that the NPA can be forced to divulge why they made certain decisions not to prosecute has been established by the High Court.

The man now stuck between a rock and a very hard place is new NPA head Mxolisi Nxasana. On the one hand there is immense pressure from Zuma's men; on the other the knowledge that civil society won't hesitate to go to the courts again if he does anything suspicious.

That, in the final analysis, is Zuma's problem: our courts are still independent and functional, and the Constitutional Court is still a fierce and credible watchdog over the Constitution.

Nxasana's job is to restore faith in the NPA as an independent and professional body, and thus the credibility of the criminal justice system. Mxolisi, after all, means 'bringer of peace'.

But it won't be easy and appeals to his Zulu loyalty are inevitable. I sincerely hope he has no dirt in his private life. Zuma has made sure that his 'security cluster' is headed by loyal 'homeboys' from KwaZulu-Natal: justice minister Jeff Radebe, police minister Nathi Mthethwa and state security minister Siyabonga Cwele. Bheki Cele was his hand-picked commissioner of police from the home province, but when rumours started flying that Cele wasn't exactly blindly loyal, he was axed.

Perhaps Nxasana will take a leaf or two out of the book of South Africa's brave and stubborn Public Protector, Advocate Thuli Madonsela.

Not so tough at the top, or is it?

Zuma was clearly not a wealthy man – relative to most other top ANC leaders – when he accepted millions from Schabir Shaik. But his fortunes, or at least those of his family and his clan, improved spectacularly after his Polokwane victory. Six years after Polokwane there were probably more Zuma millionaires than any others sharing a surname. Zuma Economic Empowerment, as a Young Communist League leader, David Masondo, called it, was in full swing.

The *Mail & Guardian* reported in March 2010, just after it became known that Zuma's wives cost the taxpayer more than R15 million a year, that fifteen people close to Zuma were in business and had 134 company directorships or memberships of close corporations. More than 80 per cent of these were registered in the years since Polokwane.

Adriaan Basson reports in his book *Zuma Exposed* that Zuma's sons Edward and Saady, his twins Duduzane and Duduzile, and his nephew Khulubuse are the ones who have benefited most. 'Between the five of them, they accumulated eighty-nine new business interests since Zuma's Polokwane victory.' Khulubuse Zuma, famous for his lavish lifestyle and super-expensive cars, has added twenty companies to his name since 2008. In 2013 it was reported that Edward Zuma was part of a consortium planning to start a new low-cost airline in South Africa, Fastjet.

Khulubuse and a Mandela grandson, Zondwa Mandela, owned Aurora Investment, which had acquired the Pamodzi mines. It was a disaster. They treated the mines almost like a Ponzi scheme, a liquidator said after Aurora was liquidated. Trade unions said that once Aurora took over the mines, 3 500 jobs were lost and 42 000 people became impoverished. And yet Khulubuse and Zondwa kept on living like billionaires, with Khulubuse even donating R1 million to the ANC.

Zuma Incorporated, as Basson calls it, really blossomed when three shrewd brothers from India, Atul, Rajesh and Ajay Gupta, realised that the new South African president would be amenable to a mutually beneficial relationship. Six months after Polokwane, Duduzile and Duduzane Zuma were given jobs in the Gupta's company Sahara Computers. Shortly afterwards, Duduzile, then twenty-six, became a director of Sahara and Duduzane a director of the Gupta-owned brokerage firm JIC Mining Services and of Mabengela Investments. Duduzane looked set to become a billionaire when he and the Guptas got a fat iron-ore tender, but the deal ran into too much opposition.

In January 2013 Zuma told an ANC anniversary gala in Durban: 'I have always said a wise businessman will support the ANC because supporting the ANC means investing very well in your business.'

South Africa was slowly getting used to their president behaving more like a powerful traditional chief than the head of state of a modern country.

Zuma married his fourth wife, Nompumelelo Ntuli, in January 2008; his fifth, Tobeka Madiba, a year later; and his sixth, Gloria Ngema, in April 2012. He told Ngema at the wedding ceremony not to 'close the door' behind her, signalling his intentions to perhaps marry a seventh wife. (Ntuli and Madiba own or have interests in large numbers of companies.)

Embarrassing stories appeared in the newspapers about how his second and fourth wives 'went berserk' when he announced that he was going to marry again. Then it became clear that his four current wives (one of his wives committed suicide and another divorced him) were not the only women he attended to. In 2010 he impregnated the thirty-nine-year-old daughter of soccer supremo Irvin Khoza, Sonono. The baby was officially his twentieth child (he had another child with one of his wives later, bringing the number to twenty-one), but persistent rumour has it that there could be several more.

Khoza was furious and felt betrayed by his friend, who was six years older than him. Khoza is a powerful man: a multimillionaire, chairman of the iconic Orlando Pirates soccer club and chairman of the 2010 Soccer World Cup organising committee. Zuma awarded him the Order of Ikhamanga Gold in April 2011.

But Luthuli House was probably even more outraged. They were spending a considerable part of their time and energy in spinning him out of trouble with his legal challenges, luxurious lifestyle, bad decisions and regular embarrassing gaffes, and here he was reinforcing the one thing South Africans loved to talk about behind closed doors, his rampant libido.

After a huge public outcry and a lot of tasteless jokes doing the rounds, Zuma was forced to issue a statement acknowledging the birth of his baby with Sonono Khoza. But instead of admitting his mistake and apologising, he attacked the media and lectured them about the protection of children.

The outcry continued, and Luthuli House noticed. Zuma's office announced that he was taking two days off. Three days after his first statement, he issued another one, this one clearly written for him by Luthuli House. 'The matter, though private, has been a subject of much public discussion and debate,' he said. 'It has put a lot of pressure on my family and my organisation, the ANC. I also acknowledge and understand the reaction of many South Africans. I deeply regret the pain that I have caused to my family, the ANC, the Alliance and South Africans in general.'

The script he was given added: 'I reaffirm my commitment and that of my movement to the importance of the family as an institution. I also reaffirm my commitment and that of my movement to the values of personal responsibility, respect and dignity.'

As I said earlier, I'm not in favour of the media digging into politicians' sex lives. I have learnt in more than three decades in journalism here and abroad that the urge to sleep around is inherent in most male politicians. Political power and conquering women seem to go hand in hand – think of Pierre Trudeau, Bill Clinton, Silvio Berlusconi and Dominique Strauss-Kahn. It was also true of many NP politicians during the last two decades of apartheid rule.

But this was a proper scandal that had to be exposed, and not only because Zuma was once the chief patron of the Moral Regeneration Movement. In a country with close to the highest HIV-infection rate in the world, the government, spearheaded by Zuma himself, was urging citizens not to have multiple sex partners and to use condoms. Yet here he was, the president, having unprotected casual sex with young women – one of whom we know was HIV-positive.

In fact, in his first statement after his baby with Sonono Khoza was born, he said: 'It is mischievous to argue that I have changed or undermined government's stance on the HIV and AIDS campaign. I will not compromise on the campaign. Rather we will intensify our efforts to promote prevention.'

Huh?

In 2012 Zuma told talk-show host Dali Tambo that he was happy that his daughter Duduzile was going to get married 'because I wouldn't want to stay with daughters who are not getting married, because that in itself is a problem in society'. (He added that it was important for women to have children because being a mother gives 'extra training to a woman'.)

In August 2012 Zuma's office released a green paper on families aimed at creating a new dispensation that 'deliberately supports and strengthens families in the country by eliminating all conditions eroding the family'.

Says Adriaan Basson, formerly assistant editor of *City Press* and now editor of *Beeld*: 'While Zuma was preaching conservative family values, newspapers around the country remained on "baby watch" as rumours reached us about more Zuma babies.'

In May 2012 an art exhibition showed a painting by Brett Murray. It featured Zuma in the iconic Lenin pose, but with his genitals exposed, and was called *The Spear*. It was rude and utterly disrespectful, but in my view a legitimate comment.

When *City Press* published a picture of the painting, Luthuli House went mad – their leader's sex life was their biggest headache. ANC secretary-general Gwede Mantashe, spokesperson Jackson Mthembu and SACP leader Blade Nzimande led the hysterical onslaught on Murray, *City Press* and the art gallery that teetered on the brink of mob violence. It was so patently a complete overreaction that it was clear there was another agenda. A boycott of *City Press* was called with the chant from public platforms 'Don't buy *City Press*, don't buy!' It was quickly turned into a race issue.

Here are my notes on the incident:

A lot of noise, smoke and mirrors again this week in our beloved land. But despite the smog of opportunism, expediency, incitement and rabble-rousing, I think we'll one day look back at the Zuma Spear saga as a helpful one in our project of building a stronger democracy.

The three people who will stand judged by history after this week for their recklessness and irresponsibility are President Jacob Zuma himself, ANC secretary-general Gwede Mantashe and SACP leader Blade Nzimande. Not artist Brett Murray, the editor of *City Press* or the owners of the Goodman Gallery.

Mantashe and Nzimande, acting as Zuma's re-election battering rams, took what was at most going to be a debate about satirical art and cynically and with no regard for the consequences turned it into a race war and an assault on all black people's dignity.

What they wanted, I think, was for the nation to talk about something other than Zuma's sexual indiscretions, the shameful protection of another Zuma storm trooper, former SAPS intelligence chief General Richard Mdluli, and other government failures, and to make Zuma the victim once again, a position that previously helped him become president. If you're black and proud, you would rally around Zuma, was the message.

Brett Murray's depiction of the South African president as a fake revolutionary with an open fly was rude, offensive and disrespectful. But there was no racial element in it. If it was relevant that Murray was a white man, then we have to scrutinise his record as an artist to see whether he has been racist during his long career as a creator of satirical art. It would have taken Mantashe and Nzimande, and their Rottweiler Jackson Mthembu, three minutes on Google to establish that he established himself first as an artist viciously attacking apartheid and its leaders in the 1980s.

Of course, once Mantashe, Nzimande and Mthembu had sold the idea that Murray (and those who defended him) were racists and that the painting was meant to offend every black person in the country, it generated a lot of genuine anger and dormant resentment – even calls by a religious leader for Murray to be stoned to death. The more the temperature rose, the more the ANC trio whipped up the frenzy.

It is completely acceptable to disrespect Jacob Zuma, as it is to disrespect Helen Zille or Bantu Holomisa or Terror Lekota. Many people disrespect Zuma, including the ANC Youth League and others wanting him to be replaced at Mangaung. Disrespecting the person doesn't translate in any way into disrespecting the country, our democracy or the nation.

Insulting one politician is in no way equal to insulting the race, culture or language group that politician belongs to. No, an injury to one is not an injury to all. Zille has been insulted often, and in very crude ways, even by senior ANC leaders, but that didn't amount to insults to other white people. Mosiuoa Lekota was called a dog and a snake when he broke away from the ANC.

There were two almost comical incidents during last week's controversy underscoring the absurdity of the event. The first was Mthembu saying on eNCA that the size of the depicted penis was also a very sensitive issue. The second was Zuma complaining in court papers that Murray was painting him as a 'womaniser and philanderer'. Enough said.

Murray's painting of Zuma can never be divorced from the fact that Zuma's sexual antics have often been in the public domain, more so than any politician's in living memory. It would be unthinkable for Murray to have painted any of Zuma's predecessors or other politicians in this way.

We are a very conservative society, white and black, and I suspect most would not agree with the depiction of a phallus in public art – just as most citizens are probably against gay marriages and abortion and for the death penalty. But this is where responsible political leadership should come in and give guidance on what is principle and what is constitutional. In this, the ANC failed miserably.

I don't think the ploy by Zuma and his lieutenants worked. The best minds in the ANC itself, including the cabinet, think the campaign and boycotts were wrong and irresponsible. Most black intellectuals expressed their discomfort with the Zuma/Mantashe/Nzimande propaganda war. *City Press* received a strong surge in its circulation because of the call for it to be boycotted. And Zuma's public image didn't improve one iota; it probably took a further dive.

But we've learnt some good lessons here about who we are as a nation, what makes us angry and what leaders should and shouldn't do. White South Africans have hopefully taken proper notice of how raw their black compatriots' emotions and memories still are. And even the most ignorant among us now know that there is something like satirical art.

The rocky road to Mangaung

In 2012 Zuma was faced with the reality of a new ANC congress, where leaders would be elected, at the end of the year. Although he was on record four years earlier saying that he would not be interested in a second term, it was now clear that being re-elected was crucial if he wanted to stay out of jail and continue to enjoy his lavish lifestyle and that of his family and clan.

An ANC insider told me that he had attended a meeting of the Zuma clan – brothers, uncles, cousins – where it was decided that Zuma would not be allowed to drop out of the race for the presidency of the ANC at Mangaung in December 2012 because the clan needed another term to accumulate more wealth and power. I have no way of corroborating this information, but I do trust my informant and I know how close he was to the ANC inner circle.

Despite Zuma's popularity at Polokwane, his re-election was far from a done deal. Unhappiness about his messy private life, the enrichment of his family and clan, his suspect relationship with the Gupta family, the rise of corruption and tenderpreneurship, and the increasing likelihood that his criminal charges wouldn't just go away as thought earlier were just part of the reason.

There was a deeper cause for the growing discontent in the ANC alliance. Polokwane was seen as a move to the left, a shift towards a greater focus on economic transformation and an improved life for the poor. That shift didn't happen. A deep anger among the dispossessed in the townships and squatter camps was evidence that the post-Mbeki ANC was simply doing business as usual.

Some of his most committed supporters during the Polokwane period, such as COSATU general secretary Zwelinzima Vavi and ANC Youth League leader Julius Malema, started openly criticising Zuma's leadership. Vavi was the one who coined the phrase 'Zunami' and Malema famously said he was prepared to 'kill for Zuma'. Vavi now said things like: 'We are heading rapidly in the direction of a full-blown predator state in which a powerful, corrupt and demagogic elite of political hyenas increasingly controls the state as a vehicle for accumulation.'

Malema and Vavi would pay dearly for their criticism.

The black middle classes and educated elite were also becoming visibly critical of Zuma and his weak leadership, and black journalists and commentators said harsh things about him.

Struggle veterans too started voicing their discomfort publicly. For instance, Rivonia trialist Andrew Mlangeni, who spent twenty-six years in jail with Mandela, said in an interview that the Rivonia accused did not go to jail so that ANC leaders could reap the rewards of freedom through self-enrichment and greed. 'You put people into leading positions in government because you know them to be trustworthy. You know that they are going to carry out the policy of the ANC of helping the people of South Africa. They start off being good people, but ultimately they change and start filling their pockets with money through these tenders. Tenderism [sic] has destroyed many of our honest people.'

One of the ANC's foremost intellectuals and former head of the policy and coordination advisory unit in the presidency, Joel Netshitenzhe, said in the 2012 Harold Wolpe Lecture that failure to organise itself into an effective instrument of rapid growth and development will lead to the state becoming irrelevant, rejected as a mere dispenser of patronage, 'mocked as an instrument of pork-barrel regional and ethnic delivery', and 'attacked as a defender of super-exploitation'. He criticised the lack of a coherent economic policy and an indecisiveness when it came to taking hard decisions.

But it was young Julius Malema who posed the biggest public threat to Zuma, the man who once called the Youth League firebrand 'the next president of South Africa'. Zuma sat back and allowed 'Juju' to accumulate tremendous wealth through his political connections, insult and threaten minorities and opponents of the ANC, and successfully dominate the front pages and television screens with his militant talk of nationalisation and land invasion. The reckless but very clever young populist redefined the public discourse and dragged the hitherto fairly decent political culture in the country to unknown depths. He let a genie out of the bottle that we'll probably never get back in again.

Malema's antics suited Zuma. He was Zuma's strongest supporter, after all, and here he was galvanising the support of the youth and the marginalised while at the same time diverting attention away from the Zuma administration's failures.

The editor of the *Sunday Times*, Phylicia Oppelt, wrote in September 2012: 'If anyone is to be held accountable for encouraging the rise of Malema and his cohorts, it is the president. And if there is anyone to whom blame must be assigned for what journalist Kerry Cullinan describes as the "misogynist, racist, nationalist, populist fraud" that is Malema, then it is Zuma ... The confidence that Malema displays, the relentless picking of the festering wounds of the poor, the militancy, the insults and taunts habitually flung at his former mentor – all these can be largely blamed on Zuma.'

Of course it had to end in acrimony. Malema became more and more frustrated that Zuma refused to support his siren call for nationalisation, always downplaying it as simply a young man's views. Malema was furious when he found out that his private financial affairs were being investigated – he thought his dominance of the media meant that he was virtually untouchable – and he became increasingly critical of Zuma. (Mandy Rossouw said: 'His aides tell of how he never actually read the newspapers himself, but unfailingly every day asked, "Where are we in the newspapers?" Nothing made him happier than being the centre of attention.')

Malema embarrassed the government and most South Africans when his tirade at a BBC journalist, Jonah Fisher, who was attending a press conference in Luthuli House, was broadcast to the world. Fisher dared to ask Malema how his lavish lifestyle correlated with his calls for economic empowerment and his championing of the poor. Malema chased him out of the room, calling him a 'bloody agent' and a 'boy' with 'rubbish in his pants'.

But Malema's cardinal sin was when he compared Zuma unfavourably with Mbeki. On top of that, he proclaimed his support for Robert Mugabe while Zuma was the mediator between ZANU-PF and the Movement for Democratic Change, and announced that the Youth League would actively work towards the overthrow of the Botswana government.

Malema was hauled before disciplinary hearings. On 25 April 2012 he lost his last appeal to have his expulsion from the ANC overturned and his expulsion took immediate effect. In September 2012 he was charged with fraud and money laundering.

Malema became so arrogant and power-drunk that he made the fatal mistake of crossing the man once in charge of the ANC's security machinery, the man who smiles in your face while causing you harm.

The June 2012 policy conference of the ANC at Gallagher Estate in Midrand was a prelude to the elective conference at Mangaung six months later. Zuma was getting nervous about the possibility that his deputy was going to challenge him for the presidency.

Zuma saw the conference as an opportunity to bolster his image as a man of change and made his rallying call 'the second transition' – 'the first transition' obviously referring to the start of democracy in 1994. He thought it would send the message that his second term would see a meaningful shift towards pro-poor policies and actions, a new beginning after the disappointing performance of the ANC governments since 1994. He was reading the signs of the time.

But few were buying it. Deputy President Kgalema Motlanthe asked: 'From when to when is the second transition? And when did the first one end?'

Zuma's opening speech was full of revolutionary bluster around land reform and ownership of the economy. But the divisions in the ANC soon became clear. The idea of a second transition, from which Zuma now tried to distance himself, and the issue of the nationalisation of mines, which he had conveniently allowed to dominate the discourse for two years, were debated with much heat and passion, to the point that fist fights broke out in the queue at the microphone.

Zuma quickly left the room and came back when order was restored. Another ugly confrontation was avoided when Motlanthe took a walk through the exhibition centre and a large group of Zuma supporters, singing pro-Zuma songs and showing two fingers, signalling a second term for Zuma, almost confronted him. He ducked and they passed, but outside supporters of the two men were engaged in a sing-off. It was shades of Polokwane.

It was clear from the press conference at the end of the policy conference that there would be no jump to the left, despite the rhetoric. It was a complete damp squib.

The ANC regions then started nominating their candidates for Mangaung. When it became clear to the Zuma camp that Motlanthe was going to oppose Zuma, they formally offered him the position of deputy president on their slate. He declined, saying he had to respect the branches that had chosen him. 'I do not want any backroom arrangement,' he was reported to have said. The powerful Johannesburg region of the ANC was one of those that nominated Motlanthe – one of the leaders there told the *Sunday Independent* that they thought Zuma had displayed 'scandalous, embarrassing' leadership during his first term and was 'unfit' to lead.

There were many reports of manipulation, vote rigging and money changing hands during the nomination process, and two court cases ensued. An ANC Youth League leader told the *Mail & Guardian*: 'The behaviour of comrades in this campaign has been characterised by money, be it in the JZ or Motlanthe camps. Others are getting money as individuals and others as a group or factions. The money is thrown around at big parties with scantily clad women, first-class commercial flights and fancy German cars. The difference is that the JZ camp is also using state resources while Motlanthe's people are using money from private individuals.'

But in the end, Motlanthe hardly fought a campaign, while Zuma's team, which included SACP leader Blade Nzimande, COSATU president Sdumo Dlamini and at least five cabinet ministers, worked the branches and the regions. Their message was a strong one: Polokwane had torn the ANC apart and created COPE. It was now time for unity and for the ANC to consolidate, not for new candidates with ambitions.

But the stroke of genius was to propose the charismatic Cyril Ramaphosa as Zuma's running mate. He had been out of politics for sixteen years and was thus untainted by the infighting, although he remained active in the ANC. He was the head of the disciplinary appeals committee that finally expelled Malema from the ANC. Importantly, Ramaphosa was first proposed by the ANC's strongest province, KwaZulu-Natal.

People were reminded that Ramaphosa was the man who had built the National Union of Mineworkers; that he was instrumental in the formation of COSATU; that he was the man standing next to Nelson Mandela when Mandela made his first speech after his release; that he was the one who had outmanoeuvred F.W. de Klerk and Roelf Meyer during the negotiations; and that he was the chairman of the constituent assembly that gave South Africa its Constitution in 1996.

Ramaphosa was a *rara avis* in the ANC top ranks: his private life was clean and he had never been accused of any corrupt deals or tenders. On top of that, he was one of the few BEE beneficiaries that had actually grown his business, so he had proved his managerial skills.

Motlanthe didn't have an exciting, fresh name like that. He just had politicians on his slate who had been part of the infighting for years, people such as Tokyo Sexwale and Mathews Phosa.

If critics of the ANC had hoped for yet another chaotic conference at Mangaung along the lines of Polokwane or the earlier Esselen Park policy conference, they were deeply disappointed. The rabble-rousers of the Youth League were not seen or heard. It was an orderly, disciplined and, by all standards, successful conference. Part of the reason was probably that the Motlanthe supporters didn't behave like the Zuma supporters had at Polokwane.

In the end the Zuma–Ramaphosa slate won overwhelmingly. This was probably more a mandate for continuity and unity, and for people like Ramaphosa, Mantashe and treasurer Zweli Mkhize, than a mandate for Zuma himself.

Zuma was magnanimous in his acceptance speech, warning that the election shouldn't divide the ANC. He kept Motlanthe as deputy president of the country, although he purged or sidelined many of his other opponents during the months that followed.

Mangaung was completely dominated by the leadership election, which took attention away from some other important decisions that were made there. Large-scale nationalisation was finally taken off the table as a policy option, and the National Development Plan was accepted as the ANC's official plan for growth and development in the period up to 2030.

Ramaphosa's election made a lot of sceptics think again about abandoning the ANC. Says *City Press* editor Ferial Haffajee: 'He is gloss and credibility for the party, and he helped bring the business sector back into the national fold of citizenship – from the confused and marginal space it has occupied for the past five years.'

One commentator who didn't buy the version that the ANC had 'self-corrected' and 'restored its soul' at Mangaung was Mondli Makhanya, commentator and former editor. Writing shortly after the conference, he said: 'Most leaders who go for re-election with the stench and baggage that Zuma carried into Mangaung would be assured of a lynching by the party faithful. But those are not the ways of this post-Polokwane ANC. Whatever wild spirits were released in Polokwane are now the defining character of the party. There is no going back.'

I think events since then have proved Makhanya correct.

He continued: 'The culture of the organisation is set by its leader and the members have clearly said they like Zuma the way he is and they want to be like him. A cult of personality has developed around Zuma and it has been expediently encouraged by party mandarins whose political futures depend on him. Ramaphosa and the band of reasonable men and women in the NEC will find it hard going in a structure loaded with worshippers, some of them very dodgy ... South Africa should brace itself for life under an ANC that will be impervious to public opinion and obsessively protective of its president.'

I find it hard to disagree with Makhanya. But two scandals unfolding in 2013 could mean that the Zuma cult is no longer as unshakeable as he had thought: Nkandla and Guptagate. And, of course, the aftermath of the Marikana massacre.

Manor, villa or compound?

As president, Zuma has the use of three official residences: Groote Schuur in Cape Town, Mahlamba Ndlopfu in Pretoria and Dr John L. Dube House in Durban, all fit for any president of any country.

Most presidents also have a private residence that they can retire to or use to maintain a presence in their home region. Zuma's is Nkandla in rural KwaZulu-Natal.

But other presidents of democracies pay for their own private houses, apart from perhaps limited security measures. Not Zuma. His Nkandla home will most likely end up costing the South African taxpayer well over R200 million. And he gets to keep it when he is no longer president.

When pushed during a debate in Parliament, a visibly angry Zuma said: 'There are two different things: my homes that are built by me and my family, and the security features that the government wanted. These are matters that the government ... don't ask me, don't ask me.'

But he didn't tell Parliament that the state was also paying millions for air conditioning, elevators, fire-fighting equipment, landscaping (R14.3 million), a tree nursery, houses and two AstroTurf soccer fields for security guards, an underground bunker, a hospital complex, roads, a helipad and a tuck shop for his wife MaKhumalo. Oh, and a cattle kraal that cost more than R1 million.

All these developments will cost him and his family (or his benefactors from the business sector) only about R10 million.

When Zuma said he didn't know what the state was going to build for him or how his estate was going to be 'secured', he was not being truthful. Documents obtained by the *Mail & Guardian* show that he was consulted or gave instructions on many occasions during the construction work – these documents referred to him as 'the principal'. In any case, Zuma spent many weekends at Nkandla while some of the construction was still ongoing. (On most weekends, he flies to Durban and is then transported by police or air-force helicopter, often two helicopters, to Nkandla.)

Government's first reaction to queries from the media and the opposition was that Nkandla was a national key point and that the documentation was classified. An investigation was launched into possible irregularities in the tendering process and invoicing by contractors. Its findings have not been made public.

On the day in July 2013 when they published some of the Nkandla documents that they were given after a Promotion of Access to Information Act application, the *Mail & Guardian* wrote: 'What we have been able to obtain … demonstrates how an administrative culture of grovelling sycophancy has grown up around Zuma, and that this culture is responsible for ballooning costs, unjustified secrecy, and spending decisions that bear no relation to rationality or to the regulations surrounding presidential perks. There is one person responsible for this Big Man culture, and that is the man at its centre. If the criminal justice system can be made to serve at his pleasure, after all, with acting bosses who survive on sufferance, what is it to reach into the public purse for the building of a country house?'

Professor Njabulo Ndebele was one of those asking the hard questions about Nkandla. 'Nkandla is carving its place in our history as a major test of a people's character,' he wrote in an opinion piece. 'Few things in recent times will test the capacity of the people of South Africa to honour the truth. Public and private institutions all face the test. The highest tree in the land, the president of the republic and head of state, is at the centre of it all. Will he, his government and the Parliament his party numerically dominates give the truth a place of honour? Or will they honour the lie?' He concluded: 'Nkandla manifests an advanced stage in the systemic nature of corruption in South Africa that has been growing over an eighteen-year period and gathered momentum in the past five years. It presents all South Africans with a slippery slope they can descend in anguish, or climb with hope.'

Nkandla is a real scandal in the eyes of most South Africans, not just opponents of the ANC. Spending so much state money on such luxury at one man's private home while millions live in shacks and hardly have food to eat is outrageous in anyone's book. Not even the men and women in Luthuli House are trying to justify it.

This is the kind of thing corrupt dictators like Zaire's Mobutu Sese Seko and Ivory Coast's Félix Houphouët-Boigny did. It is completely alien to South Africa.

At the time of writing there was still a chance that Public Protector Thuli Madonsela would be given enough access to the secret documentation to make a credible finding on Nkandla.

Weddings for pals

Another scandal that severely tainted Zuma's reputation among most South Africans was the way his Gupta friends treated South Africa as their own private fiefdom when they illegally used Air Force Base Waterkloof to land a plane full of wedding guests from India and then had them transported in blue-light convoys to Sun City in April 2013.

These are my notes at the time:

> The last time South African cabinet ministers lined up to solemnly declare 'I didn't know' and then watched civil servants take the rap was when F.W. de Klerk, Magnus Malan and Adriaan Vlok appeared before the Truth and Reconciliation Commission in 1997.

> I didn't believe De Klerk and Co. then and I don't believe Jacob Zuma, Jeff Radebe, Maite Nkoana-Mashabane, Siyabonga Cwele and Nosiviwe Mapisa-Nqakula when they feign outrage at the insult to our national pride that was the Gupta wedding plane flying into our top air-force base.

> These politicians had known for months that the Gupta wedding was going to take place and that it was going to be a grand affair – they were, after all, invited to attend as guests of honour. They had all been dined and wined by the Gupta family on many occasions.

> They, or at least Nkoana-Mashabane (international relations), Mapisa-Nqakula (defence) and Cwele (state security), knew early in February that the Guptas had applied for special landing rights for their plane full of guests in South Africa. The ministers had denied these requests, says Radebe.

> So what did they think was going to happen next, one wonders. That the Gupta guests were going to come by ship? That the wedding was going to be cancelled? Surely as invitees they would have been told?

> Zuma himself, as well as his wives, his son and his cousin, both in business with the Guptas, had all accepted invitations to the Sun City wedding.

> Then, according to Radebe, there followed a secret conspiracy between the Indian high commissioner, the head of protocol of Nkoana-Mashabane's department and a senior officer in Mapisa-Nqakula's department to wangle permission anyway to land at Air Force Base Waterkloof.

A large number of other officials from home affairs, the defence force and the police, 194 people according to Radebe, were drawn into the conspiracy that was concocted over weeks.

And yet not one of the ministers or Zuma himself, not even Cwele as minister of state security, got wind of it. What is it that state security does, then?

A plane full of civilians and a number of private helicopters were breaking every rule in the book by landing at an air-force base, and dozens of policemen and traffic officers took time off to take them to Sun City in convoy – and it remained a secret right until after they landed and a journalist got wind of it? Not agents of the National Intelligence Agency, crime intelligence or military intelligence. No, a news reporter.

Not one of the 194 officials and officers (or the 296 private-security people) involved in the conspiracy ever said a word to any of their superiors? Not even the dozens of customs officials who had to check the guests' passports? Not a single one of all these people told their colleagues or friends or wives or husbands about their involvement in the celebrity wedding of the year?

Yes, this is what Radebe and Co. wants us to believe. Two hundred foreigners fly into South Africa's main air-force base and get a friendly reception from many dozens of officials and no one in state security or intelligence got wind of it until after the fact, is what they're saying.

They also appear to want us to believe that the two central figures in the conspiracy, an air-force colonel and the head of protocol, thought they would get away with their dirty secret.

That follows, doesn't it? Or could it be that these two senior career civil servants thought they were simply doing the right thing, that what they were doing was what the president and the government wanted? That they would have been stopped if that wasn't the case?

There was a lot of name-dropping, says Radebe, Zuma's name among them. And that explains it all.

When the news about the plane and the blue-light brigade leaked out, it provoked national outrage, even from Luthuli House. And yet several cabinet ministers and several members of the Zuma clan attended the wedding days after they realised that the people of South Africa regarded the event as a national insult.

Despite all the smoke and mirrors, the simple, undeniable truth is that Zuma is at the heart of Guptagate and he should be the one facing Parliament this week.

Cwele should stand right next to him. Not only because he says his many hundreds of spooks knew nothing of this affair, but also because he stopped an earlier investigation into the Gupta family and fired senior people who had instituted it, clearly only to protect Zuma's and his clan's interests.

Richard Nixon did not have to resign because of what happened at the Watergate office complex, but because of the way he lied to cover it up.

During the investigation into the incident, the chief of protocol, Bruce Koloane, admitted to telling the officials at Waterkloof that 'Number One' wanted the Gupta plane to land there. But, he said, he didn't actually get the order from Number One himself. He was demoted and sent back to work.

The military officers at the base were hauled before a military board of inquiry where Lieutenant Colonel Christine Anderson, Waterkloof's movement control officer, said Koloane had explicitly told her that Zuma had been aware of the plan and had personally inquired about progress before the wedding. Emails from the base commander suggested that seven helicopters carrying some of the Gupta guests had been authorised to fly from Waterkloof because the 'Indian delegation' was to meet 'No. 1' at Sun City. The tribunal had not made a finding at the time of writing.

Zuma afterwards denied any involvement in getting permission for the plane to land at a key air-force base and condemned 'the practice of using his name and that of cabinet ministers to secure privileges or flout government procedures'.

ANC heavyweight and former cabinet minister Pallo Jordan wrote:

No one is questioning the president's right to choose his friends. In that respect, African National Congress secretary-general Gwede Mantashe is correct. President Jacob Zuma, like the rest of us, has the untrammelled right to choose his own friends. But, just as mention of a name can suggest approval, another name might invite disapprobation. (If one associates with X, then one must share the same character flaws.)

A private citizen's associates might be of no significance beyond the individual and his family, but those of a head of state are of great relevance to the nation. The friends a person chooses are both matters of taste and of judgement. If the actions of your friends suggest a lack of respect for you and a tendency to abuse your name, we would not be remiss in questioning your own judgement.

Until all the questions about this humiliating incident are adequately answered, the Gupta jet incident will corrode Zuma's credibility, leaving serious questions about his judgement.

Ironically, Nkandla and Guptagate probably undermined Zuma's standing in society and in the ANC more than his alleged corrupt relationship with Schabir Shaik.

Can the ANC afford for him to be president for five more years after 2014? More importantly, can South Africa afford it?

It could have been very different. When Zuma became president in 2009, he must have known, like most South Africans knew, that the one crisis that needed fixing, and fast, was the education of South Africa's black youth. If he had committed himself to that and had some success, history would have remembered him as the president who saved the youth instead of the president who tried to stay out of jail.

PART II
The big issues

8

An undeclared war
on our own children

Primary and high school education has without doubt been democratic South Africa's greatest and most depressing failure and the brightest flashing red light.

If there is indeed a time bomb ticking and about to blast South Africa into a new era of instability, it has been made by our disastrous education system.

We have been dumping hundreds of thousands of black youngsters who have failed to reach matric and who have little hope of ever finding a meaningful job or a rewarding, dignified life into the townships and squatter camps every year for decades.

Some 745 000, or almost two-thirds, of pupils who enrolled in Grade 1 as six-year-olds, the first so-called Born Frees to go to school, either did not make it to or did not pass their matric exams in 2012.

Twenty years of disastrous education in mainly black schools have fundamentally undermined any possibility of significantly improving the persistent, growing racial inequality in the country.

According to Statistics South Africa, 76 per cent of whites aged twenty and older had completed Grade 12 by 2011, compared to 31 per cent of blacks, 35 per cent of coloureds and 64 per cent of Indian South Africans.

Almost all white youngsters attend what are known as 'former Model C schools' (schools in the areas formerly reserved for whites) or expensive private schools. Almost all of these schools are functioning well and many have standards of education on a par with the best in the world. But more than eight out of ten schools in townships, squatter camps and traditional rural areas are dysfunctional.

Formerly white Model C schools produce about half of all graduates, despite the fact that the vast majority of pupils go to black schools.

Those youngsters who do make it to university are ill-prepared for tertiary education. Some 45 per cent of students at universities and 66 per cent

---

Former Model C schools

- By far the majority of the top-performing schools in South Africa are the 5145 'Model C schools' in the former white suburbs. They make up 20.8 per cent of all state schools and have more than 2.4 million pupils, 56 per cent of whom are black.
- Parents contribute more than R10 billion in school fees, paying for about 37 000 additional teachers.
- Almost 97 per cent of the pupils at General Smuts High School in Vereeniging, a former Afrikaans Model C school, are black Africans. Smuts outperforms many, mostly white, Model C schools.

---

at universities of technology leave before graduating. Business studies are a clear indication of the inequality: only 33 per cent of black students graduate within five years, while 83 per cent of white students do.

The reality is ugly. 'A third of Grade 6 students are functionally illiterate; they cannot read a simple paragraph and extract meaning from it. Forty per cent of Grade 6 students are functionally innumerate,' says Nicholas Spaull, a much-published specialist in education research at Stellenbosch University.

Spaull: 'I can go on for ages about the shocking statistics emerging from many local and international assessments. The pieces of evidence together reveal the predicament we are in – there is an ongoing crisis in the quality of education in South Africa, yet few people are willing to treat it as such.'

The various assessment figures for learner competency are skewed because the top 20 per cent of schools do really well and push the figures up. The figures for the bottom 50 per cent are much, much worse.

Almost all white kids going into Grade 1 have already spent a year or more in a preparatory school or kindergarten. Most black kids do not have this kick-start to primary school, although this is improving. Very few white youngsters go to school hungry or suffer from malnutrition. Many black youngsters do.

How are the black youngsters supposed to compete with their white counterparts in the job market? It simply entrenches further inequality and fuels more black anger and frustration.

Most South Africans, excluding only the white right wing, support sensible affirmative action to correct the imbalances caused by apartheid measures. If we do not drastically improve the education we provide to black youngsters, we will soon run out of young black people with basic numeracy and literacy skills to fill affirmative-action positions.

Education by the numbers

- Despite the fact that South Africa spends 6 per cent of our much bigger GDP on education, R234 billion (20 per cent of total government spending), we have had the worst performance of all sub-Saharan African countries in science and mathematics.
- There are nearly 400 000 teachers in South Africa.
- There are roughly twelve million pupils attending 27 000 schools.
- About half of South Africans are under the age of twenty-five and a third are under fifteen.
- Today, 20.8 per cent of whites have a tertiary qualification, compared with 2.9 per cent of blacks (1.7 in 2002), 4 per cent of coloureds (1.8 per cent) and 11.8 percent of Indians (7.7 percent).

The doors of learning and culture shall be opened?

A good education for our black youth, the children of those who were oppressed and held back by apartheid, was supposed to be our first democratic government's top priority. Producing educated, self-assured and competent young people with good job prospects is clearly the surest way to fulfil the dream of complete liberation of the people of South Africa; it is the obvious way in difficult economic times to ensure a dignified and fulfilling life for new generations and to build a successful, progressive society.

The Freedom Charter of 1955, the professed lodestar of the ANC and its allies COSATU and the SACP, declares under the heading 'The doors of learning and culture shall be opened!': 'Education should be free, compulsory, universal and equal for all children.' The preamble to our Constitution states that we, the people, shall 'improve the quality of life of all citizens and free the potential of each person'. The right to education is part of the Constitution's Bill of Rights.

More than white intransigence or 'white monopoly capital' could ever have done, our education system has been perpetuating apartheid. The children of the white middle and upper classes still get a good education and go

---

No Rights Day

12 March 2013. While South Africa celebrates Human Rights Month, Eastern Cape education MEC Mandla Makupula tells hundreds of students at the Bhisho legislature that they are not entitled to any rights: 'For you, rights come later in life when you are independent, finished studying and have your own place to stay and your own car. That's when you can start talking about rights.'

---

on to have good careers. The education we have given black children since 1994 is close to the worst in the entire world.

The United Nations Educational, Scientific and Cultural Organization (UNESCO) Education for All Campaign says better learning outcomes 'are closely related to higher earnings in the labour market; thus, differences in quality are likely to indicate differences in individual worker productivity'. The impact of education quality appears to be stronger for workers in developing countries compared to those in industrialised societies.

'Empirical research has also demonstrated that good schooling improves national economic potential – the quality of the labour force, as measured by test scores, appears to be an important determinant of economic growth, and thus of the ability of governments to alleviate poverty,' UNESCO says.

Educationist Graeme Bloch, who was banned and detained several times as a UDF and education activist in the 1980s, says in his book *The Toxic Mix: What's Wrong with South Africa's Schools and How to Fix It*: 'If we fixed our schools, education could contribute far more to build a shared citizenship, a respect for diversity, a tolerance for each other and for a range of views and customs.' He says most children find that the education system fails and penalises them 'and almost rationalises their ongoing exclusion from the fruits of democracy and change. Education seems to reinforce inequality and shuts children out rather than being inclusive in its aspirations and effect.'

Nick Taylor, research fellow at the NGO JET Education Services (quoted by Bloch), says: 'Hundreds of thousands of our children leave our schools every year without the foundation skills needed to benefit from further education or to secure anything but the most menial jobs. More disturbing is that dysfunctional schools are unable to socialise young people into the attitudes of mind required for citizenship in a democracy … school leavers are easy prey to a life of crime, poverty, corruption and inefficiency.' And there you have most of the ills of our society.

Businesswoman and former vice-chancellor of UCT Mamphela Ramphele told a conference on education just days before she launched her new political party, Agang, in June 2013: 'Our country is at a crossroads: the government's mismanagement of our education system is robbing our youth of their rightful future as well as handicapping the prospects of our country ... We have a second-class system that accepts second-rate results – 30 per cent or 40 per cent is not a pass. No one wants a nurse, teacher or plumber who only knows 40 per cent of the requirements in the field.

'What dismays me is that these falling standards are not caused by a failure of policy and it isn't down to a lack of spending on education in South Africa. It is a failure of political will to live the values of human dignity, equality and true freedom for all in our beloved country.'

The Department of Basic Education hit back in a statement a few days later, accusing her of 'reckless and desperate cheap politicking' and 'unfounded rants'. 'We have uplifted our people from disadvantaged communities more than she can ever imagine,' it stated.

The statement then mentioned the department's achievements: over eight million children from poor communities in more than 82 per cent of public schools now receive free education in no-fees schools. Many learners benefit from the more than R5 billion put into the National School Nutrition Programme. The number of learners who achieved university exemption almost doubled over the last twelve years, it said.

The department also uses the improvement in matric results as proof of progress. On the surface, these do look good: the national pass rate improved from 60.6 per cent in 2009 to 70.2 per cent in 2011 and 73.9 per cent in 2012.

But this is a problematic barometer of improvement. It reflects only those pupils who wrote the exams and not those who dropped out. As Spaull explains: 'The matric pass rate is calculated as a percentage of students that are enrolled in Grade 12. Most drop-out takes place between Grade 10 and Grade 12. The students are pushed through the system until Grade 10, and then schools realise that if they put these kids through, they are not going to pass Grade 12. The evidence suggests that the problems are rooted in primary school, but because there are no matric-type exams in primary school, they proceeded to higher grades. Getting low pass rates in matric is problematic for schools, so they weed out these students. If you only look at half of a cohort, those passing matric, to see if the quality of education is improving or deteriorating over time, there is no indication of how the other 50 per cent is doing.'

Spaull adds that another factor that makes a comparison of annual pass rates problematic is that pupils are choosing easier subjects. For instance, in 2009, 51 per cent of pupils took maths and 49 per cent the much easier maths literacy, but in 2012, 44 per cent of pupils who passed took maths and 56 per cent maths literacy. NGO Equal Education's Doron Isaacs agrees: 'The pass rate can go up because there is a genuine improvement, or because there is a shift of students out of physical science and into easier subjects like business studies or tourism or consumer studies.'

'Slow learners'

The minister of basic education's admission in Parliament that a passing standard of 30 per cent for subjects in the National Senior Certificate was applied created quite an uproar. She explained that it allowed 'slow learners' to exit the system with dignity.

One of the great heroes of education in South Africa, Free State University rector Jonathan Jansen, was one of those outraged. Referring to past intellectuals/activists like Steve Biko and Neville Alexander, he said he 'wondered how their restless spirits must be choking when they hear this kind of utterance by an irresponsible and reckless class of politicians. These educated activists all agitated for the black child, and they would say there is no connection between a 30 per cent pass and human dignity. They would argue, no doubt, that providing a high-quality education to the first generation of high school graduates not to live under apartheid was in fact a sacred commitment of that long and costly struggle for freedom ... To call them "slow learners" is an insult for they faced two problems: one is poor educational inputs in their twelve years of schooling (poor teaching, lack of textbooks, limited instruction time, and more) and another is the low expectations by the officials serving them. Thirty per cent does not offer dignity; it offers a dead-end street to the children of the poor – no job, no further education, no skills. It is, in fact, a massive indignity being suffered.'

At a loss for an explanation as to why the ANC government has neglected and mismanaged education so badly since 1994, several commentators have wondered out loud whether the ANC actually wants to keep the population uneducated so they won't end up doing what Zimbabwe's well-educated people did: they started standing up to the ruling party.

Of course this is complete nonsense. The explanation for the state of school education in South Africa is much more complex: the legacy of a fractured and neglected system inherited from the apartheid era; gross bureaucratic incompetence and corruption; badly trained teachers; lazy and irresponsible teachers protected by their politically connected trade union; terrible curriculum mistakes; cadre deployment; the sudden loss of a large number of experienced (mostly white) teachers; the scrapping of the system of school inspectors; many black pupils' poor circumstances at home; and lack of parent participation in school affairs.

In fact, I feel confident in stating that the main reason why most South Africans feel that our education system is failing is because success or failure can actually be measured easily through pass rates and numeracy and literacy tests. The way government has been handling education is probably not worse than the performance of most other departments, but most other departments' success or failure can't be so easily measured and compared – think of foreign affairs, defence, sport, culture, trade and industry, justice, energy, and so on.

And South Africans are angrier about mismanaged education because it involves children, especially the children of the former victims of apartheid, and thus our nation's future prospects for stability, growth and development.

We have had quite a few truly incompetent members of cabinet since 1994, but, curiously, our education ministers were not among them: Sibusiso Bengu, Kader Asmal, Naledi Pandor and Angie Motshekga. The explanation is twofold. The first is that education is primarily run by the provincial governments and, with the exception of Gauteng and the Western Cape (and to some degree KwaZulu-Natal), they have been national disasters.

The second explanation is that these national cabinet ministers, being members of the ANC leadership, did not have the political freedom to do what they knew would save the education system. They were restricted by the ANC's partnership with the trade-union movement, COSATU; by the incessant power struggles in the ANC; by the influence some provincial leaders have in Luthuli House (ANC headquarters); and by a lack of vision and strong leadership in the party and the presidency.

It's not about the money

We do know for sure that state spending on education is not the problem. From 2010/2011 onwards, education was the largest single line item in the budget: 20 per cent, about 6 per cent of GDP. This is significantly higher than in any other African state and a whole lot more than in some countries that consistently outperform South African pupils.

The apartheid-era pattern of spending more on white than on black pupils was reversed in 1994 and now more is spent on schools in poor communities. Professor of economics at Stellenbosch University and South African National Research Chair in the Economics of Social Policy Servaas van der Berg says almost half of the education spending on salaries went to the poorest 40 per cent of communities. Non-salary spending on the poorest 20 per cent of schools was about six times higher than on the richest 20 per cent. According to Spaull, by 2011 struggling Limpopo province had the highest public expenditure per pupil in the country. (It should always be kept in mind, though, that schools in wealthier communities, especially former Model C schools, augment their budgets through higher school fees.)

In May 2013 the National Education Evaluation and Development Unit (NEEDU) released a telling report called 'The State of Literacy Teaching and Learning in the Foundation Phase', painting a very bleak picture. (The foundation phase is Grades 1 to 3.)

It came to the conclusion that too many teachers cannot teach and many don't make much effort to do so. This conclusion was supported by the results of a test conducted by the Southern and Eastern Africa Consortium for Monitoring Educational Quality: more than half of Grade 6 teachers failed a Grade 6 language and mathematics test. They lacked pedagogical teaching skills and an understanding of the broader curriculum. It also identified latecoming and absenteeism of teachers and pupils as additional problems.

This topic always gets DA leader and Western Cape premier Helen Zille, a passionate educationist herself, going. Referring to the NEEDU report, she said: 'Most educational experts have known this for a long time, but the government has been in denial because most of South Africa's under-performing teachers belong to the South African Democratic Teachers Union (SADTU), one of the largest COSATU affiliates and a pillar of support to President Jacob Zuma and in his battle against Zwelinzima Vavi.

'Confronting South Africa's education crisis requires the political will to face down SADTU. The NEEDU report is path-breaking because it confronts this issue head-on. It names the elephant in the room. It highlights how SADTU has paralysed education in some provinces, particularly in the Eastern Cape and Limpopo, and is responsible for the poor discipline and the widespread collusion and nepotism in the recruitment and promotion of staff in the schools it "controls" ... The question that arises is whether the government will now have the courage to act on the report's recommendations and implement measures, like merit-based appointments and competency testing, which SADTU opposes.'

SADTU, COSATU and some elements in the ANC have angrily accused Zille of racism because of her criticism of the teachers union.

When the government announced its intentions to declare education an essential service, meaning industrial action would be severely curtailed, COSATU forced it to back down.

In March 2012 basic education minister Angie Motshekga told Parliament that teachers were absent for a national average of nineteen days a year, the highest in the southern African region. This amounts to a full month of teaching days in a year that already has four school holidays of roughly ten weeks in total.

Motshekga plans to install fingerprint machines in schools to monitor teachers' attendance, but SADTU is opposing the move, saying it will 'deprofessionalise' teachers.

I have a family member who is a teacher at a huge township school. She tells shocking tales of teacher absenteeism. She once was left with one other teacher running the entire school of seven hundred pupils while other teachers took days off to go to the funeral of a colleague's spouse. All the teachers were SADTU members.

SADTU is most ordinary South Africans' pet hate. For years they have built a reputation as a reckless bunch with concern for their pupils low on their agenda. Time and again they have chosen to go on strike or launch protest action just before important school exams, even the crucial Grade 12 finals.

Take the case of Ronald Nyathi, spokesperson of SADTU in Gauteng. In 2008 he defended teachers guilty of having sex with pupils, saying the department had not run workshops on the topic. Shortly afterwards, when Alexandra pupils complained about teacher absenteeism and child abuse, he led a strike by teachers and threatened the pupils with violence if they went to school. In 2009 he warned the minister that schools would remain unstable until Jacob Zuma was elected president and that teachers would hold political meetings in school time if they thought it was necessary.

Before the SADTU strike in August 2010, Nyathi warned: 'Any school that stays open is declaring war on 1.3 million workers. We will crush you because we are many.' In September 2011 he threatened that all Soweto schools would be closed down if a principal accused of assault on a pupil was not reinstated.

Relying on their political clout in COSATU and thus the ruling Tripartite

Alliance, SADTU have for years blamed the departments of education, the ministers and the senior managers for the failures of the education system. The first minister to actually stand up to them was Motshekga, and SADTU launched a national campaign to get her and her director-general, Bobby Soobryan, fired. At one of these rallies in March 2013, protestors held up an oversized pair of panties with the words 'Puluma ya Angie' (Angie's panties) written on them.

But the ANC and government leadership has never had the guts to take SADTU head-on. Jonathan Jansen does. The problem, he told a meeting of educators in May 2013, is not one of education – it is one of politics and power, and as such it can only be resolved politically: 'We need our president to step in and tell his partners in the unions, specifically COSATU and the South African Democratic Teachers Union, that the government is taking back the schools. The government then needs to run our schools in a way that does not undermine the children of the poorest of the poor.'

He expressed his anger at SADTU's ongoing strikes and the go-slow that has affected schools across the country. 'It is immoral for our union leaders to disrupt schools for the vast number of poor children in our country, while their children attend schools which are undisturbed.'

In *The Toxic Mix*, Bloch asks: 'What happened to the democratic teachers' unions of the 1980s, who could not be silenced from their concerns and debates round People's Education? Fighting for immediate rights and benefits of teachers seems to have taken precedence over questions of their social role and contribution to development. Labour trumps development every time.'

Panyaza Lesufi, head of communications at the Department of Basic Education, expressed the increasing irritation of the ministry in an opinion piece in the *Sunday Independent* on 28 April 2013: 'Teachers are the cornerstone of our children's future, and when an organisation like SADTU blatantly disregards the rights of the African child, one is left wondering if it is truly committed to a better nation through improved education.'

No education before liberation
But teachers aren't the only ones to blame. This is what Mosibudi Mangena, president of the Azanian People's Organisation (AZAPO) and former deputy minister of education and later minister of science and technology, said when he received an honorary doctorate from the University of South Africa (UNISA): 'There is absolutely nothing wrong with our children, but there is a lot wrong with our society. We are, indeed, a strange society that wages an

undeclared war against our own children. If we are not parents who don't care when our children go to school at nine o'clock and come back at eleven, we are teachers who won't teach.

'If we are not officials who could not deliver learning materials in schools, we are thieves who steal chairs, desks and computers from their schools. If we are not a community that burns down its schools because we are campaigning for a road, we are another community that prevents them from going to school because we, the adults, are toyi-toying and quarrelling about something. We are indeed a strange society that, instead of keeping its children safe in the background, uses them to fight adult battles.

'The tragedy is not that we are incapable of teaching our children, but that we won't.'

Mangena was probably referring in part to the extraordinary events in the Northern Cape in 2012. Communities in a wide area from Olifantshoek to Kuruman decided to stop their children from going to school to force the provincial authorities to meet their demands – some wanted a new mayor, others wanted tarred roads. Thousands of pupils at sixty-five schools with more than six hundred teachers lost an entire year of education. Matriculants were taken away to study at a special camp, but ended up doing very badly. Several schools were burnt down.

Brigette Mulepa from Cassel near Kuruman told a *City Press* reporter the community felt that if children went to school normally, the government would not listen to them. Lucas Botha of Olifantshoek said parents and children had decided together to boycott school because they wanted a new mayor. Shoes Obuseng said the pupils were staying home of their own volition: 'They do not see why they should go to school if there's no future for them in this place.'

This madness reminds one of the disastrous 'no education before liberation' campaigns of the 1980s.

As I've already suggested, most of the problems with education mirror those in other spheres of governance: corruption, bad and fast-changing policies and decisions, bureaucratic incompetence, and political expediency counting more than productivity.

It seems South Africa can build five world-class soccer stadiums on time and host one of the best Soccer World Cups ever – we can even build a R300 million private villa for the president – but we cannot deliver textbooks to schools on time. The 2012 Limpopo textbook debacle, when most pupils had not received their essential books by July, was one of the most shameful chapters of mismanagement since 1994.

A Corruption Watch report for the first quarter of 2013 stated that school principals and school governing bodies were robbing pupils of resources at an alarming rate. Between January and April the NGO had received 513 reports of such corruption.

'It is, sadly, steadily increasing,' says the executive director of Corruption Watch, David Lewis. 'When you have reports of corruption at one hundred schools it is difficult to believe that it is not widespread.' He pointed to the example of Thubelihle Intermediate School in Soweto, where the principal had allegedly written cheques worth about R176 000 to herself and the former chairman of the school's governing body.

The Port Elizabeth *Herald* conducted a two-month investigation into the management of education in the Eastern Cape in 2012. It revealed, the newspaper reported on 28 November 2012, 'that the department is being run by a corrupt clique using blackmail and intimidation to swing tenders fraudulently and withdraw millions of rands from the department's banking accounts. Dubbed the Education Mafia by colleagues, this clique includes senior officials together with well-connected politicians who use intimidation, threats and bribery to force staff members in key positions to do their dirty work.' It found that a mind-boggling R9 billion could not be accounted for in the previous nine years.

The newspaper was devastating in its comment: 'Crippled by rampant corruption, wide-scale inefficiency and almost non-existent financial management, the Eastern Cape Education Department is stealing our children's future.'

The Eastern Cape is probably the worst province in the country in terms of education management, but education in provinces such as Limpopo, Mpumalanga, North West and the Free State is not a lot better. The same problems occur: bureaucratic inefficiency, weak financial management, corruption, tender manipulation, cadre deployment and nepotism, and lazy and undereducated teachers.

One of a long list of bad, if not disastrous, decisions by government that have impacted on education was to close down the existing 120 teacher training colleges between 1994 and 2000 – a decision aimed at 'overcoming the educational inequalities of apartheid and reducing an identified oversupply of primary school teachers'. Teacher training was henceforth to take place at

Mud school

For the children of the Eastern Cape, twenty years after Freedom

Minister Motshekga, your name is mud. Let's see
what we can do with you. We can fire you and make
of you a brick, and add you to our school, maybe
as the corner stone. In rain you'll turn into a turd.
We'll skip over you and laugh. We can smear
you thickly on our walls and watch you crumble
in the summer wind, we'll use your flakes to learn
subtraction until there is nothing left to reckon with.
We can bake a cake with you and pretend we're eating
lunch, or mould you to a wafer to serve us as a thin,
melting sacrament. We can press you in a frame
to form a wet slate and write this poem on you
with a twig and send the president a truck of sun-
baked tiles to read until he weeps. But maybe he
will only grin and say, why complain? Look where I
have gotten to with only standard six, I hold an honorary
doctorate from Beijing! Mrs Mud, we could erect for you
a headstone in every school and every morning march
around it chanting, till it falls down like the walls of Jericho.
But will it help if the element is air, or song, or pristine hope?
Mud is a multi-purpose substance, Minister, we can fling
it in your face, if you would show it to us, but you rarely come.
A grateful word for rhyming, too, this mud that is your name,
for chewing on, like a dumb beast on its cud, until one day –
having baked, skipped, eaten, written, reckoned,
ruminated, marched, prayed and chanted in its medium,
inhabited its frailty and studied well its force – we mix our blood
in it, and turn it into rock, and fan it into flame and furl
it into smoke and shout and tread under our feet the very buds
of spring, the things you should have nurtured,
the flowers of fresh learning, that we should have been.

(A protest poem by Marlene van Niekerk published in many newspapers
with the invitation for others to contribute poems about education)

universities. This was an immature, irresponsible and political rather than educational decision. For one, there was never an oversupply of teachers. It took government until 2012 to reverse this decision, with the first new training colleges starting in 2013.

An even more disastrous decision, also motivated by political immaturity rather than the interests of education, was the voluntary severance package and teacher redeployment scheme of the mid-1990s – to encourage white teachers to quit the profession. According to Helen Zille, this 'was aimed at appeasing the teacher unions rather than improving education' and 'the consequences for education were predictably disastrous'.

Bloch says the exercise was meant 'to ensure teacher rationalisation and equalisation across race groups'. But even he agrees that it had a detrimental effect: 'Many of the more entrepreneurial and more experienced teachers took "the package" and left the system. What this meant was further desta-bilisation of the profession and the loss of an older, more committed layer among teachers.'

The move quickly stripped the public school system of much of its skills and experience. In KwaZulu-Natal alone, 514 principals, 223 deputy principals, 925 heads of department and 1 465 senior teachers took voluntary severance packages during 1996/1997.

I grew up in an education system in which principals, teachers and pupils knew that their performance and progress would be checked regularly by regional school inspectors – and that there would be consequences if these were not up to standard. But in 1990 and 1991 black teachers literally chased inspectors out of their schools and the system was not replicated after 1994.

Bloch again: 'It is likely that these moves, and this particular destruction of a relation to authority, were the strongest influences to be carried into the democratic period. Teachers thereafter fought tooth and nail to ensure that accountability systems and external controls on them were not enforced, coupling these with strong demands concerning pay and other labour rela-tions issues. As the wider education movement (including students and parents) became demobilised in terms of direction and activities, with con-sequently less pressure on teachers, these more "pure" union demands were to prevail over other developmental or educational goals.'

Outcomes? What outcomes?

The next ill-conceived decision was to throw the traditional content-based method of teaching out the window and to import outcomes-based education

(OBE). It was first proposed by COSATU and announced with great fanfare in 1997 by then minister of education Sibusiso Bengu as the post-apartheid government's first big change to the curriculum since 1994. Curriculum 2005, as it was called, was implemented in Grade 1 classes countrywide in 1998.

The theory behind OBE is great. Where traditional education focuses on sources available to the pupil, on content coverage, OBE proposes pupil-centred learning with a focus on the broad competencies a pupil should have at the end of the year – 'a collaborative, flexible, transdisciplinary, outcomes-based, open-system, empowerment-oriented approach to learning', in the words of the National Curriculum Development Committee in 1996. It was going to produce great citizens that could transform the South African economy.

It was doomed to fail from the start, as many educationists, such as Jonathan Jansen, warned before it was implemented. OBE is a very complex system and presupposes highly skilled teachers with a proper understanding of its philosophical underpinnings. OBE can't succeed in schools where resources and teaching abilities are already very poor. It means a continuous assessment of pupils, which wasn't happening at all at the time, and places a huge administrative burden on teachers. It also demands they spend a lot more time with pupils – and yet the department knew beforehand that out of a township or rural school's workweek of 41 hours, on average 15.18 hours were spent on teaching and the rest on strikes or go-slows, on administration, sport and simply slacking off. (Teachers in former Model C schools spend on average 19.11 hours teaching.)

Needless to say, OBE failed miserably and was dropped in 2010. (It was dropped in Australia in 2007.)

There is universal consensus that mother-tongue instruction at primary school level benefits children significantly. It helps a child tremendously to learn the foundations of conceptual development and basic literacy and numeracy in his or her home language. English- and Afrikaans-speaking children, white, brown and black, have clearly benefited from this over the decades.

One of my personal heroes and one of the foremost public intellectuals of the last few decades, Neville Alexander, made the argument for mother-tongue instruction very convincingly.

'It may sound melodramatic,' he wrote in 2005, 'but a moment's thought will convince you that the following statement is true: one of the fundamental reasons for the economic failure of post-colonial Africa south of the Arabic zone is the fact that, with a few important exceptions, mother-tongue (home language) education is not practised in any of the independent African states.

'Moreover, contrary to conventional wisdom, it is not true that only "monolingual" countries have been economically successful in the modern world.

'These two statements lie at the heart of the language issue in Africa, including post-apartheid South Africa. It is a fact that a child, or any other learner, can be taught and can learn in any language provided she or he has a sufficient command of the language concerned. For most people and in most practical situations, that language is the mother tongue – that is, the language(s) in which the child first meets the world, forms concepts and learns to expand and deepen thinking, feeling and imagining. Nothing is more opposed to the achievement of quality education than having to "learn" in a language one does not know well enough.'

Professor Russell Kaschula of Rhodes University's School of Languages agrees: 'Although our situation is complex, one of the key reasons for the drop-out rate from school … is language. Children become disillusioned because they have no idea what is going on in the classroom and they drop out.'

Alexander again: 'The self-esteem, self-confidence, creativity, engagement and participation that come with being taught in one's home language are irreplaceable assets of a system based on the mother tongue(s) of the learners. In South Africa, because of the legacy of apartheid education, it is necessary for the foreseeable future to establish a mother-tongue-based bilingual educational system on the assumption that most people will inevitably choose English as the other language to be learnt and/or to learn in.'

But in the reality of post-apartheid South Africa this is not a simple matter. One of the worst legacies of Bantu Education is the rejection of mother-tongue education by most black parents. Exacerbating this is the belief that the elite and powerful all speak English, so tuition in English empowers kids. This, says Kaschula, 'suggests South Africa is liberated as a country but our languages remain in bondage. We are still unable to free ourselves from our colonial and apartheid past.'

There are two other complicating factors. In many, probably even most, township schools children speak a variety of local languages, even languages from elsewhere in Africa. Which one should be chosen as the language of instruction in such a class? And then there is the problem of the class teacher's home language. 'With the best intentions in the world,' says author and educationist Gillian Godsell, 'a multilingual teacher may revert to a blended or "pidgin" English to clarify a concept. Psycholinguistically, this messes up a child's conceptual development even more.'

But in many primary schools, especially in the rural areas, most pupils and teachers share the same mother tongue. The idea put forward by many experts like Alexander is that pupils be taught English in a way that would make them able to handle English as a language of instruction by senior school and university.

The post-1994 government's commitment to mother-tongue education and to the advancement of indigenous languages in general has been weak and puzzling. At least Motshekga announced in early 2013 that an indigenous language will be taught at Grade 1 level at all schools from 2014 and increase incrementally grade by grade thereafter.

Mud schools

The poor infrastructure at township and rural schools is as shocking as the poor teaching. For example, 15 per cent of schools don't have access to electricity; 75 per cent don't have libraries; 60 per cent have no computers; and 60 per cent have no sewerage systems. These figures cover all schools, which means that when one takes the better urban and Model C schools out of the equation, the picture is much uglier. In the Eastern Cape, for instance, only 3 per cent of schools have libraries and 4 per cent have computer rooms.

Some schools have virtually no buildings at all and pupils get taught under trees or in rooms provided by local residents. There are hundreds and hundreds of mud schools, schools not built with brick and mortar.

Hundreds of schools have no desks or chairs. *City Press* visited Meyisi Senior Secondary School in Flagstaff in the Eastern Cape in January 2013 and found 153 pupils having to share one classroom. In another classroom they found eighty-seven pupils and only three desks. There were only eleven teachers for roughly eight hundred pupils. There is a national shortage of more than 500 000 desks and chairs.

The *Mail & Guardian* visited Putuma Junior Secondary School in the Eastern Cape in March 2013 and found 140 Grade 2s in one classroom. Pupils use the veld as a toilet. There are many similar stories in Limpopo, Mpumalanga and the Free State.

So where did the billions and billions of rands the state spent on education in the last twenty years go to? Billions were stolen, we know. Hundreds of millions went to ghost teachers. Billions went to the hugely bloated and

---

Promised promises

President Thabo Mbeki, 2004: 'By the end of this year, we shall ensure that there is no learner learning under a tree or in a mud school.'

Former Eastern Cape education MEC Mkhangeli Matomela, 2006: 'I'm confident that we will eradicate mud schools in the next two financial years.'

Former education minister Naledi Pandor, 2007: 'Fifty per cent of the mud schools will be rebuilt between 2007 and 2009.'

Former Eastern Cape education MEC Mahlubandile Qwase, 2008: 'It is my plan that the eradication of mud schools must be fast-tracked in the 2010/2011 financial year.'

Basic education minister Angie Motshekga, 2011: 'By 2014, we will have eradicated all mud schools in the [Eastern Cape] province.'

Motshekga again, 2013: 'By 2015, in terms of mud schools, we should be done.'

Actual position in mid-2013: There are still more than four hundred mud schools in the Eastern Cape.

(Quotes supplied by Equal Education)

---

inefficient bureaucracies. After the salaries of legitimate teachers were paid, little was left.

Civil society bodies such as the Legal Resources Centre, Equal Education and Section 27 have taken the government to court to force it to improve school infrastructure. In the latest move, Equal Education is trying to force the Department of Basic Education to subscribe to a binding and ambitious set of norms and standards. Thank goodness for civil activism.

But I was touched by a statement made by a pupil at Tolweni Senior Secondary School in Mount Frere when interviewed by a *Mail & Guardian* reporter. The school is totally overcrowded, with few desks and virtually unusable toilets. The reporter asked Ayanda Mndwetywa what her dream school would be. She answered: 'It would just give me a good education. Good teachers.'

She's right, I think. Of course the state of the township and rural schools is a bloody scandal and should be fixed urgently. But there are many examples of mud schools and others with almost no facilities that have done extremely well academically – because they have good teachers and good principals.

Minister Motshekga was reluctant to endorse the minimum norms and standards, and she was crucified for it. And then Helen Zille came to her defence. While agreeing that decent school infrastructure is a necessity, she said the norms-and-standards approach runs the risk of pouring billions of rands into interventions that will not necessarily advance the top priority of improving education outcomes. In fact, Zille said, 'there is a risk of diverting resources away from strategies designed to achieve such outcomes'.

Every year-end, newspapers tell us the unlikely success stories – poor

---

Lessons in leadership

School principal Edward Gabada has been fighting for his vision for Mpondombini Senior Secondary School in deep rural Eastern Cape since his arrival in 2001. He is tough on his pupils, engages with their parents and holds teachers accountable.

'When I came here, the school was hopeless,' he says. Only 23 per cent of matriculants passed their exams. It was one of the most dysfunctional schools in the country, in one of the poorest communities.

In 2012, with virtually no improvement in the school or the community's infrastructure, Mpondombini had a 100 per cent matric pass rate. The only explanation is its principal's vigorous leadership.

'I realised it's not the teachers who weren't working; it's the management that was not making them work,' he says.

The success of the school has given the community of Lubunde near Bizana a renewed sense of hope. There is very limited running water, no electricity, high unemployment and many child-headed households. 'The one thing we do have is a good school,' says Grade 12 pupil Akhona Mate.

(From documentary film-maker Molly Blank's reports in the *Mail & Guardian* on her video series Schools that Work)

---

schools and even mud schools that perform on par with the better Model C schools because they have a good principal and committed teachers.

A no-fee school in Limpopo, Dendron Secondary, is one of the top maths and science schools. Batswana Commercial Secondary School in a poor community in Mahikeng had a 96.4 per cent matric pass rate in 2012 and believes it will reach 100 per cent in 2013. In a remote KwaZulu-Natal village, a maths and science teacher built himself a mud hut on the grounds of the Slang River Primary School and two other teachers live in a dilapidated caravan to be able to spend more time with their pupils.

Privatise?

Could private schools, schools not subjected to SADTU's recklessness or the state's bungling bureaucracy and confused policy-making, be a part of the answer? If so many South Africans are using private security companies to do the work the police aren't doing, why not do the same with education?

I'm not talking about the elite private schools like Kearsney College, Hilton or St Stithians, or even the less-expensive Montessori or Waldorf schools. These schools have produced brilliant results and very successful citizens over the years and certainly deserve their place in our society.

But the new phenomenon is low-fee or medium-fee independent schools, something that has blossomed in recent years in countries such as Nigeria, Ghana, Kenya, Colombia, Chile and India. These are schools that ordinary lower-middle-class and working-class people can afford.

Whenever I meet or speak to groups of business people, I ask them what they regard as the biggest problem South Africa is facing. All of them mention poor education in the top three. And then I confront them: 'Guys, if you know our education system is such a threat to our growth and stability, two things crucial to your businesses growing, why haven't you invested in education yourself to deal with the problem? Why do you wait for government to fail and then enjoy blaming them?' I feel strongly that it is critical for the private sector to become more involved in education, through adopting struggling schools, supporting initiatives to better education and by starting low-fee private schools.

PSG, Old Mutual Investment Group and Advtech are among the companies investing in education and their investments are paying off. (A R10 000 investment in PSG's Curro in 2011 was worth R29 160 in 2013.) Cyril Ramaphosa's Shanduka Foundation has partnered with the education NGO Kagiso Trust with a R400 million investment in new schools. Among the groups already operating independent schools in South Africa are Curro, Advtech, Spark Schools, Nova Schools and BASA Educational Institute Trust.

Private or independent schools have been growing rapidly in the last few years and the growth curve is continuing sharply upwards. The Independent Schools Association of Southern Africa (ISASA) said in January 2013 that more than 120 000 pupils had crossed from public to private schools in the last three years – most of them black.

ISASA's Jane Hofmeyr said the seven hundred schools her association represents (there are about 1 500 registered independent schools) had 256 283 pupils in 2000 and 504 395 in 2012. She said the fastest enrolment growth was from black families, ranging from the elite to the working class. Most of the independent schools, even the most expensive ones, have long waiting lists. Curro Holdings CEO Chris van der Merwe says their schools enrolled 12 500 pupils in 2012 and 21 000 in 2013. Classes are limited to thirty pupils each.

Private-school fees range from about R200 000 a year (Hilton College) to as little as R12 000. The fees at most of the low-fee private schools compare favourably with those at many Model C state schools. Some non-commercial independent schools charge much less.

A new concept is 'contract' schools, publicly funded schools that are privately managed. The Centre for Development and Enterprise's (CDE) Ann Bernstein explains: 'Government provides funding and clearly defined goals for pupils and private providers to come up with innovative ways of delivering schooling to them. A performance contract is signed between the two, and if the school underperforms it is closed down. If pupil outcomes improve, according to the performance contract, then the school continues to get funding.'

The CDE proposes that pupils at these schools get the same per-child funding that other state schools get. The schools should be regulated by a public authority, and management should be free to appoint and dismiss teachers and principals. The advantage is that they would be free of the red tape and bureaucratic bungling that occurs at other state schools.

I hope many more low-fee independent schools will be established in the next few years, and that government ignores the calls made by the likes of the SACP, COSATU and the ANC Youth League for these schools to be nationalised. (Trade-union leader Irvin Jim recently demanded the abolition of 'the white colonial and racist three-tier structure of the education system which features private institutions, Model C schools and ordinary public schools in order to redistribute resources towards ordinary public schools in working-class and poor communities and to equalise quality of education'.)

But if one keeps in mind that there are more than 27 000 state schools in the country, it is clear that private schools will not be able to make a significant dent in the short or medium term. The solution to South Africa's education crisis is to be found in public schools.

No-fee schools

Sixty-three per cent of state schools, or 15 567 out of 24 532, charged no school fees in 2010. In 2008 this figure was 58 per cent. The Free State had the highest percentage of no-fee schools in 2010, at 83 per cent. Of the 1 636 public schools in the Free State, 1 354 were no-fee schools, up 34 per cent from 2008. It was followed by Limpopo, at 71 per cent in 2008 and 77 per cent in 2010.

What is to be done?

The National Development Plan, adopted in 2012 by the ANC as its blueprint for development towards 2030, identifies poor black-school education as one of nine major challenges facing South Africa, and makes several proposals for how the quality of education could be improved.

It proposes proper nutrition and diet for young children and at least two years of preschool education for all.

It wants the layers of bureaucracy to be reduced so more resources will be available to support schools and teachers.

It wants a campaign to improve infrastructure in poor schools.

'The common feature of all well-run schools is leadership,' the NDP declares. It supports proposals to measure the competencies of principals based on learner scores. It says principals should be selected purely on merit, be given greater powers over school management and be held accountable for performance.

The NDP believes teachers, both individually and at school level, should be held accountable for learner performance. Professional development, peer review, and the provision of learner-support materials and teacher-support systems need to be strengthened.

But we know that the NDP has subsequently been torn to shreds by COSATU and the SACP. This includes the parts of the plan with proposals for future education policies. And even if it hadn't been, the present government's capacity and political will to implement the plan with urgency and energy were very low anyway.

In the beginning of this book, I talked about the difference between using apartheid as an excuse for bad governance rather than as an explanation for persistent problematic trends.

Perhaps I have not focused enough on the shambles and distortions the government of 1994 inherited from the apartheid-era education system. There can be no denying that the past still has an impact on today's education and attitudes to it. Examples are the poor development of young children due to malnutrition and the failure of black communities and parents to mobilise in support of schools, compared to white communities. And of course black schools inherited a massive infrastructure backlog compared to most of the Model C schools.

Sadly, the ruling alliance, from President Zuma himself to COSATU and the SACP, has, over the last twenty years, consistently been blaming apartheid for the tragic state of education rather than explaining and analysing the implications of the legacies of apartheid for the rebuilding of the education system.

There is no or very little introspection about the bad policy decisions, the driving out of experienced and highly skilled teachers because they were white, the criminal neglect and corruption of bureaucracies, or the appalling attitude of SADTU-aligned teachers.

Let's consider, for instance, a lengthy statement made by NUMSA, issued on 10 February 2013 in reaction to the proposals that teaching should be declared an essential service. It makes for very depressing reading – the denialism is absolutely shocking. I use the NUMSA statement because the views therein correspond with broader ANC-aligned analyses. NUMSA is also one of COSATU's strongest and most influential unions.

NUMSA correctly locates the crisis in the 'Black, especially African' part of the education system. It correctly asks: 'How is it that, almost twenty years in a democracy, the education system in the Black community is extremely dysfunctional while in the white community it works almost as well as in any other European country?'

But then it also asks: 'Why is it that "good principals" are hard to come by in African schools and are plenty in white schools? Why are teachers in

African schools spending less time and in white schools they spend more time?'

Now brace yourselves, here is NUMSA's answer to its questions: 'To answer these questions, we must never refuse to be bullied into pretending that post-1994 South Africa has suddenly disappeared the past, has no historic causes of the continuing drivers of the crisis of development in general and the crisis in education in particular. To do so is to yield to the powerful continuing white supremacist, racist, false psychological and shallow behavioural analysis of post-1994 South Africa.'

It is white-supremacist analysis, says NUMSA, 'which places the blame of failure to resolve and transform the South African education system at the feet of Black and African teachers in general and ultimately at the Black and African population in particular'.

Referring to proposals to make it more difficult for teachers to go on strike, NUMSA declares: 'By proposing to declare education an essential service, the ANC succumbs to the demands of the white supremacist DA which seeks to perpetuate the colonial status of Africans everywhere and especially in education.'

Is this DA that NUMSA is referring to, I am tempted to ask, the same as the DA that is in power in the Western Cape, where black education is in a much better condition than in most other, ANC-run provinces?

NUMSA, as part of COSATU and hence a partner in government, is clear on why black education was designed to fail: 'We challenge anyone to dispute the most obvious fact about the South African education system: that the inferior colonial education of Africans in South Africa is good for sustaining the superior racist position of the white population and its small sprinkling of Black and African elite.'

And then it goes into 'no education before liberation' mode: 'Thus ideally we should have just about all the children in African schools in African working class communities and rural areas permanently on strike demanding to see evidence of revolutionary measures being put in place to transform the quality of lives in their communities and schools.'

If you ask me what is to be done to fix education in South Africa, my first response would be: get rid of this disempowering attitude. This mentality of blaming everyone but oneself prevents true introspection and mobilisation. It is paralysing and stops us from getting to grips with the massive job of fundamentally transforming our society.

What is to be done? Focus on the worst-performing schools, but don't mess with what works. Most private schools and most Model C schools work well enough. They need continued support from the state and the state should make it easier, not more difficult as is often the case, for new private schools to be established. And we need thousands more low-fee private schools.

There are a number of initiatives by the Department of Basic Education and by civil society organisations to help teachers teach better and to provide better support for school principals. These initiatives need more urgency and commitment to make a noticeable impact.

A large consulting firm was contracted in 2013 to help fix education in the Eastern Cape – to clear out the present systems, to identify problems and problem people, and to put new systems and guidelines in place. It's expensive, but we've seen this work at the Department of Home Affairs some years ago. We need the same in the other dysfunctional regions so that the lack of accountability and efficiency in provincial administrations can be addressed.

Some in the ANC alliance are pushing for education to be taken away from provincial governments and for the establishment of one national department. This will need a change to the Constitution. The other problem is that this could negatively affect the two provinces where education is working well, the Western Cape and Gauteng. Such a new national department will be massive and the same bureaucrats will be used to staff it. This is not a viable solution.

Some activists are proposing a National Education Charter to spell out priorities and expectations of teachers and principals. This is a good idea, but it could easily just be another document and an exercise that would fool us into thinking we have made progress.

Almost all educationists say it is essential for parents and communities to get more involved with schools. I agree, but how does one make this happen? Who will mobilise these communities? Perhaps churches and faith groups could play a role.

The role of activists and NGOs is absolutely crucial in mobilising public opinion and putting pressure on government, but also to make smaller interventions in schools and communities. They have made quite a difference in the last two years.

I'm trying hard, but I'm not convincing myself. After twenty years of neglect, fixing education is going to be a mammoth task that will demand a new national obsession – and it will take a very long time.

I simply cannot see the present ANC government getting its act together to whip civil servants into shape; to re-establish accountability, oversight and assessments; to root out corruption; and to confront the SADTU monster.

The administration of Jacob Zuma seems to have other priorities than to save our children.

9

The land shall be shared

No national issue elicits as much anger, fear and fiery confrontation as the ownership of land.

At the same time, few, if any, other national issues are as misunderstood, misrepresented and mismanaged as the land question.

We are nothing without our land, we hear black voices say. It was at the heart of our long struggle for liberation. Africans can't have their dignity back until they get their land back. Landownership is the gateway to the prosperity we have been denied by colonialism and apartheid.

We bought the land legitimately, we hear white voices respond, and we can't undo three hundred years of history. There was little real agriculture going on when we took it over. We produce food for you and we provide revenue for the state and employment to millions.

The noise around land seemed fairly low-key during Nelson Mandela's presidency, and even as Thabo Mbeki took over from him. But after Robert Mugabe's ZANU-PF government sanctioned violent land grabs in Zimbabwe from 2000 onwards, the issue again took centre stage in South Africa.

Some 245 000 black Zimbabweans were eventually established on land previously worked by some six thousand white farmers. This sent cold shivers down the spine of the white South African community. It was the manifestation of their oldest fear.

By 2013, the centenary of the legislation that finally robbed black South Africans of most of the land, the 1913 Natives Land Act, the demand for a wholesale redistribution of land in South Africa had reached a crescendo. It was also the year Mugabe and ZANU-PF were re-elected once again, despite the fact that they had damaged the Zimbabwean economy almost beyond repair.

Many now warned ominously that unless black South Africans got their land back, and quickly, the country would face a bloody revolution.

When Julius Malema's EFF launched its Founding Manifesto in July 2013, the first of seven 'pillars for economic freedom in our lifetime' stated that the state should expropriate all land without compensation and then lease it to suitable applicants under temporary licences.

Malema told a gathering of ZANU-PF's youth wing in Harare that the Zimbabwean way of getting the land back was an inspiration and would be followed in South Africa, by violent means, if necessary, because whites had acquired the land violently. 'Actually they killed people to get that land and those minerals. We are not going to give them money when we take the land back because it will be like we are thanking them with money for killing our people.'

Another icy shiver down the white spine. Malema became Mugabe's Mini-me, white South Africa's chief bogeyman. 'We're becoming a Zimbabwe' became the refrain.

The white community reacted strongly to these threats because land expropriation went to the heart of their oldest fear: they don't belong in Africa; they're still regarded as 'colonialists of a special kind'; they will never be fully accepted as fellow Africans.

Among white farmers the added fear and insecurity was that they would lose their livelihood and their lifestyle. In many cases they and their parents and grandparents had been bonded emotionally with their land for generations.

What many black and white South Africans, especially Afrikaners, have in common is an irrational, primal feeling that owning a piece of the land is an essential precondition for full citizenship. This kind of sentiment disappeared almost completely from urbanised North American and European societies generations ago.

Perhaps the use of the word 'irrational' is not entirely appropriate here. I use the word because most of those agitating publicly around the land issue live in cities with no desire to be farmers; and hundreds of thousands of people with land available to them in the old Bantustans abandon the land in search of work in the cities.

The emotions around land, says prominent ANC intellectual and former cabinet minister Pallo Jordan, 'are even more firmly embedded by the various associations with which the land is embellished. We speak of the "mother-land", evocative of the unequivocal love of a mother for her children. "Mother" is associated with birth, caring and nurturing, all of which inspire warm, positive feelings. Every national movement claims its inspiration is the struggle to reclaim land lost to oppressors or conquerors. Virtually all the nationalist slogans in the South African freedom struggle invoke the land and assert its primacy among the objectives of the struggle itself.'

It is thus important to understand how strong the symbolism around landownership is before we get into the nitty-gritty of the land question. It is more about history, justice and belonging – and nostalgia? – than it is about making a living off the land.

The total surface area of South Africa is 122 081 300 hectares. A quarter of that is controlled by the state: 15 per cent or eighteen million hectares black communal land, and 10 per cent conservation areas or property of the SANDF, SAPS, or provincial or national government departments. Commercial farmland constitutes 67 per cent of the land.

Of the 80 000 land-restitution claims received by 1998, only 5 856 claimants preferred land; the rest preferred cash payouts, totalling R6 billion.

The amount of money spent on land reform since 1994 could have bought 37 per cent of all commercial farmland, 7 per cent more than the government's yet unmet target.

Two-thirds of black South Africans say they don't need to own land. Two-thirds of those who say they do, live in rural areas.

In 2010, 62.2 per cent of South Africans were living in cities, the highest urbanisation rate in sub-Saharan Africa. Gauteng's population grew by 31 per cent to 12.8 million between 2000 and 2010, up from 9.4 million. The Western Cape's population grew by 29 per cent between 2000 and 2010, from 4.5 to 5.8 million.

The eight metropolitan areas account for 2 per cent of the land, but are home to 37 per cent of the population.

The number of commercial farmers in South Africa declined from 120 000 in 1994 to less than 36 000 in 2013.

Settlers and trekkers

Many white South Africans find it uncomfortable and thus they are very reluctant to confront the realities of the history of landownership in the country. Let me personalise the history; perhaps that will make it more palatable.

My paternal ancestor, Hercule des Pres (semi-literate Dutch clerks changed his surname to Du Preez), arrived at the Cape on board the Dutch ship *De Schelde* in 1688 with a group of other French Huguenots fleeing religious persecution. It was only thirty-six years after the first Dutch settlers under the leadership of Dutch East India Company (or VOC) representative Jan van Riebeeck set foot on African soil and found the Khoikhoi pastoralists and Bushmen hunter-gatherers on the Cape Peninsula and surrounding regions.

Hercule was given a farm on the banks of the Berg River in the Draken-stein valley, De Zoete Inval, today still a prestigious wine estate. (Sadly, no land claims for me, even though the Du Preez family monument stands on the farm.) The land belonged to nobody, was the argument, because the Khoikhoi didn't acknowledge private landownership and the local herders, of the Cochoqua clan, constantly moved around in search of fresh pasture.

Soon so many settlers were established on farms in the fertile valley that there was little pasture left for the Khoikhoi and their cattle. (The sheer number of French settlers in the valley gave the town of Franschhoek its name.) The earliest settlers were poor and struggling, and initially could not afford slaves, so they started employing the Khoikhoi as labourers. After several violent clashes between the settlers and the Khoikhoi, and the devastating smallpox epidemic of 1713 (the virus came ashore with laundry from a visiting European ship and the indigenous people had no immunity to it), the Khoikhoi virtually disappeared as a distinct group in the Western Cape.

So there were my ancestors with their low skills and poor education, rendered homeless in their country of origin, snugly settled on their farms on land in Africa that the Khoikhoi and the Bushmen had regarded as theirs for many generations.

The new settlers were soon successful farmers and, as happened with all settler farmers, developed a thirst for more land. Hercule's offspring were among those trekboers who moved eastwards, crossed the Hottentots Holland Mountains and eventually settled in areas where Xhosa-speaking farmers had been farming and grazing their cattle for generations. (These black farmers didn't initially settle in the Western Cape, mainly because it was a winter-rainfall area not suited for growing millet and maize.)

By now the Cape had become a British colony and the new colonial power was as dismissive of the local people's land rights as its predecessor. The Xhosa groups put up a much greater fight for their land, though, and several bloody and hugely disruptive Frontier Wars followed. In 1820 the British even started importing thousands of British subjects to settle as farmers in the

Eastern Cape – among the first group of four thousand, not one had owned land before.

By the 1830s the Du Preez farmers in the Eastern Cape were among those who had had enough of British colonial interference (and the end to slavery) and decided to trek to the interior – the Great Trek, as it was later romantically called. My mother's great-great-grandfather, a farmer in Graaff-Reinet who was a descendant of Jacob Kruger, a VOC soldier who left Germany for the Cape in 1713, was also part of the Trek. These Voortrekkers, proud and independent pioneers in the eyes of their descendants, trekked by ox-wagon over the Drakensberg and eventually into what is today the provinces of KwaZulu-Natal, the Free State, Gauteng, Mpumalanga, Limpopo and North West.

My Du Preez great-grandfather was allocated a farm in the Free State on land that fell under the jurisdiction of King Moshoeshoe of the Basotho. In 1854 the area now known as the Free State was declared an independent Boer republic called the Republic of the Orange Free State. My Kruger great-grandfather was given a farm near Potchefstroom in today's North West, where the Batswana had been farming and grazing their cattle for centuries. In 1848 this area was part of the independent Boer republic called the South African (or Transvaal) Republic.

The new settlers did not buy the land they settled on. Some simply pegged out the outer perimeters and proclaimed it. Others were allocated farms by the Boer leadership after the local black groups were subjugated or local chiefs had agreed that the settlers could farm the land. In the black societies' culture at the time, land wasn't something an individual could own and keep or sell. It belonged to the people to use as they needed and fell under the jurisdiction of chiefs and kings.

So by the end of the nineteenth century, present-day South Africa was divided into four territories: the British colonies of the Cape and Natal and the two Boer republics. The various black farming groups and the descendants of the Khoikhoi, the Bushmen and the slaves had very little, if any, political voice and had most of their land taken away.

After the discovery of diamonds at Kimberley and gold at the Witwatersrand, Britain developed an interest in the Boer republics and, between 1899 and 1901, the Boers and the Brits fought a vicious war. Both my grandfathers fought as officers in the war, which the Boers lost. (Forgive my shorthand history; I'm trying to stick to the land issue.) The whole of South Africa now belonged to the British Empire.

In 1910 the British and the Boers agreed to the establishment of the self-governing Union of South Africa and our country as we know it became one state for the first time – a 'white' state, because Britain agreed that, with very few localised exemptions, only white people could vote.

While the black majority had lost most of their land during the nineteenth century, there were still some black farmers on ancestral land outside the 'tribal reserves', and black farmers with the means, as well as chiefs and communities, were still able to buy land. Many black people worked land owned by whites and paid the owners rent in cash, in labour or in a share of the harvest.

And then, just three years after the formation of the Union, Parliament passed Act 27 of 1913, the Natives Land Act. The intellectual and author Sol Plaatje famously wrote: 'Awakening on Friday morning, June 20, 1913, the South African Native found himself, not actually a slave, but a pariah in the land of his birth.'

The Act set aside 7.3 per cent of all land in South Africa for black South Africans in 'native reserves'. It made rental tenancy and black sharecropping illegal, and stopped black people from buying and owning land in 'white' South Africa – and whites from buying land in the reserves.

Historian Colin Bundy quotes the Transvaal native affairs commissioner Godfrey Lagden: 'Every rabbit has a warren where he can live and burrow and breed and every native must have a warren too.'

In short, the Act sought complete territorial segregation between black and white. It was the cornerstone on which the radical ideology of apartheid was built and formalised in a host of other legislation after 1948. It made it possible for the architects of apartheid to turn the 'reserves' into 'homelands' or Bantustans, some of which became nominally independent after 1976, and to perfect their idea that there was a white South Africa and a black South Africa – the only blacks allowed in white South Africa would be those needed as labourers on the farms, in the mines and in the factories (and nannies to raise the children of the white middle classes). The Natives Urban Areas Act of 1923 declared urban areas the preserve of white people and black people needed permission to be there, meaning the system of pass books, the *dompas*, had to be refined. This was eventually perfected in the Natives (Abolition of Passes and Co-ordination of Documents) Act of 1952.

(I lived a blissfully ignorant and privileged life as a white child in Kroonstad, but I do remember finding it bizarre as a sixteen-year-old that I could sign the passbook of my family's adult gardener, the father of children older than me, that would save him from being arrested for being in a white area.)

The Natives Land Act 'devastated the majority of people, and their descendants, both socially and economically,' says former Pan Africanist Congress (PAC) MP and now DA mayor of Cape Town Patricia de Lille. 'It expropriated land from those whose identities and livelihoods were closely bound to it. This was not only an assault on identity – it was an assault on natural justice … It was a milestone in determining the structural nature of inequality that defined twentieth-century South Africa.'

The impact of the Natives Land Act and supporting legislation on black South Africans was massive. Some seven million people were forcibly dispossessed of land in the decades after 1913, more than half of them after 1948. The Act was only repealed in 1991.

'During the nineteenth century,' says Pallo Jordan, 'peasant farmers, among them thousands of black tenant farmers, grew the fresh produce in the markets of our cities. This continued well into the twentieth century. Racist law-making destroyed that peasantry. The coup de grace was the Natives Land Act, which stripped thousands of black peasants of their land and livestock. After 1913, the terms "farmer" and "white" became joined.'

White mine owners and industrialists benefited greatly from the new dispensation, because overpopulation of the black reserves made it easier for them to recruit workers and transport them to the mines and factories without their families for most of the year. This migrant labour system wreaked havoc on black family life and social structures for generations – actually, it still does, as we know from the Marikana tragedy.

Setting targets

When the first democratically elected government took office in 1994, this great injustice starting with the dispossession of land had to be addressed as a top priority. The insults to black dignity had to be redressed.

But there were four complicating factors facing the liberation movement turned democratic government: the political allegiance of chiefs and other traditional leaders lording over communal land; the massive scale of black urbanisation in recent decades; the fact that the white agricultural sector was almost solely responsible for South Africa's food security; and the clause in the new Constitution that protected private property ownership. One can add to that the hypersensitivity in a free market and globalised economy to any tampering with property rights and asset redistribution.

The government led by President Mandela adopted a target for land reform: to redistribute 25.89 million hectares (30 per cent of agricultural land) to black people in just a few years through land-restitution and land-redistribution programmes.

But by March 2012, eighteen years later, only 8 per cent of the land, 26 per cent of the target, had been delivered.

The land-restitution programme was quite successful, though: only 4.4 per cent of restitution claims were outstanding after the claims of 31 895 households or 1.6 million beneficiaries had been settled. (Claims for restitution were reopened in 2013 after the first deadline of 1998.)

But this high figure translated into a less-than-expected amount of land, because most beneficiaries opted to be paid out rather than receive their land back. The minister of rural development and land reform, Gugile Nkwinti, said in April 2013 that government had paid out 71 292 restitution claims instead of transferring land. 'We thought everybody, when they got a chance to get land, they would jump for it. Now only 5 856 opted for land restoration.' If these payments (about R6 billion) were translated into hectares (about 1.3 million), it would reveal far greater progress than has been acknowledged.

Nkwinti explained the changing dynamics: 'The one big factor is that people have become urbanised. Number two, because of poverty and unemployment, people are opting for money. They have become de-culturised in terms of tilling land, and so on. We no longer have a peasantry; we have wage earners now.'

This is a very important point rarely mentioned by government critics or land activists.

Urbanisation is a crucial factor in the land issue, because it gives some indication of how many people need agricultural land and how many need jobs and houses. According to the United Nations' Human Development Report, 62.2 per cent of South Africans were living in cities in 2010. At the rate of urbanisation since 2010, this figure could well be a few percentage points higher in 2013, by far the highest in sub-Saharan Africa. Compare this with Zimbabwe's 33.8 per cent, Zambia's 35.9 per cent, Uganda's 13.5 per cent, Tanzania's 26.9 per cent, Kenya's 22.5 per cent, Malawi's 20.3 per cent, Mozambique's 39.2 per cent and Namibia's 38.6 per cent.

According to the 2011 census, Gauteng's population grew by 31 per cent to 12.8 million, up from 9.4 million a decade earlier. The Western Cape's population grew by 29 per cent between 2000 and 2010, from 4.5 million to 5.8 million. Most of the inflow came from the Eastern Cape.

Who owns what

Perhaps we should try to get a true picture of who owns what and how much has been transferred since 1994 before we delve deeper into the land issue.

Figures supplied by the Department of Rural Development and Land Reform, Statistics South Africa, the SAIRR's *South Africa Survey 2012*, researchers at universities, the ANC, the EFF, and political analysts and commentators are often contradictory and sometimes vary vastly.

During the debates in 2013, the old figure of 87 per cent white and 13 per cent black landownership was still bandied about by many. I can say without fear of contradiction that this is completely wrong.

The total surface area of South Africa is 122 081 300 hectares. Cities, towns and municipal commonage make up 8 per cent of that – the eight metropolitan areas account for just 2 per cent of the land, but are home to 37 per cent of the total population. Another 10 per cent is owned by national or provincial departments: conservation areas; military, police and prisons land; schools; hospitals; etc. The former Bantustans, trust land and former 'coloured reserves' represent 15 per cent. This leaves 67 per cent to commercial farmland, until 1994 owned almost exclusively by whites. (These figures were put together by the University of the Western Cape's Institute for Poverty, Land and Agrarian Studies from various sources.)

We can't even say the 67 per cent of farmland is now the figure for white-owned land, as this figure includes farms transferred to black owners or groups through the redistribution and restitution programmes. Minister Nkwinti told Parliament early in 2013 that 4 813 farms had been transferred to new black owners between 1994 and January 2013. More than 230 000 people benefited from this transaction.

An unknown number of commercial farms have also been bought privately by black farmers and black-owned companies – one of Tokyo Sexwale's companies recently bought thirty farms in the Vryburg district, for example. I was invited to speak to organised agriculture bodies in every corner of South Africa in 2012 and 2013, and at each one of these meetings I met black people who had bought their own farms. I know of quite a number of senior ANC and COPE members and cabinet ministers who have bought farms.

But farmland is not just farmland. Professor Cherryl Walker of Stellenbosch University points out that the largest block of commercial agricultural land is in the arid Northern Cape, where just over six thousand farmers own just under thirty million hectares, about a quarter of all agricultural land. It is also the least valuable land to farm on and the least capitalised.

'Thus – hypothetically – simply by directing all land-reform resources at replacing white farmers in the Northern Cape (only 10 per cent of the national total) with black farmers, it would be possible for the Department of Land Affairs to exceed the current land-reform target of 30 per cent of all agricultural land redistributed by 2015. However, it should be obvious that if this transaction were to be no more than a straight colour-coded swap, the impact, while not without social effect in the Northern Cape, would be negligible in terms of making substantial inroads on rural poverty and land hunger in that province, while leaving land issues in the rest of the country essentially untouched.

'The Northern Cape example, I think, illustrates the limitations of regarding the inadequate shorthand of 87/13 per cent (the conventional but misleading figures for white-/black-owned land) as the major indicator of inequality and exclusion in contemporary South Africa.'

Indeed. The numbers game makes no real sense. It would be more advantageous to sustainability, productivity and indeed dignity, for example, to give new farmers smaller, irrigated farms than to give them large tracts of land which they would be very unlikely to farm successfully.

Political reality

Ah, but this is not the political reality. Even settling all the aspirant black commercial farmers on viable land won't undo the anger among many or most in the black community if most of the 36 000 existing white commercial farmers kept their land and the largest chunk of land wasn't in black hands. The hurtful history of land dispossession has to be reversed if justice is to be served and black dignity is to be restored, is the feeling.

Andile Mngxitama, an EFF leader with a big media voice who styles himself as the only prophet of the legacy of Steve Biko (he once propagated violent attacks on a left-wing white activist who wrote about Biko), wrote in August 2013: 'To break the racist stranglehold on the black majority, one must overcome the fear of radical land redistribution and the nationalisation of the economy as a basis for true transformation.'

One almost gets the impression that some land activists are more interested in dispossessing whites of land than in empowering new black farmers. We witness the same sentiment in the demand from trade unions and others that all Model C and private schools be closed so most children get the same level of education. If we can't all do well, then we must all do poorly.

I can't help but notice that few of these activists show concern when emerging farmers who received land fail because of almost no technical and financial support from the state. The focus is overwhelmingly on the numbers game.

Says Walker: 'For many land activists, indeed for many South Africans, this history of dispossession is constitutive of the social and political identity of black people as a group, inclusive of people who may not themselves have experienced land loss or forced removals ... It is this historically sanctioned political identity that informs the approval shown by many black South Africans for the chaotic and corrupt land-redistribution campaign launched by President Mugabe in neighbouring Zimbabwe.'

It is also wrong to say 'the whites' own most of the land. There are 4.5 million whites in South Africa and about 36 000 white farmers – less than 1 per cent. Thus about 4.1 million whites don't own land either (besides property in towns and cities, that is).

I have often wondered why the ANC and government, even when criticised for the slow pace of land reform, do not paint the full picture of the land question for the public. This would inform their own constituency that it wasn't as easy a job as initially thought and that government has actually achieved more than they get credit for. Instead, ANC politicians regularly jump on the bandwagon and issue stark warnings about the danger of a continued situation where whites own more land than blacks.

One of the reasons for this could be simple incompetence. Another reason could be that these politicians don't fully understand all the complexities of the land issue. But I think part of the explanation could be that the ANC leadership is still, as we witness in many other spheres, stuck in liberation mode. They have not fully unlearnt, even after two decades, the sloganeering and propaganda typical of a liberation movement fighting for freedom against a formidable enemy.

Or, heaven forbid, could there be some truth in the conspiracy theory that they're dragging their feet with land redistribution so that they can use it as a propaganda tool when there's a threat that they might get voted out of power, like Robert Mugabe did after 2000?

Every single government minister or senior official I have talked to about the land issue over the last few years has blamed white intransigence and the 'willing buyer, willing seller' principle for the failure of their land-reform programme. And yet this principle was their own creation; it was not pre-scribed by any law or by the Constitution. In fact, the Constitution makes provision for the expropriation of land in the public interest; it just stipulates that there should be fair compensation.

The 'willing buyer, willing seller' principle was officially abandoned in 2007 by the Mbeki administration, but five years later it was still used as an excuse. It was again officially rejected by the Zuma administration, but is still used as propaganda by many.

The subtext is that white people should get the blame for the fact that not enough black people have been given agricultural land.

I have heard a few stories of white farmers who, when approached to sell their land for redistribution purposes, massively inflated their prices. Many even got away with it. Of course this is morally repugnant given the history of landownership, but it is also common human behaviour: why settle for R1 million if the buyer is prepared to pay R2 million? The more important question is: why did the officials of the land-reform department fall for it? Were they incompetent, were they duped or were they corrupt?

It brings me to a very simple question that has never been answered sat-isfactorily: why has there not been a focus on farms already available on the open property market? I read *Landbouweekblad* and *Farmer's Weekly* every week and always go through the 'Farms for Sale' smalls. There are hundreds of farms advertised by estate agencies and private owners every month. They're looking for a sale; they won't be asking inflated prices.

I don't often agree with Leon Louw, head of the Free Market Foundation, but here he has a point. 'Despite calls for its abolition, the willing buyer, willing seller system is spectacularly successful,' he wrote in *Business Day* on 7 August 2013. 'Thousands of willing buyers and sellers trade land daily in response to eager sellers, who advertise their willingness to sell. The only failure is that of one, single buyer, the government, which is too unwilling or incompetent to buy readily available land.'

Another question: I have personal knowledge of farmers who have bought land very cheaply from the Land Bank's stock of repossessed, bankrupt farms. Why does the state not get in first?

I realise that farms so available are not always in areas where land is needed for redistribution, but often it must be.

Now here is the astonishing truth about land redistribution, the willing buyer, willing seller principle and the target of 30 per cent: according to respected academics and Agri SA's figures, the amount of money spent on land reform since 1994 could have purchased 37 per cent of all farmland at market value.

This is worth repeating. Even if the state had been forced to use the willing buyer, willing seller guideline and never expropriated any land, we would have been well beyond the target for land redistribution by now if the money spent had been used properly. The only conclusion: billions must have been lost through bureaucratic bungling, bad management and corruption.

Pragmatists

My personal experience of white commercial farmers and organised agriculture is that most fully understand that they will face uncertainty – the very last thing a commercial farmer needs – until the land debate has been put to rest and those who really deserve to get land have got it.

White farmers are far more pragmatic on these kinds of issues than most people think. That is also true of their elected leaders, some of whom I have got to know, like Grain SA's Louw Steytler, Agri SA's Theo de Jager, Free State Agriculture's Dan Kriek and Wine Cellars SA's Henk Bruwer.

Every time I meet groups of farmers, I'm confronted with real stories of land being offered to the state, or farmers being asked to sell their land, and four, five years later nothing has happened.

An Afrikaner farmer in his seventies told me after I addressed Free State Agriculture in 2012: 'I understand that blacks are unhappy because my forefathers settled on land that wasn't strictly speaking theirs. I would have been angry too. I don't understand that black people insist that we should ignore how farming and ownership on the ground has changed the last century and more.

'I support land justice. But I run a productive farm that I bought from my uncle's bankrupt estate many years ago. I produce maize and meat for the people of South Africa. I look after the soil. I employ nine families and I look after them; they even use part of my farm to graze their own cattle. The farm next to mine has been lying fallow for eight years and nobody is interested in buying it. The government has done nothing in my district to get blacks on farms. I don't understand why the government can't tell me that my land is safe, that I can invest more in it without fear that it will be expropriated. The uncertainty is killing us.'

My message to all the agricultural gatherings I am invited to speak at is that they should make peace with the fact that they have to bear the brunt of the anger around land on behalf of the rest of white South Africans. They should accept that the land debate will always be complicated by emotions around history, dispossession and injustice, and will rarely be just about practical outcomes. They will simply have to deal with it and understand that they, rightly or wrongly, have a terrible reputation among the majority of society – but they should also do something about it.

I always advise farmers to make sure they understand the nuances and undercurrents in our political dynamics so that they can distinguish between populist rhetoric and genuine policy shifts, and know what is possible and what is not. And for this they can't just read agricultural magazines and Afrikaans newspapers; they need to hear what black South Africans really feel and think.

I always criticise organised agriculture for not doing nearly enough to communicate with the rest of society about who they are and what they do and about the difficulties and achievements of their industry. They should be far more proactive and strategically clever to shake off the image of reactionaries reluctant to accept change.

At every meeting I have with groups of farmers, they complain that the media always headline stories of abuse of farmworkers and create the impression that abuse is common. My advice to them is that organised agriculture should appoint its own inspectors to police its own members' treatment of workers and expose the bad apples themselves.

Perhaps it is time for organised agriculture to employ bold and competent reputation managers to change the image of especially white farmers from that of land thieves and violent abusers to food providers and employers.

I have also told organised agriculture on several occasions that they should consider whether it is in their interest to have the leader of a white, Afrikaner nationalist political party as their voice in government: Pieter Mulder, leader of the Freedom Front Plus and deputy minister of agriculture.

Mulder is a decent man and a hard worker. But his party still propagates a white Afrikaner *volkstaat*. He serves the narrow interests of conservative white Afrikaners and his political tone reflects that. In his speech on land reform in Parliament in February 2013, he made some very relevant points. But people only remembered his repetition of old white myths around land that provoked justified outrage. Bantu-speakers, he said, moved down from the equator at the same time as whites moved from the Cape and they met at the Kei River – the 'we're all immigrants' argument. He is dead wrong.

He also made reference to the old Afrikaner myth that the Difaqane, the tumultuous upheavals among black groups in the early nineteenth century, left the land in the northern and central regions of South Africa vacant for when the Voortrekkers arrived. The truth is much more complicated than that.

Mulder quite rightly pointed out that very few, if any, black farming groups were living in the present-day Western Cape at the time white people arrived. But he didn't say a word about the Khoisan who did regard those parts as their land. He added that this was also true of the north-western Cape, but he clearly didn't know of the Tswana-speakers who lived in parts of that region and he also made no mention of the Griqua people who had lived there well before the first whites came to those parts.

But Mulder's presence in government is typical of Zuma's approach, along the lines of 'Afrikaners are an ethnic people, like the Zulu, and I've generously invited one of their leaders into my government to be their voice. Now be happy with that.'

In my view, South Africa's agriculturalists need a strong ANC cabinet minister to deal with, so there can be hard bargaining and frank talk. While Mulder is in government, this won't happen.

Most commercial farmers probably don't even vote for the Freedom Front Plus; they vote DA. Today's successful farmers are modern and innovative entrepreneurs and business managers; they stay on top of international trends and new technology. Bearded Oom Piet with his khaki shorts and *velskoens*, his Voortrekker hat and pipe, and his dilapidated bakkie with a ridgeback in the back is not typical of the farmer of 2013, although there must still be a few of them out there.

It is not in the interest of today's agri-business to have as their 'man in government' a politician preaching virtual secession of his tribe. It has the potential to perpetuate the caricature of *'die wit boer'*. Today's Afrikaans-speaking farmers are no longer *Boere*; they're simply *boere* – actually, they're agricultural entrepreneurs. In fact, large tracts of land are being farmed not by individual farmers, but by large companies and corporations.

This image that so many still have of white farmers as wealthy Christian fundamentalist patriarchs who treat their workers as slaves is a big part of the perception problem bedevilling sound land reform.

If South Africans could see them for what most of them really are today – entrepreneurs using the soil of South Africa to produce food and other products, create employment and earn foreign currency – a lot of the heat will dissipate from the land debate.

But I'm afraid Afrikaners remain their own worst enemy. The negative image of white farmers and their perceived racism and intransigence was further entrenched by an astonishingly insensitive and ahistorical presentation on land reform given by the chairman of the Afrikanerbond (successor to the Broederbond), Pieter Vorster, to Parliament on 20 August 2013.

Vorster spent considerable time discussing a 1975 report on how unproductive black farmers were. He had not a single bad word to say about the land dispossession during the apartheid era; he instead blamed British imperialism. The allocation of land on a racial basis is wrong, he said. The market mechanism is the best mechanism to effect change.

Vorster's presentation was an extraordinary demonstration of exactly how white people and farmers should *not* conduct themselves in the debate around land reform. His remarks elicited a heated response from MPs of the ANC and the IFP. Even the DA's agriculture spokesperson, Annette Steyn, pleaded with Vorster to soften his approach.

ANC MP Mandla Mandela, a traditional chief in the Eastern Cape, came back with a predictable response: if white farmers did not cooperate on land redistribution and acknowledge the wrongs of the past, then expropriation would be the only way to resolve the issue. 'Expropriation is not the way we necessarily want to go, but at this rate this is the way we are heading.'

Vorster's view is that of the right-wing Transvaal Agricultural Union and hard-core elements among Afrikaner farmers, certainly not that of Agri SA and most regional commercial agricultural organisations. At Free State Agriculture's 2011 congress, then president Louw Steytler told delegates they should put 'a year's daylight' between themselves and the Afrikanerbond. His statement was greeted by a standing ovation from delegates. Free State Agriculture should instead align itself with people and organisations that are committed to sustainable land reform and transformation, Steytler said.

Risky business

There's another mind shift that needs to take place. Too many still see white farmers as extraordinarily wealthy and agriculture as an easy, low-risk enterprise. If that were the case, not so many farmers would have sold their land during the last decade to find new careers and more reliable incomes. In 1994 there were about 120 000 farmers; now there are less than 36 000. Since 1994, all direct and indirect subsidies to farmers have been abolished. State marketing boards with tax breaks and easy credit were closed down. Input costs such as diesel, electricity, fertiliser and labour have increased sharply. And then there's South Africa's often very unreliable rainfall. Farming is really a marginal, high-risk business.

Other African countries, and some further afield, have a more realistic view of South African farmers as innovators and tough agriculturalists.

Twenty-two African governments have offered South African farmers land. By 2013, well over two thousand of them and some agri-business companies were farming in Congo-Brazzaville, Mozambique, Tanzania, Mali, Madagascar, Zambia, Kenya, Botswana, Malawi, Benin, Egypt, Senegal, Sudan, Uganda and elsewhere. And Agri SA formed an Agri SA Africa Committee that is negotiating agreements with even more countries.

Several South African farmers are also farming in Georgia, in the Caucasus region, and another group went to investigate in late 2013. In June 2013 the Georgian deputy minister of agriculture, David Natroshvili, had a meeting with his South African counterpart, Mulder, to discuss further cooperation and a memorandum of understanding.

Deals with farmers typically include tax holidays, no import duties and long leases on large pieces of mostly idle land, in some cases even free land. What is in it for these countries? The training of their own farmers, food security, creation of employment and the boosting of exports. In a paper published by the Institute for Poverty, Land and Agrarian Studies, 'The Next Great Trek? South African Commercial Farmers Move North', Professor Ruth Hall quotes André Botha of Agri Gauteng: 'There are three main reasons why we are in the Congo. The first is, of course, to diversify our own businesses; the second is to assist local farmers to commercially develop their own land; the third reason is to assist the government of South Africa to fulfil the expectations of the world in stabilising the African continent through the exchange of skills and technology.'

The initiative has the support of the South African government – President Zuma has even bragged on occasion about the talents and resilience of South African farmers at meetings of the Southern African Development Community (SADC). The Department of Agriculture, Forestry and Fisheries has created a fund to support the new 'trekkers' and Minister Tina Joemat-Pettersson has said that 'if we can't find opportunities for white South African farmers in this country, we must do it elsewhere on the continent'.

Not all are impressed. Agang leader Mamphela Ramphele told the Land Divided 2013 conference at UCT that commercial farmers were needed to nurture and support the emergence of small South African farmers. 'It is worrisome that South Africa is losing its commercial farmers to other countries in the north. We are told that 50 per cent of the commercial farmers in Zambia are South Africans. There are eight hundred of them in Mozambique.'

One can't really blame those farmers who gloat and say that while they're not welcome in the land of their birth, they're welcome in the rest of Africa, or that other countries appreciate them while at home they're constantly bad-mouthed and threatened with expropriation. There are indeed also some who say they're trekking further north because they're feeling insecure at home.

But it is clear that most of these farmer-trekkers made a simple business decision. Says Hall: 'There is a certain poignance in what has been called the "white tribe of Africa" – predominantly white (male) Afrikaner farmers – finding or claiming they are not valued in a new South Africa, who see the expressed demand for their skills as affirming their "African-ness" and their place and role in the future of Africa as a whole.'

Hall again quotes Botha: 'This is not running away – it is a calculated process of helping Africa take up its rightful place in the world. All over Africa the message we get is: we are looking for South African farmers, which is incredibly important to us. It means that our contribution to the future of this continent is valued.'

Hall continues: 'This discourse is useful to them – and perhaps true in the view of some – but a far more economically and politically nuanced strategy seems to be at work: on the economic side, farmers are diversifying rather than leaving South Africa. None of the farmers signing up for land in the Congo intend to sell their South African operations, and of those considering Libya [in 2010], most intend to remain based in South Africa and employ managers ... to manage their operations.'

Grow, Africa

There is great enthusiasm in Africa for increased agricultural output as the most likely way to erode poverty and malnutrition and to drive economic growth, an enthusiasm I don't see in South African government circles – perhaps they're taking it for granted that we have the best agricultural sector on the continent.

Former UN chief Kofi Annan is one of the champions of new farming in Africa. He is the chairman of the board of the Alliance for a Green Revolution in Africa, partly funded by the Bill and Melinda Gates Foundation. 'Africa is the only region where overall food security and livelihoods are deteriorating. We will reverse this trend by working to create an environmentally sustainable, uniquely African Green Revolution,' he said recently. 'When our poorest farmers finally prosper, all of Africa will benefit.'

The late president Meles Zenawi of Ethiopia and President Jakaya Kikwete of Tanzania are also strong proponents of agriculture as a driver of growth. Zenawi had considerable success in establishing about a million families on small tracts of land and Ethiopia showed consistent economic growth of more than 10 per cent over a few years because of it.

I interviewed Zenawi in Addis Ababa in 2011 on his vision and then visited some of these peasant farmers. The system really works and has stemmed the tide of urbanisation while also providing employment and good nutrition to children.

The Ethiopians did it with much conviction and energy. Thousands of agricultural extension officers were trained and dispatched; farmers were assisted to form cooperatives to help with buying and selling; seed and fertiliser were provided. Some of the cooperatives were clubbing together to buy tractors and other equipment when I visited.

Ethiopia doesn't rely only on peasant farmers. The government has also leased, controversially I might add, large tracts of land to foreign agri-business concerns to farm intensively. This model is getting traction elsewhere, and in some countries this is where South African farmers enter the picture.

Smallholder farmers or peasant farmers thrive in other parts of the world, despite serious challenges and some failures. Small-scale farmers in Romania are responsible for one of the highest self-sufficiency rates in Europe, *Farmer's Weekly* reported in August 2013. I visited successful peasant farmers growing maize in the Novi Sad region of Serbia in 2010. I watched them harvest by hand with just a cheap two-stroke engine and trailer to transport the maize. I'm told some smallholder farming projects in India and Ghana also work well.

But in South Africa, smallholder farming is mostly scoffed at. The future is mechanised agri-business, the naysayers maintain. Small-scale farming means going back centuries. Economy of scale is what counts. What we need is faster urbanisation, because it's easier to care for people in the cities. And so on.

I concede that smallholder farming is sometimes romanticised by some do-gooders. I agree that it is not the most efficient way to produce large amounts of food.

But I have no doubt that with our history and demographics it should be an essential element in dealing with land dispossession, self-sustainability of rural communities, and extreme poverty and malnutrition.

We do have rapid urbanisation, but we can't generate jobs for the new arrivals and we can't even give them proper homes, services and education. If you're a proponent of this argument, please visit the vast, squalid squatter camps outside every one of our cities and big towns. They are breeding grounds for crime, abuse, resentment and instability. So there goes that argument.

Former cabinet minister and trade-union boss Jay Naidoo is one of South Africa's few supporters of small-scale farming, having investigated it in India. At a recent workshop in Polokwane, Naidoo told delegates about the cooperative model used there. 'I am looking to help the victims of the 1913 land dispossession to make a living out of the land. Through this model 90 per cent of the profits go back to the farmers. In our country this model could act as a true black empowerment.'

But smallholder farming can't work without proper support from the state to get things going, without advice from established farmers or technical officers, or without forming cooperatives with good deals with the retail sector. Peasant farmers are also more vulnerable at times of drought and disease, so they would need a bit of a security net.

One such initiative was recently launched by a former farmer turned military general. When he discovered that all military bases were buying their vegetables and meat from supermarkets, he organised small farmers in the vicinity of these bases to supply the military instead. This means the farmers have a ready market for their surplus produce, and no middleman.

I once drove between Pretoria and Pelindaba and noticed two-metre high maize growing next to the double highway and in the space between the two roads. I stopped and a woman working the field told me the soil was rich, the rainfall high and she had had three excellent crops already. She and her husband and friends have a thriving business selling green mealie cobs to nearby townships and they mill their own mealie meal. Between them, they have seven children, all well clothed and well fed and going to a good school. How's that for successful small-scale farming?

Landbouweekblad recently interviewed the influential secretary-general of the ANC, Gwede Mantashe, on his farm in the Elliot district in the Eastern Cape. He told them he believed that farming the communal land of the former Transkei and Ciskei had huge potential, but that the provincial agriculture department wasn't doing anything to promote it. He said the small farmers in the area had no implements and no knowledge of management, and added that he had pleaded with the minister of agriculture to 'get the information officers out of the office so they could show these farmers how it should be done'.

I spent several weeks in the former Transkei in 2012 working on television documentaries. We went off the main roads to the more remote villages.

Everywhere I went, I saw rolling hill upon rolling hill – and almost no cattle, sheep or goats, and almost no cultivated land apart from patches of plantings around houses.

I asked a local chief in the Mvezo district why no one was using the land while there was such an outcry about land redistribution. He almost had tears in his eyes when he told me that people didn't want to work the land any longer. They wanted to work in the government offices in Mthatha and Bhisho or they wanted to go to Cape Town or Johannesburg. 'They look down upon us who stayed here on the land,' he said. He later explained that some young men leave the area to find work as farmworkers elsewhere because they get housing, food and a salary every month.

The old Bantustans would surely have been the best and easiest way to start land reform and get black farmers going. Instead, these areas remain the undeveloped backwaters of the country.

The NDP recognises this and states that insufficient tenure security – access to land is strictly controlled by traditional chiefs and the land remains the property of the group – is the most important risk to integrated and inclusive rural economies. 'As long as these farmers (especially women farmers) do not have secure tenure, they will not invest, and agricultural production will not grow at the rate and pattern required for growth in employment.' Better land use in the communal areas, the plan states, 'has the potential to improve the livelihoods of at least 370 000 people'.

Writing in the DA's online newsletter in January 2013, DA leader and Western Cape premier Helen Zille remarks: 'If the ANC simply applied the NDP's proposals for transforming communal land tenure, it would more than quadruple the yields of the most fertile land in the country, meet its numerical reform targets, create thousands of jobs, and extend food security. This surely must be a priority, rather than the continued destruction of once productive farms in an escalating race to the bottom.'

Political will

Ah, but one would need the political will to take on the abuse of power and patronage of traditional leaders, and that the ANC doesn't have. Not under Mandela or Mbeki, and certainly not under arch-traditionalist Zuma. And it isn't going to change any time soon. The ANC has lost support to the DA, COPE and possibly even Agang in the Eastern Cape (the Thembu king is now a DA member), and will do nothing to alienate chiefs in that region.

KwaZulu-Natal is now the ANC's strongest power base and Zulu-speakers are the most traditional-minded group in the country.

Says Pallo Jordan: 'In the former Bantustans, the ANC's own political tactics have persuaded it to find accommodation with the chiefs, in whom colonial/apartheid law vested the power to determine access to arable land and grazing. Consequently, the ANC's practice vacillates between asserting the rights of rural dwellers as set out in the Constitution and acknowledging the claims of chiefs, rooted in pre-colonial traditions that are of little relevance in the twenty-first century.'

Aninka Claassens, veteran land-rights activist and senior researcher in the Law, Race and Gender Research Unit at UCT, is more blunt in a piece written in 2012: 'To overturn the Land Act's legacy requires confronting autocratic chiefly power and the denial of black landownership. The post-apartheid government has chosen to do the opposite. Its package of traditional leadership laws vests far-reaching unilateral powers in chiefs, including apartheid-era appointees, while re-entrenching the deeply contested tribal boundaries of the former Bantustans.'

This package includes the Traditional Leadership and Governance Framework Act of 2003; the Communal Land Rights Act of 2004, which was declared unconstitutional by the Constitutional Court six years later; eight provincial laws on traditional leadership; and, lately, the Traditional Courts Bill, which enables chiefs to punish people by stripping them of customary entitlements such as access to land, and the National Traditional Affairs Bill. 'These laws bolster the Bantustan-era arrogance and power of traditional leaders towards their "subjects". Community meetings are banned, tribal levies extorted and landownership rights denied,' says Claassens.

Traditional leaders know they will lose their power and privilege once land rights in the former homelands are recognised, and thus they argue that customary law prohibits it. It would be 'un-African' and 'a slap in the face of the ancestors', one said. Even legitimate restitution claims of people who were forcibly removed from their land have been turned down because authority over land now resides with chiefs.

Claassens: 'We have come full circle. One hundred years after the Land Act denied black ownership, the ANC government is supporting traditional leaders in upholding this "tradition". Now, as in the past, a ruling elite has reached for the law to bolster its contested authority and monopolise land and other resources at the expense of the poorest.'

This is Free Market Foundation executive director Leon Louw's take: 'Converting all black-occupied land to full, freely tradable ownership un-compromised by the Expropriation Bill would be more transforming and empowering than anything else proposed so far by pseudo-radicals.'

And the communal land is not a tiny slice: 18 023 102 hectares, which include 1 277 926 hectares of former 'coloured areas'.

A popular argument among land-reform critics is that state-owned land should be redistributed first and that this would meet the targets. This is not true. Only 2 per cent of the 12.6 million hectares of state land is available for redistribution – that is, if we can trust available figures, because there still is no definitive audit of state land. Almost 30 per cent of state land is used by national parks and other protected areas, for instance, and land used by the South African National Defence Force (SANDF), Water and Environmental Affairs, Correctional Services, schools and hospitals can't be redistributed either.

There is one form of state land, though, that could make a huge contri-bution to alleviate landlessness and add to the livelihoods of the poor outside the big cities: municipal commonages, the agricultural land most munici-palities own around towns. This is ideal for part-time farming to augment incomes and to satisfy desires to engage in agricultural activities like cattle farming and crop planting. According to the Institute for Poverty, Land and Agrarian Studies, the incomes of over 10 per cent of households in three Eastern Cape towns would drop below the poverty line if contributions from commonage activities were excluded.

Unfortunately there is no clear information on municipal land. The bits of information available suggest it could amount to a substantial number of hectares: in the Free State, for instance, municipal commonage comprised around 113 000 hectares in 2003.

It is crucial to know who actually wants land. A 2001 survey estimated that 9 per cent of black South Africans not already farming had aspirations to do so. The most comprehensive survey was done by Michael Aliber, Maxine Reitzes and Marlene Roefs and published by the Human Sciences Research Council (HSRC) in 2006. It found that a third of all black adults want access to land for food production, while another 12 per cent want land for other purposes.

This means that 66 per cent of black adults don't want to engage in agricultural activities. As significantly, 48 per cent of those who wanted land said they would be satisfied with one hectare or less. A piece of land smaller than a hectare is just a big vegetable garden. A further 25 per cent said they would be happy with less than five hectares. (Almost 60 per cent of those dispossessed of land said they would prefer financial compensation rather than land, according to the survey.)

Here's the view of former *Sunday Times* editor Mondli Makhanya in a column in 2010: 'We are wasting valuable time and energy trying to restore people to their peasant ways. Ordinary South Africans either do not want land or just don't have the capacity to work it. They want to go to cities and work in the modern economy ... Large-scale, highly mechanised commercial farming is now the way of the world. You cannot turn the clock back four decades. Furthermore, the young people would, as has happened elsewhere, have simply upped and headed for the towns and cities. Yet we continue to nurse the notion that we can reverse the inevitable march to an urban future. We keep wanting to fight the logic of large-scale commercial farming.'

Failures

The government's land-reform programme has been tainted not only by bad management and wrong decisions, but by the failures of many of those new farmers established on land. Some of these are truly heartbreaking and represent a spectacular waste of millions in taxpayer money. An example is the twenty productive dairy and crop farms, bought for R12 million in the Eastern Cape, where all production had ceased. Many of these redistributed farms deteriorated into squatter camps. (*Farmer's Weekly* recently ran a story about a new farmer, Ziphilele Matinise of the Ncera district in the Eastern Cape, who was prevented from farming by people who just arrived and squatted on his land with no reaction from the authorities.)

These failures are too often used as arguments against land redistribution. But in many of the cases I have come across, the cause of the failure was a complete lack of financial and technical support for the new farmers from the national and provincial departments of agriculture. Any experienced farmer will tell you it's impossible to make a success of farming if all you have is the land, especially if you're a novice. Other causes of failure include power struggles and infighting, where land was given to a whole group of people, and, in some cases, new beneficiaries keeping their jobs in the cities and towns and not focusing on their farming businesses.

There are a good number of success stories too, though. In many of these cases, the new farmers had the support and advice of neighbouring farmers or were part of a programme run by organised agriculture or NGOs. I have

---

Best and worst

Here is Free State Agriculture president Dan Kriek on what would be
the best and worst decisions on land reform over the next twenty years:

> Best case: we have real political leadership, as was the case in the
> Mandela era, when a concerted effort was made in terms of rec-
> onciliation and nation building. Unity in agriculture is achieved
> within the next two years. The relationship of trust between
> government and the private sector is restored to such an extent that
> government enables the agri-business sector, as well as commodity
> organisations, to conduct land reform on its behalf. Property rights
> are fiercely protected. Government creates an enabling environ-
> ment for agriculture to flourish, which will enable us to create jobs
> and deliver on rural development. The National Development Plan
> for agriculture comes to fruition.
>
> The worst-case scenario would be to carry on with the same
> situation we are experiencing at present. While playing political
> games with sensitive issues such as land reform, government creates
> massive uncertainty that seriously affects investor confidence in
> the sector. Populist economic and constitutional doctrine becomes
> the norm. Property rights are diluted further, seriously affecting
> sustainable, profitable food production. Food price hikes lead to
> ever-increasing levels of social instability.
>
> What follows could be as destructive for South Africans as
> apartheid was.

(From *Farmer's Weekly*, 2 August 2013)

---

also come across a few successful new farms where the owners had enough
of their own capital, in many cases pension money, to get through the first
difficult years.

I see no evidence yet of a marked change of attitude from government
departments towards technical and financial support for emerging farmers.
This is simply part of the general malaise from which our governments have
suffered over the years. I can't see new smallholder farmers making a great
success either, because of this lack of interest, energy, commitment and man-

agement by the state. There will simply have to be a greater input by civil society, especially established farmers.

But there are other schemes and models that have proved to be workable and successful, and we'll simply have to have more of these. One of the most successful land-reform schemes to date is the equity-share schemes in especially the Western Cape, where farmworkers and farmers co-own the land, and productivity and management levels are kept high.

The NDP contains very ambitious proposals for land, rural and agricultural reform in the period to 2030 – all great ideas in my view, but not ideas I can see a faltering state machinery implementing any day soon.

But it does have one very interesting, concrete proposal for more efficient land redistribution that I can see working if commercial farmers and their organisations, business, civil society and opposition politicians put enough pressure on municipalities, provincial governments and national government. This is it:

> Each district municipality with commercial farming land in South Africa should convene a committee (the district lands committee) with all agricultural landowners in the district, including stakeholders such as the private sector (the commercial banks, agribusiness), government (departments of Rural Development and Land Reform, the provincial departments of agriculture, water affairs and so on) and government agencies (Land Bank, the Agricultural Research Council and so on).
>
> This committee will be responsible for identifying 20 per cent of the commercial agricultural land in the district, and giving the commercial farmers the option of assisting in its transfer to black farmers.
>
> This can be done as follows: Identify land readily available from the following categories: land already in the market; land where the farmer is already under severe financial pressure; land held by an absentee landlord willing to exit; and land in a deceased estate. In this way, land could be found without distorting markets.
>
> Obtain the land through the state at 50 per cent of market value (which is closer to its fair productive value). The 50 per cent shortfall of the current owner is made up by cash or in-kind contributions from commercial farmers who volunteer to participate.
>
> In exchange, commercial farmers are protected from losing their land in future and they gain black economic empowerment status. This should

remove the uncertainty and mistrust that surrounds land reform and the related loss of investor confidence.

Helen Zille supports the plan's ideas, but isn't overcome with optimism: 'The NDP's proposals should be the centrepiece of public debate during this centenary commemoration [of the Natives Land Act], so we can avoid the tempting detours of political expedience that has resulted in past failures … But given the emotive value of the land issue in achieving the ANC's goal of mobilising its electoral support base by exacerbating racial divisions, this may be too much to hope for. The odds are greater that President Zuma will continue to duck the issues, blame the past to avoid dealing with the realities of the present and destroy one of the most important pillars of our economy.'

I hope Zille is wrong. It is entirely possible for us to satisfy the land needs of those genuinely needing a small patch of land, a medium patch or an actual farm. There are enough tested models and schemes that we know work properly; we need to shift towards those and stop the ones we know don't work.

There is enough goodwill among white farmers to get them to play a much bigger role, although politicians and activists need to stop bad-mouthing them as a group, or this goodwill will also evaporate.

We need the media, organised agriculture, civil action groups and the political opposition to bring perspective to the public debate on what the real issues are and to expose political opportunism.

We need the business community and civil society to become more actively involved in land-reform initiatives. We cannot afford to leave the entire land-redistribution process to the bungling state bureaucracy any longer.

It is possible to find a balance between genuine agrarian reform that will lead to better productivity, sound communities and employment on the one hand, and the angry demands around land dispossession being satisfied on the other.

Organised commercial agriculture will have to clearly distance itself from the likes of Afrikanerbond chairman Piet Vorster, the Transvaal Agricultural Union and other reactionary voices arguing against a fair dispensation. It will have to clean up its own house, also in terms of conditions on farms, be far more proactive and come with more of its own initiatives to redistribute land, as has happened in some regions.

If we cannot achieve visible progress and in good time, we will most certainly be faced with Malema's option of large-scale expropriation of land and the disasters it will bring.

10

Crime and policing

Crime is the one topic that you're guaranteed to see on the front pages of South African newspapers every single week of the year. You can count yourself lucky if you go to any social occasion and crime stories don't dominate.

South Africans are obsessed with crime. Not only do most of us, or people close to us, have personal experience of criminal actions, but many of us also use crime as a barometer of how generally well or badly we're doing as a country and/or of the state of our race relations. In the process, the picture often gets completely distorted, especially by fearful white people and by some right-wingers who use it to express their inner racism and to turn whites into the victims of an imaginary black onslaught.

In this way, greater Johannesburg and Cape Town are regularly labelled the world capitals of murder, rape, car hijacking and robbery. Yet there are several cities in countries such as Sierra Leone, Mexico, Brazil, Colombia, El Salvador, Honduras and Russia that are equally or more dangerous, as well as American cities such as Detroit and Chicago. (Admittedly, I have been burgled in South Africa, but I have also been mugged in Philadelphia and Los Angeles on two different visits to the US.) Broadly speaking, South African citizens are not much more likely to become victims of crime than those of most other countries, apart from the few very safe ones such as Austria, Ireland, Sweden and Finland.

But it does appear that we are top of the heap when it comes to *violent* crime. We may not have many more burglars than other places in the world, but here they don't just rough up their victims and steal their stuff; they also kill and sometimes rape and torture their victims. Violent or contact crimes make up a third of all crimes reported to the police. Between April 2011 and March 2012, there were 15 940 murders, 14 859 attempted murders, 192 651 serious assaults, 64 514 sexual offences and 101 000 cases of aggravated robbery recorded in South Africa.

I couldn't find any definitive comparative statistics or reliable studies, but

Farm murders

Right-wing white South Africans launched a national and international offensive that describes whites as the victims of a massive, racially motivated criminal assault. Some even used the word genocide.

Farm murders especially are used emotionally to prove this new white victimhood. Popular Afrikaans musician Steve Hofmeyr, for example, wrote on his Facebook page and his website in 2013: 'My people are being killed like flies.' He added that a white farmer was murdered every five days. Tens of thousands of Afrikaners rallied behind Hofmeyr, some urging him to start a political party and 'lead the Afrikaners'.

But virtually every single statistic Hofmeyr quoted was quickly refuted and his sources discredited, among others by an investigation by Africa Check.

The Institute for Security Studies said that white South Africans are far less likely to be murdered than their black or coloured counterparts. An analysis of some 1 400 police murder dockets in 2009, for instance, revealed that whites accounted for only 1.8 per cent of the cases, despite making up almost 9 per cent of the population.

Hofmeyr declared that the number of whites murdered by blacks since 1994 would fill one of the country's largest football stadiums (thus sixty thousand plus). The real figure of murdered whites is probably around seven thousand, almost certainly less than ten thousand. Africa Check found that the current murder rate of white South Africans is equivalent to or lower than murder rates for whites between 1979 and 1991.

Hofmeyr's insistence that a white farmer was 'slaughtered' every five days was also wrong. According to the police, at least 38 per cent of farm-attack victims are black, coloured or Indian. Several studies over the last few years have found that farm attacks are, with possibly a few isolated exceptions, not politically motivated, but can be blamed on the vulnerability of people living far from neighbours.

The right-wing hysteria about farm murders and the claim of genocide has had the unfortunate effect of making many people dismiss the phenomenon of farm murders as propaganda. But it is a serious problem. According to the SAIRR and the activist group AfriForum, farmers are three times more likely to become murder victims than ordinary South Africans – their murder rate is 98.8 per 100 000 per year. In addition, anecdotal evidence suggests that farm attacks are often more brutal than other murders and assaults.

AfriForum's campaign for the minister of police to recognise farm murders as a crisis and a 'unique crime', and to prioritise it, is thus not unreasonable, in my view.

my guess is also that our police service must be among the most corrupt, inefficient and brutal in the democratic world.

Rather than dwell on the myriad crime statistics, which are often contested, I would rather explore the possible explanations for why our crime rate is so high, why our crime is so violent and what has gone wrong with our police service.

Any analysis of the root causes of our high rate of violent crime should start in our violent past. Nation-forming in the eastern and central parts of South Africa in the early nineteenth century was violent and was hardly over when the Voortrekkers arrived and triggered more bloody conflict as they established themselves on the land. Apartheid was a violent ideology, and practices such as influx control, migrant labour and forced removal deeply traumatised communities, families and individuals.

The resistance against oppression was also violent, not only the armed struggle waged by MK and AZAPO, but also during the 1980s with the enforced consumer boycotts, which rendered the townships ungovernable, the practice of necklacing, and the bloody conflict between the ANC/UDF and the IFP.

During this period, political violence was glorified and romanticised by both black and white society. The SADF troops 'on the border', actually referring to Angola and Namibia, and the policemen (and later soldiers) in the townships were heroes fighting for white survival. Extrajudicial kidnapping, torture and assassination by death squads such as the Vlakplaas unit, the Civil Cooperation Bureau and the Directorate of Covert Collection, and the Third Force activities fomenting violence between black groupings, continued with impunity even into the early 1990s.

The language of violence is still used when the ANC sings its struggle songs at rallies and gatherings. Zuma's trademark song, although he's not singing it as often any more, is 'Awuleth' Umshini Wami' (bring me my machine gun). More often than not, strikes by COSATU unions turn violent and the killing of scabs or of members of opposing unions is common, and receives little rebuke from the political leadership. About two hundred people, mostly non-strikers, were killed, mostly by striking workers, during industrial action in the last thirteen years. Some four hundred were injured.

I think it is safe to say that the sanctity of human life is not valued as highly in South Africa as it is in most other societies.

Liberation and democracy didn't live up to the dreams of ordinary people and many still live in squalor. Unemployment is extremely high with no prospects of improving soon. Rapid urbanisation since 1994 has brought millions of people to unfamiliar surroundings, often tearing families apart. Simultaneously, the failing education system has been dumping millions of teenagers who fail to pass matric back into the townships. There isn't a lot of hope in the country's townships and squatter camps, but rather a feeling of helplessness, marginalisation and rage, which can't but contribute to violence and criminality.

And then there is the gross inequality in society, which some analysts say contributes more to crime than poverty itself. Again, the absence of hope that this will change any time soon leads to anger and frustration. A further complication is the racial overtones of the divide between rich and poor.

One of South Africa's clearest thinkers on criminality is academic and author Antony Altbeker. He acknowledges the legacies of the past, poverty and inequality as factors contributing to the high crime rate, but he also asks serious questions about them.

He points out that other societies that went through long periods of oppression and violence and other societies with serious poverty problems do not have the same culture of violent crime as we do. He asks why it is that, at the height of apartheid and thus of exclusion and marginalisation, the number of murders was about two-thirds lower than the 2009 figure of 19 000, and why in the early 1960s fewer than four hundred murders were committed annually.

Altbeker's theory is that violence is contagious. He cites an American study that found strong and statistically significant correlations between one person's weight gain and the weight gains of their friends and relatives. He paraphrases the study's finding by applying it to violence: 'Having violent social contacts might change a person's tolerance for using violence or might influence his or her adoption of specific behaviours (e.g. assaulting, robbing, raping, killing).'

High crime levels in some social environments thus breed more violent crime, because it becomes 'normal' and is seen as inevitable. The failure to arrest and jail violent criminals perpetuates this culture. This theory certainly fits the situation on the Cape Flats for as much as I'm familiar with it.

Theories and policies on crime and policing come and go, but the reality remains that a society in which would-be criminals believe they're going to get away with their crimes will always have a high crime rate. Catching criminals, especially the serious ones making a life out of crime, prosecuting them successfully and putting them in prison remain the most important litmus test for any criminal justice system.

From a mid-2013 prison population of 156 400, we can extrapolate a prison population rate of 294 per 100 000 of the population.

Our ratio of one police official for every 303 citizens is not low compared to international standards. In April 2013 there were 157 518 members of the South African Police Service (SAPS) and about 6 000 Metro Police officers, who also do some police work.

But here's a sobering fact: There are nearly nine thousand private security companies registered in South Africa and they employ about 400 000 registered security guards – more than the police and the military combined. They're not police officers, but without them our crime rate would undoubtedly be much higher. Strictly speaking, though, they're not part of the criminal justice system and that's where South Africa falls dismally short.

It all started so well after 1994. The South African Police became the South African Police Service and the military ranks were changed to typical police ranks. 'We're a caring nation now; unlike the apartheid police, our new men and women in blue will serve the people' was the thinking. We had to make sure our new police service had more legitimacy than their pre-liberation counterparts.

Along with it came a new approach of *crime prevention* rather than *law enforcement*. Community policing. We have too many people in jail, most of them young black men, and it would be better to prevent people from committing crime than to catch and lock them up after they have done so.

This policy shift from catching criminals, prosecuting and giving them stiff jail sentences to preventing crime before it happens led to a terrible neglect of our criminal justice system.

I was a crime reporter in my early twenties. The hierarchy then was that the security policemen were on top, followed by the detectives and then the riot squads, with the men and women (mostly men then) in their neat blue uniforms at the bottom. The leadership of the police was drawn mostly from the ranks of the security branch and the detectives.

The security police were the political police and their job was primarily to spy on, harass and jail anti-apartheid activists.

My heroes as a crime reporter were the detectives – that subculture of committed men in shabby civilian clothes; chain-smokers and hard drinkers most of them. They were not really political. They lived to figure out who had committed what crimes, building cases that would stand up in court and working with the prosecutors to ensure convictions. They were proud of their job and always competed against one another; over a drink or around the braai at home, they still talked only about their cases (and about rugby, of course). The uniformed police didn't like them much, these guys with their moustaches, scruffy shoes and cheap cologne, always scurrying about with a brown docket cover under the arm.

A few years ago, my house was invaded by three gun-wielding crimi-nals. One held a pistol to my head while his partners carried out virtually everything I owned. When the detectives came the next morning to take my statement and to lift fingerprints, I realised that the detectives of my crime-reporting days no longer existed.

These ones didn't appear very keen to look for clues or to interview the witnesses across the street – in fact, they didn't talk to anyone but me. And they were bossed around by the uniformed guys. The two detectives more or less made it clear to me that their main job was to create a file with details of all my stolen property so that I could claim from my insurance company. Not even the fact that the same criminals had struck a house down the street a few days earlier could get their enthusiasm up. In short, my experience of these detectives was in stark contrast to the confident, competent and keen detectives I knew as a crime reporter.

On investigation, the reasons became clear. In 1996 the detectives were put under the command of local station commanders with the uniformed police. They lost their status as specialists and were often starved of resources because most station commanders were from the uniformed branch. The next step was almost inevitable: the specialised units in the detective service were scrapped. It wasn't such a desirable job to become a detective now, which meant the detective service ceased to attract most of the best human material.

Specialised detective training, I was told, also suffered from this loss of status. The once highly efficient (and often politically abused) forensics department of the old SAP virtually collapsed and became so dysfunctional that investigators and detectives almost could not bank on them for assistance. This sad state of affairs was beginning to change in 2012 with new laboratories and an increased staff complement of about 1500.

Let's return to Altbeker's analogy between crime and obesity, the theory that violence and crime are 'contagious'. A major step forward obviously would be to drastically reduce the levels of poverty and unemployment, but at the same time catching and incarcerating criminals could have a significant impact.

Altbeker refers to research done by a criminologist and former policeman who interviewed thirty convicted hijackers in Gauteng. Eighteen of these criminals gave details of their careers in crime over the preceding five years. Between them, they acknowledged 1889 crimes, including 423 hijackings, 295 cases of car theft, 198 burglaries, 7 robberies and 3 rapes. All the work of just eighteen men.

'Imagine if they'd been caught five years earlier than they were,' says Altbeker. 'And now consider something else: in 2008, the SAPS recorded a total of about 47000 hijackings, business robberies and home invasions, about 75 per cent more than five years earlier. That's a lot of incidents, and, if you consider that the average crime of this kind involves something like five perpetrators, then there were nearly 250000 man-incidents that year. But now consider something else: these crimes are almost always committed by repeat offenders. These are not the drunken brawls or the rage-fuelled murders into which someone might stumble once in his life; these are crimes committed by groups of people who commit them reasonably frequently. If that is so, and if we can assume – conservatively, I think – that the average person involved in these crimes commits only one crime a month, then we're dealing with a population of offenders that is about 20000 strong.'

I find this fascinating. To change poverty and unemployment or social norms can take a generation, but to zoom in on a group of 20000 or so criminals and put them in jail could have a huge impact in the short term.

Altbeker suggests the active mining of cellphone data to see who talks to whom, school and home address data to see who grew up with whom, and prison records to see who met whom in prison. 'Add to that the cellphone records of their girlfriends, and it's hard not to believe that a dedicated team of detectives, supported by sophisticated data-mining, couldn't identify large numbers against whom cases could then be built. I'd bet that if they arrested a quarter of the active offenders, most of the rest would commit far fewer crimes.'

This makes a lot of sense to me. But there are several 'if onlys'. If only our detectives were all clean of corruption, well trained and committed. If only our police service could be better managed and without political interference.

Even ordinary South Africans know the names of several of South Africa's greatest crime bosses – especially those of Italian, Russian, Czech and Nigerian origin – and local gang leaders. They are in and out of court and feature regularly on newspaper pages. Many have been named in recently written books about organised crime. Men such as Yuri Ulianitski, assassinated in 2007, and Cyril Beeka, assassinated in 2011.

And yet most of them (those not killed by their adversaries, that is) are still free men. Take Vito Palazzolo, for instance. He was convicted of Mafia activities in Italy and fled to South Africa in 1986, where he quickly corrupted at least one NP politician and, in the years since 1994, several senior policemen. He would still be living the life of a billionaire outside Franschhoek if he hadn't been arrested in Thailand in 2012.

The first post-apartheid police commissioner coming from inside ANC ranks, Jackie Selebi, was convicted of corruption in 2010 when his dealings with Glenn Agliotti, a self-confessed criminal with friends in very high places, became public. Agliotti told the court he had been a go-between for Selebi and mining tycoon Brett Kebble, who had wanted Selebi to stop an investigation into his company and have charges against his father, Roger Kebble, dropped.

Selebi was responsible for the closing down of the SAPS Anti-Corruption Unit in 2001. According to the Africa Check website, the unit had received 20 779 allegations of police corruption between 1996 and 2001. Between 1995 and 1999, an average of 1 320 police officers were convicted each year on criminal charges.

The Selebi saga was riddled with political intrigue, and was one of the first symptoms of party political abuse of the criminal justice system post-1994. The well-respected head of the NPA, Vusi Pikoli, was fired by then president Thabo Mbeki in September 2007, because he wouldn't let go of the NPA's investigation of Selebi for fraud, corruption and racketeering. Three years later, Selebi was sent to jail for corruption (but was granted medical parole) and Pikoli's reputation remained intact. The police received a bill of R17.5 million for Selebi's legal costs.

Selebi's successor, Bheki Cele, was an ANC strongman in KwaZulu-Natal and a Zuma insider, but also not a professional policeman. He was suspended in October 2011 for his role in the irregular awarding of a R1.3 billion contract for police accommodation and fired as commissioner in June 2012. (He was succeeded by Riah Phiyega, a former director of companies with no policing experience whatsoever.)

The rot didn't stop at the top. In July 2013 the police disclosed that an internal audit had revealed that 1448 serving police officers were convicted criminals, all guilty of serious crimes such as murder, attempted murder, rape, assault, corruption, theft, robbery, housebreaking, drug trafficking and aiding prisoner escapes. A number of them had been convicted of multiple crimes, resulting in a total of 3204 convictions. The audit was completed in 2009, so quite a few new convictions could have been added since then. It would take well over a year to review all these cases, the police said, because fitness boards would have to hear 'representations as to why they believe they remain fit to serve in the SAPS'.

Among the convicted criminals still serving in the SAPS were a major-general, 10 brigadiers, 21 colonels, 10 majors, 43 lieutenant-colonels, 163 captains, 84 lieutenants and 716 warrant officers.

Here's another recent example of how weak the SAPS's vetting procedures are. In August 2013, Phiyega appointed General Bethuel Mondli Zuma as the new Gauteng provincial commissioner of police, just to withdraw the appointment a few days later when a reporter Googled Zuma's name and found that he was being charged with drunken driving, resisting arrest and refusing to have his alcohol levels tested.

Now consider the case of Morris Tshabalala. He was convicted of armed robbery and possession of an unlicensed firearm in 1996, but lodged an appeal after two weeks in jail. In 1998 he abandoned the appeal and a warrant for his rearrest was issued. But before he could be arrested, someone in the police illegally cancelled the warrant.

So what is a convicted bank robber to do? Join the police, of course. Tshabalala became a captain and a rising star in the elite crime-intelligence unit with top security clearance, earning the nickname Captain KGB. Ten years after he joined the police, he was nabbed for a cash-in-transit heist in Sasolburg. The 'cancelled' warrant for his arrest was produced and he was sent back to jail. He is now being investigated for his alleged role in seven heists in which more than R30 million was stolen.

A *City Press* editorial in June 2013 stated: 'Of course all police officers aren't corrupt criminals, but Tshabalala's story leads to the inescapable conclusion that certain sections of the SAPS have been infiltrated by sophisticated criminal syndicates. The degree of infiltration is anyone's guess.'

The crime-intelligence unit, a critical unit in combating crime, has been in the news the last year for all the wrong reasons. Part of the problem is that the senior officers in the unit are extremely powerful because they have information on virtually every prominent politician, which makes them immune to just about any control or discipline. The other part of the problem is that the unit has a substantial slush fund that we know has been abused several times over the last few years. Three of the unit's top officers have been charged with corruption.

The Civilian Secretariat for Police stated in a green paper in June 2013: 'One of the main problems faced by crime intelligence is that it has had a bit of a "blank cheque". This has allowed officers to operate in areas that traditionally fall within the domain of the State Security Agency. This blurring of the lines between crime intelligence and state security has led to serious tensions and issues relating to a lack of accountability within crime intelligence.'

The real number of corrupt cops is almost certainly much higher than the figure of 1448. Between 1998 and 2012, more than 21780 criminal cases against police officers were reported to the Independent Complaints Directorate (now called the Independent Police Investigative Directorate, or IPID), and these excluded cases involving police action. Africa Watch reports that critics believe that IPID is a toothless watchdog, understaffed, underfunded and routinely ignored or lied to by police. The SAPS performance plan for 2013/14 states that there were 8846 criminal cases pending against the police by 31 March 2013. Another scary statistic: the police were facing civil claims of R15 billion in 2013 arising from cases of assault, accidents, shootings and damage to property.

Let me give you an example of the kind of stuff going on. In 2006 a criminal gang stole R100 million worth of banknotes at O.R. Tambo International Airport. The thieves were caught and some of the money recovered was kept in a safe at the Benoni police station, from where it went missing. A British company sued the police and, in July 2013, Justice Nigel Willis determined that the thieves could only have been police officers and ordered the police minister to pay the company the missing money with seven years' interest plus legal costs, an amount of almost R40 million.

Three police officers were criminally charged with the theft, but these charges were withdrawn after a number of the witnesses were killed under mysterious circumstances. The officers are still in the SAPS. This case is just one of several in the last few years in which witnesses called to testify against corrupt cops were murdered before the case reached court.

Transparency International's Global Corruption Barometer 2013 put South

Africa among thirty-six countries in which the police were seen as the most corrupt institution. About 83 per cent of South Africans believed that the police were corrupt, while 36 per cent admitted to having paid bribes to police.

The executive director of Corruption Watch, David Lewis, said the finding confirmed that the increase in corruption was not a mere perception. 'We solicit public experiences of corruption and we are getting a significant number of reports of bribery and other acts of corruption, especially from poor communities,' he said.

Crime facts 2012/13

After a gradual decline over the last few years, the crime statistics for 2012/13 released by the SAPS on 19 September 2013 showed an increase in serious and violent crimes, countering claims that the police are winning the war against crime.

The murder rate was up by 4.2 per cent to 16 259 cases or forty-five murders a day. This is four and a half times higher than the global average of 6.9 per 100 000 people. Murder rates are the most accurate of all crime statistics. Attempted murder rates increased by 6.5 per cent to 16 363 cases.

The likelihood of falling victim to crime depends largely on race, gender, age, economic profile and residential area. According to the Institute for Security Studies, most murder victims are young black men. Most murdered women are killed by their intimate partners. Men are six times more likely to be murdered than women.

More murders were recorded in Cape Town than in Johannesburg and Pretoria combined, but two-thirds of Cape Town's murders took place in just ten of the sixty police precincts. Mitchells Plain experienced the highest number of violent and property crimes in the country, while Nyanga, Khayelitsha and Gugulethu had the highest murder rates.

Half of South Africa's murders occurred in only 13 per cent or 143 out of 1 127 precincts. Three in four murders occurred in just a quarter of the country's police-station districts.

House robbery increased by 3.5 per cent in 2012/13, carjacking by 5.4 per cent, truck hijacking by 14.9 per cent, residential burglary by 3.3 per cent and business burglary by 1.7 per cent.

Where did it all go wrong?

Perhaps we should pause and consider where matters went wrong. The old SAP was a crucial tool used by the apartheid governments to enforce apartheid and, as such, was deeply resented by most South Africans. There was a racist culture in the force and the emphasis was on keeping white citizens safe and the NP in power. Uniformed police were the ones who had to check passbooks and make sure apartheid legislation was enforced. The security police focused almost exclusively on harassing, capturing and often torturing anti-apartheid activists. And then there was the SAP's death squad at Vlakplaas, operating completely outside the law, tasked with kidnapping and killing activists.

When the ANC took over government in 1994, law enforcement had to be completely reinvented and a new police service established in a very short time without the luxury of keeping most of the experienced staff. The new police had to serve all citizens and establish a new credibility. It did help that an old-order policeman, but one with a clean and non-political record, George Fivaz, acted as the commissioner for the first five years, but then it was over to Jackie Selebi, an ANC veteran and former ambassador, but a man with no experience of law enforcement.

The first ministers in charge of the police were not the worst cabinet members of their time, but they all fell short of overseeing the methodical establishment of an effective and accountable police: Sydney Mufamadi, Steve Tshwete, Charles Nqakula and the latest incumbent, Nathi Mthethwa. An additional problem was that crime figures exploded just before and after 1994, making their job that much more difficult. Another complication was that the initially strong civilian structures created to oversee the police lost much of their power and influence after 1999.

Scrutinising hundreds of press clippings, research studies and papers by experts on the police over the last few years makes it clear that the police suffered from much the same malaise as other state departments: bad appointments, wrong strategies, lack of vision and proper planning, cadre deployment, nepotism, political interference, bureaucratic incompetence, lack of accountability, weak discipline and laissez-faire management.

Reports abound of police stations without vehicles, police officers without driver's licences (for example, 40 per cent of officers in Gauteng in April 2013 didn't have licences), semi-literate staff unable to file proper reports or take witness statements, emergency telephone numbers going unanswered and police simply not turning up after being called to crime scenes.

An example: In mid-2013, only thirteen of the SAPS's thirty-seven helicopters were serviceable, meaning its helicopter capabilities were curbed by 62 per cent. This seriously impedes the police's ability to react quickly to serious crimes such as cash-in-transit heists and bank robberies, and leaves them flat-footed in the case of large-scale disturbances.

Another example: More than seventy suspected criminals were killed by mobs in Khayelitsha in 2012, constituting about 20 per cent of all murders in the Cape Town township that year, because residents feel they get little support from police.

A police task team's report published in 2012 paints a dismal picture of policing in that township. Suspects are generally not charged within forty-eight hours; a large number of suspects are detained but never charged; facial-identity profiles of suspects described by complainants are almost never made; witness statements are not always taken; complainants are seldom asked to view photo albums of criminals; and so on. But when Western Cape premier Helen Zille, supported by several progressive NGOs, appointed a commission of inquiry into policing in Khayelitsha, she was opposed in court by the minister of police.

The use of sophisticated technology has had an impact on crime in other countries. The electronic tracking of vehicles in South Africa has reduced the number of thefts and hijackings by about 20 per cent. But the SAPS is largely ignoring technology, especially on local station level.

Again, I have personal experience. I clearly saw the two men who robbed my office in Cape Town in 2010. When I asked the detective (at Cape Town's main police station) working the case to draw up a facial profile of the robbers, he reluctantly pulled an ancient PC from his desk and conjured up an image with completely outdated and primitive software that simply could not do the job. When I asked to look at file pictures of known Cape Town robbers, he produced a bunch of loose pages with extremely vague photographs – many of which had no names, case numbers or any other information attached to them.

When Commissioner Phiyega appeared before Parliament on 17 September 2013, she admitted that the plans for 'e-policing' and the generation of 'e-dockets' were way behind schedule and money budgeted for it had not been spent. The project started twelve years ago.

A big part of the SAPS's inefficiency seems to be its top-heavy structure and its prioritisation of looking after politicians.

In August 2012 the Police and Prisons Civil Rights Union (POPCRU) told a parliamentary committee that the overloading of the SAPS at senior management levels represented a bloated structure that affected the service's ability to employ sufficient staff at station level, where it was vitally important to combat crime.

POPCRU deputy secretary-general Lebogang Phepheng said there were too many senior positions at the pinnacle of the structure, at the level of deputy director-general, and that most of these positions were a duplication of services with adverse effects on the budget. 'Each one of these senior officers draws a salary of above R1.2 million per annum from the budget of SAPS. There are thirteen divisional commissioners, nine provincial commissioners, and seven deputy national commissioners. POPCRU's submission is that the department would and should do much better with a lean and mean top structure with more personnel where the actual work takes place for the proper delivery of the required services.' He said there were nearly 20 000 employees at the SAPS national head office, where the bulk of the budget was consumed. This resulted in a huge deadlock in middle management and in the junior ranks, where officers were being deprived of promotions.

Institute for Security Studies director and senior crime researcher Johan Burger agreed, saying deploying major-generals could be an advantage to the police stations, especially those experiencing problems. Trimming the top-heavy structures and placing major-generals at cluster level and at police stations could help to beef up the fight against crime, as they would contribute their expertise and experience, he said.

Here's a more shocking example of skewed SAPS priorities. According to Gareth Newham of the Institute for Security Studies, the VIP Protection Unit got 23 per cent of the total police budget of R68 billion in 2012/13. This unit doesn't fight crime. It guards the president, cabinet ministers and provincial executive committee members. We have all seen blue-light convoys, some numbering ten vehicles, speeding through the traffic.

Shoot to kill

The government was embarrassed about its inability to stem the massive surge in crime in the country and went into denial. First Mbeki suggested that only white racists complained about crime, and advised them to emigrate. Then, in 2007, Commissioner Selebi asked publicly: 'What's all this fuss about crime?'

When the ANC's own primary constituency started voicing their unhappiness with the wave of crime and violence, the attitude changed. But instead of jacking up training, management and efficiency at local stations, the reaction was to chuck the whole rights-based approach of the new police out the window and replace it with macho talk about maximum force.

In April 2008, the deputy minister of safety and security, Susan Shabangu, told police officers: 'You must kill the bastards if they threaten your community. You must not worry about the regulations. I want no warning shots. You have one shot and it must be a kill shot. I want to assure the police station commissioners and policemen and women from these areas that they have permission to kill these criminals. I will not tolerate any pathetic excuses for you not being able to deal with crime; you have been given guns, now use them. If criminals dare to threaten the police or the livelihood or lives of innocent men, women and children, then they must be killed.'

The president of the ANC (who became president of the country four months later), Jacob Zuma, was asked two days later what he thought of Shabangu's outrageously provocative statement. This is what he said: 'If you have a deputy minister saying the kinds of things that the deputy minister was saying, this is what we need to happen. What the deputy minister is saying is: what we are to be doing is dealing with the criminals rather than talking about it.'

In November 2008, the minister of safety and security, Nathi Mthethwa, took the aggressive language further. He didn't want police officers faced with armed criminals 'to take out some human rights charter', he told Parliament. He wanted the police to 'teach these people a lesson – fight fire with fire'.

In 2012, an amendment to the Criminal Procedure Act that Mthethwa had proposed came into effect, broadening the powers of the police to use lethal force. It contributed to an atmosphere of impunity, said constitutional law expert Pierre de Vos at the time.

Bheki Cele, who became commissioner of police in 2009, quickly became known for his fighting talk, as did the then deputy minister, Fikile Mbalula, who famously said that the police should 'shoot the bastards'.

The results of this new macho approach soon became evident: brutality cases recorded against police officers increased by 313 per cent between 2001/02 and 2011/12, according to the Gareth Newham.

Political analyst and journalist Karima Brown wrote in a column in March 2013: 'Zuma, unlike Mbeki, did not accuse those complaining about crime of being whingers who were only negative about South Africa. He listened and took action. The kind of action, however, saw a return to old-style jackboot policing. Suddenly it became fashionable to say "shoot to kill" and "an eye for an eye". This remilitarisation of the police became acceptable as securocrats tried to use the need to deal decisively with rising crime as a cover to encourage a style and ethos that paid little mind to rights and service. Consequently, the climb in instances of police brutality hardly comes as a surprise.'

Newham gave Parliament's Portfolio Committee on Police more information on the growing problem of police brutality in March 2013. The SAPS was facing civil claims of R1.1 billion relating to shooting incidents and assault cases of more than R800 million; civil claims against the police had doubled in the preceding two years to R14.8 billion; 35 per cent of citizens interviewed in 2012 were scared of the police and about 41 per cent did not trust the police; and only one out of every fifty people who experienced or witnessed police abuse reported it.

'Senior police management have to take full responsibility and be held directly responsible for changing the culture, behaviour and performance of the police,' Newham told the committee.

Allegations of police brutality have appeared in newspapers almost every week in the last few years. But three cases stand out, mostly because they were filmed and broadcast on television and thus provoked great public anger: the killing of Ficksburg activist Andries Tatane on 13 April 2011; the shooting of thirty-four miners at Marikana on 16 August 2012; and the killing of taxi driver Mido Macia on 26 February 2013.

I was one of the many South Africans who watched the SABC's evening news bulletin on Wednesday 13 April 2011. It showed the protests against the very dysfunctional municipality of Ficksburg, and a man without a shirt being led away by police. We see the man wrestle free, whereupon the policemen, six or seven of them, savagely beat him with their batons. He gets up, angry and shouting, and then first one and then another policeman shoots him at close range in the chest with rubber bullets. Moments later he dies in the arms of a friend. He was identified as Andries Tatane, a thirty-three-year-old mathematics teacher, community activist and member of COPE, husband of Rose and father of a four-year-old son.

I was stunned. My immediate reaction was that the policemen must have thought that what they were doing was acceptable, because they could not have been unaware of the SABC's cameraman (and, it turned out, several others) filming their actions.

It was abundantly clear, and witnessed as such by hundreds of thousands of South Africans, that Tatane presented no physical threat whatsoever to the police. At most he was resisting arrest, but he was unarmed and not attacking them, but rather trying to get out of their grasp.

Seven policemen were charged with Tatane's murder. On 27 March 2013 the regional court found that there wasn't enough evidence and acquitted them. I was once again stunned, along with millions of other South Africans who had by then seen several different video clips of his killing over and over again. How on earth was it possible that the criminal justice system could not deliver justice in a case that we all thought was open and shut?

So great was the public outrage that the NPA felt they had to explain: Two witnesses changed their testimony, saying that they could not identify the shooters after all. A third witness's testimony was so contradictory that it was dismissed.

A *Mail & Guardian* editorial on 5 April 2013 stated:

If three dodgy witnesses were all the NPA had in its arsenal as it went into battle, it's understandable that the case didn't stand up. The NPA says it started out with thirty-five witness statements, nineteen from members of the South African Police Service and four from what is now the Independent Police Investigative Directorate. From those thirty-five witnesses, the prosecutors came up with a mere three who claimed, initially at least, to be able to identify the killers. In court, the NPA found they could not, in fact, do so – or were no longer willing to.

The NPA seems to have been woefully underprepared for this case. There was no forensic evidence, no reference to a commanding officer who might be thought to carry ultimate responsibility, no attempt to identify the killers in any other way. Did the police and the prosecutors not do background checks on their witnesses? One at least was already under investigation on other charges.

The NPA has certainly made a hash of this case – a very important case, one of those in which the police force of a democratic South Africa is accused of doing very much what its apartheid-era predecessor did on a regular basis: using extremely heavy-handed tactics on ordinary protesting citizens.

The perception will persist that the state, its police officers and prosecutors were never really very keen on nailing the perpetrators of the Tatane murder. Civil society organisations (and Tatane was an active member of one such body) will view the outcome as proof that the government is highly intolerant of protest against it – and that its knee-jerk response is violence. Moreover, many will feel that the outcome of the Tatane case shows that the state is unable or unwilling to police itself, a situation that, first, puts all citizens at risk without offering them any recourse and, second, could end in a police state. That is a state to which South Africa does not wish to return.

I agree. My impression was that the criminal justice system was protecting the killers. And it was proved to be correct by British documentary film-maker Inigo Gilmore, whose film *South Africa's Dirty Cops* was broadcast as part of a Channel 4 Dispatches series in Britain in July 2013.

Gilmore says he learned that three cameras had captured Tatane's killing: a police camera, the SABC camera and a local activist's camera. The magistrate's courts in Ficksburg and Bethlehem and the Department of Justice frustrated all his efforts to look at the video material and the SABC refused to show it to him, citing a 'top management decision' – more evidence of a state reluctance to allow the truth to be known.

Gilmore did eventually get hold of a copy of the activist's video material. This was what he wrote in a piece for the *Daily Maverick*: 'The footage is extensive and what I discovered astonished me. Sitting in an edit suite in London, we quickly realised that by closely following the weapons of the two police officers who shot Tatane and then staying focused on those weapons, it was possible to identify who shot him.'

Gilmore explains how he succeeded in producing screen-grab still images of the two policemen who had fired on Tatane. 'If these men were brought before an ID parade they could easily be linked to the screen grabs and would be recognisable in an instant. The magistrate in the prosecution case said that the policemen were wearing helmets and that is certainly true – but their faces are still visible.' Gilmore did not even have the other two videos taken to help him, but the prosecutors did.

Gilmore asks: 'So how was it that the state prosecutors were in a unique and enviable position in such a case – where they had compelling and incriminating footage evidence to pin on the accused – but still failed to secure a conviction?' He says he was told that prosecutors didn't freeze-frame, crop or zoom in when presenting the video evidence.

Tatane's widow told Gilmore she believed that the witnesses changed their testimony because they had the backing of their political masters. 'The minister of safety in the Free State was talking on the radio, in the newspapers, all over, saying the police were just doing their job, so I started suspecting that it would end up like this, that they would walk free.' Asked to clarify this, she said: 'Because the ANC is our ruling party, so if they say anything they've got a lot of power, they've got powers, they can do everything they want.' She said she suspected that her husband was resented because he left the ANC for COPE and was questioning ANC councillors.

'We are scared from the police, we are afraid of the police, but this is the new South Africa,' Rose Tatane told Gilmore.

The afternoon of 16 August 2012, I switched on the television and changed to eNCA to check on the latest local news. Broadcast journalist Xoli Mngambi was reporting live on the wildcat strike at Lonmin's platinum mine near Rustenburg. There was a stand-off between police and strikers, and anchor Debora Patta was prodding him to explain what was happening.

The camera showed the heavily armed police standing around nervously. Suddenly a group of miners came towards them and the police started firing into them. Within a minute, one cop shouted, 'Cease fire!' and the shooting stopped. There was a heap of bodies lying in front of them.

As I was watching the shocking scenes, it dawned on me: the police of post-apartheid South Africa are killing protestors as if they're the enemy of the state, just like apartheid police did.

As I watched the footage over and over, it became clear to me that the police must have had an order to shoot to kill. If they hadn't, they would have had more protective gear; they would have used water cannons first; they certainly would have used rubber bullets rather than sharp ammunition.

The Farlam Commission of Inquiry is still trying to establish all the facts of the Marikana bloodbath, so I don't want to make definitive judgements on the behaviour of the police. But photographer and journalist Greg Marinovich, reporting for *Daily Maverick*, and five researchers from the University of Johannesburg led by Peter Alexander did proper investigations into the shootings and came to very disturbing conclusions.

It appears that only twelve miners were killed in the incident I saw on television. Eight others were killed in the vicinity. The other fourteen were killed on a nearby koppie, which the miners had earlier occupied. The investigations indicate that the miners killed here were executed in cold blood. Some were apparently shot in the back of the head; others appeared to have been killed while they were tied up. There is also evidence that some may have been run over by the police's Hippo vehicles. This is backed up by many interviews with surviving miners who escaped the police bullets.

'This was not public-order policing,' wrote the University of Johannesburg researchers in their book *Marikana: A View from the Mountain and a Case to Answer*, 'this was warfare.'

Fast-forward to 26 February 2013. An eTV news bulletin is showing cell-phone footage of police in Daveyton arresting a young man in a red T-shirt. He struggles, but they overpower him. They drag him to a police van, but instead of putting him in the back, they tie both his hands to the back of the vehicle in front of a crowd screaming in protest. The van slowly drives off with two policemen holding the man's legs, but when it increases its speed, they let go and the van disappears, dragging the man behind it.

The bulletin identified the victim as twenty-seven-year-old Mido Macia, a taxi driver from Mozambique. He died in a police cell later that day.

The astonishing feature of this sickening incident was that the policemen clearly did not mind that dozens of onlookers were witness to what they were doing. There was no way they could not have noticed that several people were filming the scene with their cellphones. They clearly did not think they would get into trouble. Could the fact that the victim was from Mozambique have played a role?

Nine policemen were eventually charged with Macia's murder. At the time of writing, they were out on bail.

These three incidents of police brutality made the front pages and created a storm, partly because they were so horrific, but mostly because the public could see exactly what had happened when the video material was broadcast on television. It goes without saying that they are the tiny, tiny tip of a massive iceberg.

To me it is obvious that a concerted and urgent effort needs to be made to give human-rights training to police officers and to combat racism, sexism and xenophobia. Policies should be clearer, discipline should be sharpened up and the IPID should be given more teeth, more status and more resources.

Current SAPS commissioner Riah Phiyega comes from the corporate world. She is probably a hard-working and decent civil servant. But her statements and her behaviour since her appointment have shown that she is utterly out of her depth as the leader of a troubled police force. Her performance before the Farlam Commission was pathetic and contradictory, perhaps even untruthful. Phiyega, I think it is safe to say, is not going to be the leader to turn the SAPS back into a disciplined, effective and credible force serving the people and enjoying their support.

There are no quick fixes or instant solutions when it comes to law enforcement and a police service with so many members and so much bad history. But a starting point could be to implement the proposals of the NDP, government's own blueprint for future development.

The NDP says that the national commissioner and deputy national commissioners should be appointed by the president on a competitive basis. At the moment, the president appoints political loyalists or people he thinks he can control, in all cases so far with inadequate skills and experience. The NDP proposes that a panel select and interview a shortlist of candidates based on objective criteria from which the commissioner and deputy commissioners should then be appointed.

The plan proposes a national policing board of experts from various disciplines to set standards for recruitment, selection, appointment and promotion, and to develop a Code of Ethics for the police. All police officers should undergo a competency assessment and no one should be considered for promotion until they reach the required level of competence.

Periodic checks should be conducted to establish whether the Police Code is understood and practised. Members who fail this test should be suspended or dismissed.

The NDP recommends that the SAPS be demilitarised and that this should happen as soon as possible. It also recommends that the organisational culture of the police should be reviewed to assess the effects of demilitarisation, remilitarisation and the 'serial crises of top management'.

Says Johan Burger of the Institute for Security Studies: 'Although some of the details remain unclear at this stage, if the political will exists to implement the NDP's recommendations, the plan can go a long way towards developing a professional police service for South Africa.'

11

Fiat justitia

South Africa is a constitutional state, a *Rechtsstaat*. The Constitution, not Parliament or the executive, is paramount. The rights of citizens are ensconced in the Constitution and they have the inalienable right to go to court if those rights are undermined by the state or anyone else. The Constitutional Court is the watchdog and arbiter of the Constitution, and thus the highest authority in the land. The Constitution is very clear about the separation of powers between the executive, legislative and judicial spheres.

And that is the unshakeable foundation of our freedom and stability, and will remain regardless of what else goes wrong in the country.

It is highly unlikely, at least in the next few decades, that any political party will gain the more than three-quarters majority in the National Assembly that would allow them to change those parts of the Constitution that guarantee constitutional supremacy and the rule of law. It is even unlikely, any time soon, that we'll see a party with the two-thirds majority needed to change other parts of the Constitution (to amend provincial boundaries and powers, or the Bill of Rights, at least six of the nine provinces must agree to it).

Alas, it is not entirely this simple. It is possible to undermine the essence of the Constitution, the independence of the judicial system and even the rule of law without changing the wording of the Constitution.

That is the danger South Africa faces right now.

An extreme example of what could happen is the undermining of the judiciary and the rule of law in Zimbabwe after ZANU-PF's popularity was seriously questioned in that country's 2000 election. Luckily South Africa is not Zimbabwe, and what Robert Mugabe and ZANU-PF have done to that country is extremely unlikely to ever happen here, but it is worth looking at what took place there and identifying the dangers. If the judiciary had not been compromised in Zimbabwe, the country would not have gone off the rails in the way it did.

A report by international lawyers in 2004 said it was clear that Zimbabwe's corruption of the legal system was directly linked to the 2000 election results and Mugabe's intention 'to keep a grip on power'. It gave examples of senior judges and magistrates who were forcibly removed from office after being jailed, beaten or threatened with violence for failing to toe the government line.

Senior jurists with a solid reputation of independence were no longer appointed as judges. A retired army general and ZANU-PF insider, George Chiweshe, was appointed judge president of the High Court. He was the judge who delayed the release of the 2008 presidential election results and refused to condemn the violence against supporters of Mugabe's opponent, Morgan Tsvangirai.

Most senior judges were given farms seized from white owners. Justice Wilson Sandura, a judge for almost thirty years, was a member of a five-bench Supreme Court that declared farm seizures illegal. He refused the offer of a farm and has since not heard any cases involving land or political matters – the judge president allocates cases to judges. Accepting free farms from the state violates the Zimbabwean Constitution that regulates the remuneration of judges to ensure their impartiality. Lawyers appearing for the Commercial Farmers Union revealed that they were threatened with contempt of court charges if they asked judges who had received farms to recuse themselves from hearing land-related cases.

Zimbabwean constitutional expert Derek Matyszak says the ZANU-PF government has violated various provisions of the Constitution and other legislation, and has got away with it.

Zimbabwean lawyer and director of the International Commission of Jurists' Africa programme Arnold Tsunga points to another trend: 'The defiance of court orders has really become an emblematic problem in Zimbabwe. The culture of defying court orders is a culture that has become an entrenchment of impunity and is directly linked to the political process of 2000 when Mugabe was trying to undermine the judiciary.'

Most High Court orders involving land or political rights have not been executed in recent years. In 2010 nine landowners won a case for compensation in the Harare High Court, but the order wasn't respected and they turned to the SADC tribunal in Windhoek, where they won their case. The tribunal ruled that the Mugabe government was in breach of the SADC treaty because it failed to execute court orders.

So these are the flashing red lights: courts loaded with judicial officers deemed government-friendly; pressure on sitting judges and magistrates to toe the government and ruling-party line; judges with their own prejudices against some sectors of society (race, gender, sexuality, faith); selective prosecutions and the abuse of courts as political instruments; and refusal by the government to execute court orders.

All these lights are beginning to flash in South Africa, albeit amber and not yet red. A huge difference between Zimbabwe and South Africa is that these controversies are being vigorously debated in the public arena by judges, lawyers, academics and the public.

War of attrition

The phenomenon of senior ANC leaders attacking the Constitution and the courts only really started with Jacob Zuma's ascendancy in 2007. Not since the dark years of apartheid oppression in the 1980s has the judiciary come under such pressure from politicians.

The subtext of the war of attrition against the judiciary is the post-Polokwane ANC's blurring of the separation of powers of the executive, legislative and judicial arms of government; and the very narrow understanding of democracy, expressed many times by Zuma, that only the will of the majority party should count.

In a November 2011 statement cabinet announced that they planned to assess 'the transformation of the judicial system' to 'ensure the judiciary conforms to the transformation mandate as envisaged in the Constitution in terms of non-racialism, gender, disability and other transformational variables' and to 'affirm the independence of the judiciary as well as that of the executive and Parliament with a view to promoting interdependence and interface that is necessary to realise transformation goals envisaged by the Constitution'. Cabinet believed mechanisms should be developed 'to facilitate ... regular interface between the three spheres of the state to enhance synergy and constructive engagement among them'.

Says political analyst Christi van der Westhuizen: 'The notion of "cooperation" between the executive, legislative and judicial arms is ANC policy. A 2007 discussion document misapplied the constitutional principle of co-operative governance to these arms, adding that they should "work in tandem with one another" and that the Constitution "envisages a system where all branches of government work in collaboration".'

And yet the separation of powers and the independence of the judiciary were not part of the ANC's compromises during the pre-1994 negotiations. Top ANC intellectual Joel Netshitenzhe says the separation of powers was 'a matter of conviction on the part of the ANC'. He points out that the ANC's

1992 Ready to Govern document stated: 'The Bill of Rights will be enforced by the courts, headed by a separate newly created Constitutional Court, which will have the task of upholding the fundamental rights and freedoms of all citizens against the state or any body or person seeking to destroy those rights. The judges will be independent and will consist of men and women drawn from all sections of the community on the basis of their integrity, skills, life experience and wisdom.'

Netshitenzhe asks his own comrades whether frustration with the intransigence of some whites moved the ANC to abandon its principles and join 'the race to the bottom'.

Nevertheless, cabinet decided to launch a review of the Constitutional Court – although, in an interview in February 2012, Zuma said: 'We don't want to review the Constitutional Court; we want to review its powers.' Here is the president's strange logic behind the move: 'It is after experience that some of the decisions are not decisions that every other judge in the Constitutional Court agrees with.' And again: 'How could you say that a judgment is absolutely correct when the judges themselves have different views about it?'

One can't help thinking that he was referring to a Constitutional Court decision that went against him, but that had one dissenting judge. He doesn't seem to appreciate that High Court decisions in all democracies are made by a *majority* of the judges on the bench.

To further support his cabinet's decision, Zuma threw in the argument that judges were being influenced by the media. So how would a judicial review remedy that, even if it could be proved to be true?

DA MP Dene Smuts reacted to Zuma's remarks by saying that he was on a path of confrontation with the Constitutional Court. 'It is apparent from the president's remarks that irritation with some of the court's judgments lies at the root of the desire for a review,' she said.

The minister of justice, Jeff Radebe, told Parliament in May 2013 that the assessment of judgments by the Constitutional Court and the Supreme Court of Appeal would be ready by March 2014. In August 2013 he announced that the HSRC and Fort Hare University's law school had got the tender to do a comprehensive analysis of the decisions of the two courts in the post-apartheid era and how they had contributed to the reform of South African jurisprudence and addressing inequality.

The review would also evaluate the accessibility of the Constitutional Court and the speed at which it finalised cases. Crucially, the study would also look into the implementation of both courts' decisions and 'the capacity of the state within the available resources to realise the outcome envisaged by such court decisions,' Radebe said.

Zuma's legal problems

Much of the vitriol relates in one way or another to Zuma's own legal problems and his bad decision-making.

One Constitutional Court decision that particularly angered Zuma and his cheering commando was its dismissal in July 2008 of his leave to appeal two judgments of the Supreme Court of Appeal handed down in November 2007, concerning the lawfulness of various search-and-seizure operations carried out at his premises in 2005 by the investigative unit the Scorpions. With his lawyer, Michael Hulley, and French arms company Thint, Zuma questioned the lawfulness of the Scorpions' actions and asked for all documents to be returned. Ten of the eleven judges signed the judgment, with Justice Sandile Ngcobo dissenting. Furthermore, the full bench dismissed an application by Zuma and Thint that challenged the lawfulness of the state's request to the attorney-general of Mauritius for documents held there.

Patricia de Lille, one of the driving forces behind the arms-deal probe and then leader of the Independent Democrats, reacted, saying: 'The ANC must now stop their orchestrated attack on the courts and allow justice to take its course.'

However, the case became even more controversial when Chief Justice Pius Langa announced that he and his fellow judges had laid a complaint against Cape judge president John Hlophe for improperly trying to influence two of them to find in Zuma's favour. 'The judgment however affirms that the alleged attempt was unsuccessful,' Langa said. The Judicial Service Commission (JSC) later set the complaint aside, a move which the Supreme Court of Appeal found to be unlawful. The Constitutional Court then refused to allow an appeal against this decision. (By late 2013, the Hlophe matter was still not resolved.)

Other court decisions that irritated Zuma and his cabinet included declaring his appointment of Menzi Simelane as national director of public prosecutions invalid; declaring his unilateral extension of Constitutional Court judges' terms to have Justice Ngcobo stay on as chief justice invalid; and finding that the Hawks, which replaced the Scorpions that were involved in the charges against him, were not properly insulated against political interference.

Shortly after the National Prosecuting Authority announced its decision to drop the corruption charges against Zuma in April 2009, he was quoted as saying: 'If I sit here and I look at the chief justice of the Constitutional Court, that is the ultimate authority. I think we need to look at it, because I don't think we should have people who are almost like God in a democracy. Why? Are they not human beings?'

The *Mail & Guardian* reported that the Constitutional Court judges were 'deeply concerned and perturbed' about Zuma's remarks and agreed among themselves that they would make no public response, given what they saw as the gravity of his attack on the court. The newspaper quoted 'an insider' as saying: 'Who does Zuma suggest should be the highest judicial authority in the land? Two judges have ruled in his favour; some twenty-odd have ruled against him. He can't attack the entire system because he's angry. It's very dangerous.' A senior advocate told the paper: 'He is clearly, constitutionally speaking, illiterate and it's dangerous because it's subversive.'

At the heart of the ANC's criticism of the judiciary at the time was their perception that the judiciary prevented the democratically elected government from governing as they deemed fit. Zuma actually asked: 'We were elected by the majority of the people. Who elected the judges of the Constitutional Court?' At a conference on Access to Justice in July 2011, he said that the independence of the judiciary was adequately protected by the Constitution, but argued that the executive wasn't sufficiently protected from interference by the judiciary. This prompted DA leader Helen Zille to say: 'In arguing that the courts could not supersede the voters' political mandate, he missed the point that no matter how powerful a ruling party is, it cannot do what it likes. It must abide by the Constitution. A popular mandate does not place a governing party above the law. The threat to our criminal justice system is not the judiciary's interference in the executive. It is the other way around.'

But it wasn't only Zuma. The secretary-general of the ANC, Gwede Mantashe, accused the Constitutional Court judges of having a 'counter-revolutionary agenda' – this while struggle stalwarts such as Pius Langa, Dikgang Moseneke, Albie Sachs and Zac Yacoob were serving on that bench. The ANC's then spokesperson, Jessie Duarte, defended Mantashe's statement, saying his views were the ANC's views. Referring to the Constitutional Court judges' complaints against Hlophe, Mantashe also remarked that it was a 'pursuit by some people of a vendetta against the ANC president'.

A deputy minister in Zuma's government and former Limpopo premier, Ngoako Ramatlhodi, who is prone to taking regular potshots at the Constitutional Court, declared that the Constitution reflected 'a compromise heavily in favour of forces for change' and 'emptied the legislature and executive of real political power'. SACP leader Blade Nzimande was another Zuma minister who had the judiciary in his sights, accusing it of being a 'judicial dictatorship' and 'anti-majoritarian'.

Their supporters followed in their footsteps. The ANC in KwaZulu-Natal once even adopted a resolution that judges should be appointed only from the ranks of the ANC. Spokespersons for the ANC Youth League and the Young Communist League warned on several occasions that court decisions against Zuma would trigger mass protest campaigns. In June 2012 the Youth League warned that 'land-hungry mobs' would ignore the law and the courts and seize white-owned land, and then the safety of 'Mr Van der Merwe and Mr Van Tonder couldn't be guaranteed'.

Men of integrity

Former chief justice Pius Langa was often insulted personally, yet he was hailed as a great hero and a man of integrity by the government and the ANC when he died in 2013. Langa was a founding member of the National Association of Democratic Lawyers and a member of the ANC's constitutional committee during the pre-1994 negotiations. The other target of ANC venom is Deputy Chief Justice Dikgang Moseneke, who, despite spending years on Robben Island, has a PAC rather than an ANC political background. During remarks he made at his private sixtieth birthday party, reported to the ANC leadership immediately afterwards, he said the law should be applied impartially in the interests of the entire society: 'It is not what the ANC wants or what the delegates want. It is about what is good for our people.' He was crucified by Luthuli House for this 'anti-ANC' stance and his ability as an impartial judge was questioned. He paid for his remark when he was overlooked for promotion to chief justice some time later.

When it became clear that the ANC wasn't going to be successful in its court bid (in May 2012) to have Brett Murray's painting *The Spear* removed from the art gallery and various websites, Mantashe ominously warned: 'What we can't win in the courts, we'll win on the streets.' Not long afterward, Ramatlhodi said that the Constitution 'would be interpreted on the streets' – rather than by the Constitutional Court.

How close is this to inviting mob rule? And it can't be a reaction to a white, old-order domination of the judiciary – all the country's regional judge presidents are black, as is the chief justice and eight out of the ten Constitutional Court judges (all appointed after 1994).

Senior jurists with a long history of association with the ANC, such as former chief justice Arthur Chaskalson and veteran senior counsel George Bizos, came out strongly to warn against these attacks on the judiciary. The South African Law Deans Association said in a statement: 'Political attempts at controlling the judiciary, be it by statute or by means of mob conduct, amount to an assault on an essential instrument and guarantee of democracy. We therefore call upon the political leaders of our country to set an example to the citizenry in upholding and defending the Constitution.'

Pius Langa, delivering the Ismail Mohamed Memorial Lecture in 2008, said the public and the media had the right to critique the judiciary, but such criticism 'should not degenerate to uninformed and unfair personal attacks'. He said criticism should be informed 'and not reactionary and alarmist, because that is set to undermine the rule of law which is so fundamental to the stability of our democracy'.

Mantashe reacted to Langa's lecture: 'The timing of the lecture where Chief Justice Pius Langa spoke, which was attended by Judge Chris Nicholson [presiding judge in a Zuma legal challenge] and his two assessors, coupled with the timing of the Constitutional Court and the apparent mobilisation of the judiciary, is worrying for us.'

I would say a statement by the secretary-general of the ruling party that the judiciary was mobilising against its government is far more worrying.

Loading the courts

A logical reaction from a government irritated by the decisions of the courts would be to try to load those courts with judges it feels it can influence and judges who have shown that they are sympathetic to the executive branch's belief that the will of the majority should not be frustrated by the judiciary.

The Constitution established the JSC to guard against these temptations. The debate raging in legal and political circles right now is whether or not the ANC and government are in fact subverting the JSC to get sympathetic judges appointed anyway. The JSC has become a new 'site of struggle'.

The JSC's function is to select fit and proper persons for appointment as judges and to investigate complaints about judicial officers. It also advises government on any matters relating to the judiciary or to the administration of justice.

When judges have to be appointed, the JSC calls for nominations and then shortlists suitable candidates for interviews. Professional bodies and members of the public can make representations concerning the candidates to the JSC.

The interviews are conducted in public, after which the JSC deliberates and makes its decisions in private. It sends its recommendations to the president, who then makes the appointments. In the case of the chief justice and the deputy chief justice, the leaders of parties represented in the National Assembly are also consulted.

The chief justice is the chairperson of the JSC. Other members are the president of the Supreme Court of Appeal, one regional judge president, the minister of justice, two advocates and two attorneys representing the profession, one law academic, six MPs (of whom three have to be members of the opposition), four representatives of the National Council of Provinces and four people appointed by the president.

Journalist Stephen Grootes did some head counting for the *Daily Maverick* in September 2011. The ANC could count on the votes of at least fourteen out of the twenty-three JSC votes, he wrote.

The JSC was plunged into controversy when Zuma offered to extend Justice Sandile Ngcobo's term as chief justice. The extension was challenged by civil society groups because the Constitution did not allow it. Ngcobo knew that his own colleagues would have to rule against him, and so he withdrew his earlier acceptance of the president's offer. Ngcobo had served on the court since 2009 and thus had only two years left before retirement.

The JSC now had to recommend a new chief justice, who serves as head of the Constitutional Court and chair of the JSC – a very powerful position. Ngcobo's deputy, Dikgang Moseneke, was the obvious choice, also because he was generally regarded as a brilliant legal mind with impeccable independence. But perhaps he was too independent for the ANC's liking, especially after his remarks at his birthday party.

Zuma's preferred candidate was Justice Mogoeng Mogoeng, a lay preacher in the Winners' Chapel church who had served as a prosecutor in a Bophuthatswana Bantustan court between 1986 and 1990. His candidature was immediately criticised by opposition politicians and many in the legal fraternity. They pointed out that he wasn't nearly the most experienced candidate available and that he had exhibited a 'deferential approach' towards the executive branch, held homophobic views and had ruled for reduced sentences for rapists on more than one occasion.

Mogoeng's JSC interview was televised live. This is what I wrote about it on 5 September 2011:

The televised hearings of the Judicial Service Commission (JSC) on the candidature of Judge Mogoeng Mogoeng for the position of chief justice told us a lot more than just whether he was a suitable candidate or not.

It told us that our minister of justice, Jeff Radebe, is an intolerant bully with little stomach for dissent.

It told us that the quality of the commissioners of the JSC, a crucially important body, is very disappointing.

It told us that the ANC will stop at almost nothing in its quest for hegemony and will always use its majority to steamroller others.

And it told us that there are a large number of citizens, even many of those who have senior positions in society or serve as thought leaders, who have an extremely limited understanding of democracy and of our Constitution.

Let's get a few facts on the table before we proceed.

Never since 1994 has a candidate for chief justice been opposed with even remotely the same vehemence as was the case with Mogoeng – not Ismail Mohamed, Arthur Chaskalson, Pius Langa or Sandile Ngcobo.

Not a single white judge's name was even mentioned as being in the running for the job of chief justice this time. Race was completely absent in this process. The present deputy chief justice, Dikgang Moseneke, is held in very high esteem by virtually everyone in the judiciary for his knowledge of constitutional law and jurisprudence, his sharp mind, his leadership and his impartiality.

Mogoeng's suitability was questioned by the biggest trade-union federation in South Africa, by several bar associations, many legal academics, the National Association of Democratic Lawyers and several legal and gender interest groups. Never before has a judicial appointment generated such a level of opposition.

Mogoeng's critics and the media have catalogued a long list of judgments where he demonstrated a shocking insensitivity to gender violence. They also pointed to his dissenting minority view in the Constitutional Court on the question whether calling someone gay is libellous and his curious neglect to give reasons for his position.

Mogoeng was visibly livid at the criticism when he appeared before the JSC, as were Radebe and some of the ANC members of the JSC. They seemed to say that the critics and the media acted illegally or immorally when they pointed to Mogoeng's potential weakness and shortcomings – indeed, evidence that he appeared not to be in line with the Constitution he was appointed to uphold. In his last remarks on Sunday, Mogoeng even made the scary remark that he would, if he became the chief justice, see to it that no judge would ever be subjected to such a process of scrutiny again. (Mogoeng probably had reason to feel no one had the right to point out his weaknesses – according to him it was God himself who decided he should get the job, after all.)

This attitude was mirrored by several prominent commentators and columnists. Lawyer and commentator Christine Qunta, for instance, tweeted that the scrutiny of Mogoeng would never have happened to a white judge. (Her old friend and associate, Dumisa Ntsebeza, is a JSC member and has savaged quite a few white candidates for judgeships in a way not nearly equalled by the weekend's hearings.) Columnist Victor Dlamini writes that the questioning of Mogoeng's suitability was a 'witch-hunt', politically rather than judicially motivated and actually just an attempt to undermine President Jacob Zuma.

The issue should have been simple. Our democracy is still fragile and our Constitution is under attack from all quarters, even from the ruling party. The key to stability is a credible, efficient judiciary and the protection of the integrity of our Constitution, which is the job of the Constitutional Court. We need a chief justice who is respected by his peers; who fully supports all aspects of our Constitution; who has the intellectual inclination and experience to lead discussions on our developing jurisprudence; who is a good manager and administrator; and who is known for his complete independence from political influences.

Judge Mogoeng, in my view, qualifies on only one of these: he is a good manager and administrator. If the minister of justice and the rest of the ANC contingent on the JSC did not realise that before, they certainly knew that by the end of the two-day hearings. Why did they steamroller the process anyway? Why are they settling for the second (actually, the fourth) best?

There can only be one answer: they bargain that Mogoeng will be more lenient than others on the executive when one of its decisions or laws comes before him. He is going to be chief justice for at least ten years and they're hoping he will have that influence on our highest court in years to come.

But at least the hearings proved that our democracy is still very much alive – for now.

In an editorial headed 'South Africa's Zumafication continues apace', *Business Day* wrote: 'Not only is Justice Mogoeng the most inexperienced sitting Constitutional Court judge, but his unabashed social conservatism, strongly held religious convictions and tendency to side with the executive offend many in the dominant "progressive" legal establishment. And it is unfortunately likely that his influence – as head of the Constitutional Court, head of the JSC and head of the judiciary – could put the brakes on judicial reform in South Africa in all but the narrowest racial and administrative senses.'

True to form, SACP leader and minister of higher education Blade Nzimande hit back hard in a statement: 'No sooner had the president made his nomination, than a well-coordinated and orchestrated campaign was launched to try and discredit Justice Mogoeng, not so much in opposition to him, but to spite the authority of a president whose party was voted for by the overwhelming majority of our people. This was also a thoroughly dishonest campaign, largely informed by the fact that the choice of chief justice preferred by the liberals was not nominated by the president. Much as the liberal offensive pretends to be seeking a seemingly "neutral" and "objective" judge, this was all a campaign for the appointment of a chief justice not above class and political interests, but a judge sympathetic to the oppositionist (if not capitalist) agenda of the liberals.'

Fiery session

The next fiery session of the JSC that underscored the differences and debates around the appointment of judges came in April 2013.

Most in the legal establishment believed Eastern Cape High Court judge Clive Plasket was the best candidate for a position on the Supreme Court of Appeal. He had a long record of being a progressive jurist. However, in his interview before the JSC, he faced a hostile grilling as a white male.

Niren Tolsi of the *Mail & Guardian* gave his account: 'The commission inflicted inquisitorial blows on Plasket like George Foreman's punches on Muhammad Ali during the Rumble in the Jungle's early rounds. Only the action … did not land a rope-a-dope result in the judge's favour in the end. He was repeatedly asked about his understanding of transformation and the logic of a Supreme Court of Appeal ruling that had held that the commission had acted irrationally in previously not appointing white male candidates to two out of three vacancies on the Western Cape bench.'

Richard Calland, director of the Democratic Governance and Rights Unit and associate professor in UCT's law department, attended the hearings and also wrote about the unequal treatment given to the different candidates. The dominant caucus in the JSC had made up their minds beforehand on ideological and political grounds. 'These days, the ANC wants obedient judges who "know the limits of judicial power",' he wrote.

The bad blood burst into the open when JSC member and senior counsel Izak Smuts released a discussion paper titled 'Transformation and the Judiciary'. The word 'transformation' did not appear in the statutes related to the JSC, he said. The two relevant provisions in Section 174 of the Constitution declare: 'Any appropriately qualified woman or man who is a fit and proper person may be appointed as a judicial officer' and 'The need for the judiciary to reflect broadly the racial and gender composition of South Africa must be considered when judicial officers are appointed'.

Smuts said it would be dangerous to appoint candidates with issues with certain values of the Constitution simply to ensure racial and gender quota representation because, once appointed, judges are very difficult to remove.

'There exists a very real perception in certain quarters that the JSC is, in general, set against the appointment of white male candidates except in exceptional circumstances … The JSC ought to have an honest debate about its approach to the appointment of white male candidates. If the majority view is that, for the foreseeable future, white male candidates are only to be considered for appointment in exceptional circumstances (an approach I consider to be unlawful and unconstitutional), the JSC should at the very least come clean and say so, so that white male candidates are not put through the charade of an interview before being rejected.'

He said that the requirement 'to reflect broadly the racial and gender composition' of South Africa should not exclude issues such as the existing experience of judges on the particular bench under consideration, the need for special expertise and the mean ages of judges already on that bench.

Smuts's paper was discussed during a heated closed session of the JSC, but he also released it to the public, which angered his critics in the commission.

The paper had apparently set the cat among the pigeons.

Chief Justice Mogoeng described the closed meeting as 'robust'. Outside the JSC, Smuts was called a racist and an old-order relic. Law professor Ziyad Motala, a staunch supporter of Mogoeng, wrote that the position of Smuts and others like him was at its core 'a fight by angry white men with a particular ideological disposition accustomed to getting their way'.

Smuts then resigned from the JSC. He said in a statement: 'It has become increasingly apparent to me, and has been made devastatingly clear during the proceedings of the commission this past week, that my understanding of the constitutional values, the constitutional role and duty of the commission, and even of the basic rights such as those of human dignity and freedom of speech, is so far removed from the understanding of the majority of the commission that it is not possible for me to play an effective role on the commission.'

He said the JSC had 'left a trail of wasted forensic talent in its wake which would be remarkable in a society rich in human resources, and is unintelligible in a society such as ours in which, for reasons of our discriminatory history, such resources are scarce'. He mentioned several white men as 'examples of intellectual forensic excellence' who had been overlooked by the commission, including advocates Geoff Budlender, Jeremy Gauntlett and Torquil Paterson. By rejecting them, the JSC had illustrated 'something deeply concerning about the commission's approach to the intellectual leadership of our legal community. The approach has resulted in a massive loss to our courts of the opportunity to utilise optimally the finest intellectual prowess.'

JSC spokesperson Dumisa Ntsebeza reacted to Smuts's resignation by saying the JSC was better off without him. 'I don't regret that he has decided to leave the commission, because it is untenable that we have someone on the JSC who, whenever he does not agree with the majority, he gets upset.'

Mogoeng's reaction was that there was no requirement to appoint only 'the best of the best' as judges.

Retired Constitutional Court judge Johann Kriegler criticised the JSC's attitude and said that gender and race now appeared to be the primary concerns when appointing judges. 'Are you promoting transformation or are you appointing people to staff the highest courts of the country?'

In an opinion piece in the *Sunday Times*, Kriegler wrote about the taxing and lonely life of a judge. 'If a surgeon, architect or pilot takes chances, the result is often too clear. They get caught out. An intellectually dishonest judge can get away with it indefinitely.

'None of us would dream of boarding an airliner commanded by a beginner, even one with their paperwork in order,' he wrote. 'We wouldn't dream of allowing a medical intern to perform neurosurgery on our child. Yet there are people, some of whom should know better, who seriously suggest that transformation requires lawyers without adequate exposure to High Court work to be appointed to the bench, to pick up skills as they go. This does nobody, including the unduly promoted candidate, a favour.'

Sobering advice

This important debate about what values the JSC should attach to merit and transformation became vicious, and raged on talk radio and in newspapers, and in political forums and legal circles. It was time for the chief justice, head of the judiciary in South Africa, to be wise, and to give calming and sobering counsel.

But Mogoeng instead turned into a poison-tongued political firebrand. At a retirement function for Judge President Bernard Ngoepe in October 2012, Mogoeng warned judges against being fearful of 'what vocal and well-resourced opposition party leaders can do to you, what resources and forces the rich and powerful can mobilise against you, and what ridicule, recycled criticism and misinformation campaigns the media and others could subject you to'.

He said judicial independence would be limping if it only meant independence from the ANC. 'If for fear of being labelled pro-executive or conservative you feel intimidated into toeing a particular line so that you can earn the categorisation of progressiveness, whatever it means these days, then you are not independent,' he said.

In July 2013 Mogoeng delivered another blistering attack on the critics of the JSC when he spoke at the annual general meeting of Advocates for Transformation. *City Press* legal reporter Charl du Plessis wrote about the speech: 'It contained sixteen references to unnamed "personalities and NGOs" involved in an "illegitimate neo-political campaign to have certain people appointed" to the bench. These unnamed forces of darkness (or is that whiteness?), he says, are dead set on the "protection of white male dominance in the (legal) professions and the bench, and the equation of the appointment of black and women practitioners to the institutionalisation of mediocrity". Heavy stuff indeed.'

Du Plessis concluded: 'Perhaps the chairperson of the JSC should have greater regard for the chorus of voices asking questions about the way the JSC goes about doing its business, rather than dismiss them as a "well-coordinated network of individuals and entities often pretending to be working in isolation from each other".'

In an opinion piece Mogoeng later wrote for *City Press*, he said the discomfort with transformation of the judiciary had to be dealt with decisively. 'The point to be emphasised, though, is that a deliberate attempt is being made to delegitimise the JSC and through some scare tactics intimidate or mock the JSC into recommending, without proper reflection, certain white men and at times certain women, for reasons best known to those who are campaigning for them.'

This campaign to have certain people appointed, Mogoeng wrote, must be strongly opposed. But this is not for the faint-hearted. 'The defence of genuine transformation, as was the case during apartheid, inevitably attracts mockery, being labelled conservative and a tool of the executive.'

Mogoeng's supporters hailed him as a brave man who spoke the uncomfortable truth. Professor Motala called his critics 'right-wing ideologues' and said '(m)any of those screaming were either lapdogs of apartheid or silent beneficiaries', adding that 'their false narratives are desperate acts of self-preservation'.

But Mogoeng was savaged by others, including members of the JSC, who accused him of 'conduct unbecoming a chief justice', of 'becoming personally involved in the boxing match' and of 'entering the political battlefield'.

Advocate Paul Hoffman of the Institute for Accountability in Southern Africa, a vocal critic of Mogoeng, even laid an official complaint with the JSC. He accused Mogoeng of descending 'into the arena of contestation and controversy' and involving himself 'in the politics and policy aspects of affirmative action in a matter unbecoming of a sitting judge'. Hoffman charged Mogoeng with contempt of court, attempting to defeat the ends of justice (referring to a pending application to the High Court by the Helen Suzman Foundation challenging the approach of the JSC), bringing the judiciary into disrepute and breaching the Code of Judicial Conduct for judges.

Hoffman's complaint, in turn, was called racist and anti-transformation by many, and simply added to the divisions.

Gravitas

My own view is that the appointment of Mogoeng as chief justice was a huge and costly mistake. He is an insecure and petty man, made worse by his own admission that he lacks experience and gravitas and wasn't the best-qualified person for the position. He is clearly still angry at what he experienced as a humiliation during the JSC hearings before his appointment, and will no doubt keep on lashing out at his critics. It doesn't help his confidence that, unlike the other potential candidates, he has no struggle credentials; instead, he worked as a civil servant for a Bantustan.

Judicial appointments are controversial all over the world. It is no surprise that they are so contentious here in post-apartheid South Africa. It was always going to be difficult to find a balance between the obvious need to make the judiciary more representative of the demographics of the country and the equally obvious need to appoint experienced, 'fit and proper' judges that would serve the judiciary well.

South Africa needs a judge president with obvious moral authority, gravitas, leadership qualities and judicial intelligence to lead the judiciary through difficult times and dangerous minefields – a judge president like Mogoeng's predecessors Ismail Mohamed, Arthur Chaskalson and Pius Langa. In my opinion, Justice Dikgang Moseneke would have been such a person. It is hard to imagine that he would have allowed the JSC to deteriorate into a schoolyard brawl with such strong racial overtones.

There is indeed a tendency among sections of the white legal establishment and the white community generally to be suspicious of the suitability of most aspirant black judges. There is also a tendency to overemphasise the intellectual brilliance of some white candidates, while that is surely not the only attribute a good judge should have.

But to call the likes of Johann Kriegler, Freedom Under Law, the Council for the Advancement of the South African Constitution and the Helen Suzman Foundation reactionaries hell-bent on preserving the old order and running an 'illegitimate neo-political campaign' to protect white male dominance of the judiciary is simply wrong, reckless and stupid.

The JSC, or rather the majority members in the JSC, have on occasion been guilty of blatantly victimising some of the candidates who have appeared before them because of their skin colour. The JSC has made some pretty suspect appointments while rejecting the candidature of experienced senior advocates with great records, such as Geoff Budlender and Jeremy Gauntlett. It has appointed, at least on one occasion, a white male judge with very suspect views of the Constitution and turned down a far more respected but more independent-minded candidate.

The problem with Mogoeng is that he doesn't have it in him to stand up to the race bullies and ANC heavyweights in the JSC, personalities like Jeff Radebe and Ngoako Ramatlhodi. He should be the sane voice urging consensus; instead he is a main protagonist of the transformation-above-all caucus. He should be leading an open and honest debate around the criteria for judicial appointments; instead he is playing politician and insulting all those who raise questions. And we're stuck with him for many years to come.

One calming voice in this hullabaloo has been that of Dennis Davis, judge president of the Competition Appeal Court and a judge who has never been afraid to voice his opinion. In an opinion piece in the *Mail & Guardian* in

April 2013, he addressed the criteria laid down by Section 174(1) of the Constitution, that the candidate be fit and proper, and Section 174(2), that the judiciary broadly represent the racial and gender composition of the nation.

'What is meant by "appropriately qualified"? It requires more than technical legal competence,' wrote Davis. 'Obviously, a sound knowledge of the law is required, but that alone is not sufficient ... We must lift our gaze and examine an applicant's judgement, ability to listen, understand the "Other", grasp the implications of our history, have an unbending commitment to justice and Ubuntu; he or she must possess the humanity to realise that he or she may not invariably be correct ... There will be judges, black and white, men and women, who qualify on both the technical and the other tests. Neither technical qualification nor any of the other qualities are exclusively possessed by one group.'

Davis argued that if after the consideration of 'fit and proper' the bench still remained skewed in favour of white men, Section 174(2) should then be triggered. 'Its purpose is to ensure that the journey towards a judiciary broadly reflective of our demography continues. In practical terms, if the scoring of those who were appropriately qualified produced a result subversive of the goal of broad representivity, race and gender may *then* be employed to give higher scores to some who rank lower on qualifications.'

The obvious way out of this impasse would be to change the make-up of the JSC. In fact, the NDP, accepted as policy by the ANC, says that 'judicial appointments that call the impartiality of selection processes into question must be addressed' and that the composition of the JSC should be changed because it is too big to function effectively and is seen as 'hamstrung by political interests'.

Dene Smuts has proposed a private member's bill to change the constitutional prescriptions for the JSC. She proposes culling the six political representatives from the JSC to make it more streamlined and reduce the influence of politicians. I don't hear Radebe and Co. cheering her on.

My view is that we should be true to the transformative essence of our Constitution. That means we can't ignore the directive that our judiciary should broadly reflect the composition of our people. But, more importantly, it means that we should heavily guard against any tendency to favour judges who are suspected of being weak on the separation of powers between the judiciary, the executive and the legislature and/or on the freedoms and rights ensconced in the Constitution.

We shouldn't care if it so happened that one day nine out of ten judges are black women, as long as those judges are fit and proper, not beholden to any group or section of society, and are totally committed to the letter and spirit of the Constitution.

With a judiciary like that, our democracy and stability will be able to withstand virtually any onslaught.

12

The 'national question'

Hi, my name is Max. I'm a colonialist of a special type.

I'm also delusional, because I call myself an African. Surely one can't be an African and a colonialist of any type at the same time?

Twenty years after liberation, the 'national question' – nationhood, race, identity – still dominates the national discourse. It is a difficult and highly sensitive topic to investigate in our race-conscious, unequal society. More often than not it leads to accusations, defensiveness, labels and insults. But it is so central to policy-making, societal attitudes and our country's stability that I decided to give it an honest try.

Forgive me if I personalise this chapter somewhat. By doing so, I'm saying that I know I can neither pretend to be neutral about this topic, nor pretend that I can stand in the shoes of others. My skin is pale, I am a man, my mother tongue is Afrikaans, and I grew up during apartheid and benefited from it, at least materially and in terms of education.

As I was saying, I'm a CST. Sarcasm aside, the term 'colonialists of a special type' was used by exiled ANC theorists and others to describe the position of white South Africans: they came to Africa as colonialists, but they stayed and came to see South Africa as their home. As such I suppose the term had its place, although I must say that to call someone like me a colonialist, even of a special type, feels very wrong. My white ancestors have regarded themselves as locals for more than three centuries; some even married slave and Khoi women. They did not colonise the southern tip of Africa on behalf of any European nation; in fact, very soon after their arrival, they opposed all colonial authority, especially when the British took over. My ancestors even fought their own devastating anti-colonial war against the British.

It was not a phrase I ever heard Nelson Mandela or the leaders of the internal resistance of the 1980s, the UDF, use. It was Thabo Mbeki who revived it in the post-1994 era. It was the first time most white South Africans had come across the term – very few knew that it was used widely by ANC ideologues in exile. Needless to say, most white people reacted strongly to being called any kind of colonialist.

Mbeki had another favourite phrase: South Africa is a country of 'two nations', one white and prosperous and the other black and poor. Again, as a factual statement it was correct, although a bit simplistic and in any case rapidly changing. But as an accusation against an entire community it wasn't all that helpful. Then again, wasn't it time to speak the brutal truth without all the 'nation-building' sugar-coating?

I sometimes miss Thabo Mbeki. Not his hypersensitivity to criticism, his apparent insecurity, his awkwardness in dealing with African traditionalism or the intellectual dishonesty (if that's what it was) of his interaction with African despots such as Sani Abacha and Robert Mugabe. I miss his thoughtfulness, his well-crafted speeches, his personal dignity and his aversion to cheap populism. He was accused of creating an imperial presidency, but, looking back, wasn't he perhaps correct in wanting to consolidate his power so that he could better lead a fractious party and country? Isn't that what we blame Zuma for, a lack of strong leadership and a strong hand keeping things together?

I miss Mbeki especially because his successor is his exact opposite. Mbeki carefully formulated his thoughts on social cohesion, race and the legacies of the past, whether you liked him for it or not. Jacob Zuma never does. Nobody knows what he really thinks, what his vision is. He sucks up to right-wing Afrikaners like a benevolent African chief, but then blames them for his government's own failures when it suits him. It was his rise to power that unlocked the sluice gates of cheap populism. He plays the role of the gentle father figure, the good listener and peacemaker, but uses his lackeys to insult, threaten and whip up emotions. That is his only genius, besides dodging bullets and staying in power: letting others do his dirty work while he innocently looks on.

A good example is when he sat right next to then ANC Youth League president and chief Zuma sycophant Julius Malema on a stage in Kimberley on 9 May 2011. Malema made this sweeping statement about white South Africans: 'We must take the land without paying. They took our land without paying. Once we agree they stole our land, we can agree they are criminals and must be treated as such.' Zuma just sat there, staring in front of him. What Malema had said was completely against government policy, but he wasn't repudiated.

When Black Management Forum leader and official government spokesperson Jimmy Manyi crudely insulted coloured and Indian South Africans on national television in March 2010, he was attacked by ANC veterans, but all of them from minority groups. ANC MP Ben Turok accused Manyi of 'black chauvinism', cabinet minister Trevor Manuel called him a 'racist in the mould of H.F. Verwoerd' and struggle veteran Horst Kleinschmidt said his racist comments represented a trend 'that has a well-established base in the ANC'. Zuma never rebuked Manyi, who kept his job. The ANC itself reserved its fiercest criticism for Manuel.

(The subtext, of course, as has been documented often in ANC writings, is resentment in ANC circles that most coloured and Indian South Africans have chosen not to vote for the ANC since 1994. Ungrateful bastards. During a recent informal chat with a senior ANC leader I mentioned my concern about the growth of narrow black African nationalism in the ANC. His response: 'It was inevitable. The minorities have deserted us. What do you expect?')

Zuma and his Luthuli House lieutenants also looked the other way when ANC personalities called DA leader Helen Zille a dancing monkey and a white madam who sleeps with her male colleagues in the Western Cape government.

Zille and other DA leaders, white and black, are the prime targets of racist abuse. When, in 2012, Zille used the term 'educational refugees' to describe children and parents who chose to relocate to the Western Cape because of the education meltdown in the Eastern Cape, she was met with a torrent of racist abuse. There were similar reactions when the DA marched to COSATU House to push for a youth wage subsidy. The website inside-politics.org collected some of the worst insults. Someone called Katlego, using the Twitter name @rasebitse, tweeted: 'I won't mind to rape you Zille and make SA proud. I wish you can be shot to death by Malema.' Others on Twitter called her a whore, a dog, 'Verwoerd's illegitimate child', and more. The DA's parliamentary leader, Lindiwe Mazibuko, was equally vilified and called a 'housenigger' and 'Zille's kaffirgirl'. A journalist with the Twitter name @dayjoyskillz tweeted: 'I wish that token @LindiMazibuko got hit with a brick on her pig face.'

Unbridled populism

'It is becoming more acceptable for black South Africans to scorn and abuse whites openly as a racial group,' remarked *The Economist* on 24 June 2011.

If anything, that was an understatement, at least by 2013. The post-Polokwane wave of unbridled populist politics has created an atmosphere in which it is almost required of a 'good black' to vilify and curse white people. Some, like Cape Town lawyer Christine Qunta and the 'self-anointed custodian of Biko and representative of blackness', as columnist Andile Mngxitama has been called, have turned it into a cottage industry.

It was in this climate that Zama Khumalo, a twenty-four-year-old news-paper reporter, announced on his Facebook page in early 2013 a 'Big Black Braai' to celebrate the anniversary of the deaths of forty-two white children, who were killed when their school bus plunged into the Westdene Dam in 1985. He posted the names of the victims with the comment that their deaths were 'much appreciated, my Lord!'

My reading at the time was that insults and threats to whites had become so commonplace in some sections of the black community that Khumalo genuinely thought his statement was nothing outrageous. I wanted to believe him when he apologised profusely afterwards, saying that he didn't really want to celebrate the deaths of white children. His mistake, of course, was that he wrote in English and that his Facebook page was noticed – I have heard of much worse on social media.

Just as I was writing this, I noticed that someone who had 'friended' me on Facebook, one Maleven Serage, posted: 'I hate white people with all my heart.' When I objected, he responded that he was only being truthful and that he has a tattoo on his arm that reads 'Kill the whites'.

Perhaps this behaviour wouldn't have reached such extreme levels if it hadn't been for the 'online toxic disinhibition effect' of social media. I am active on Twitter and I also put my weekly newspaper columns on Facebook. With the exception of my remarks and columns that specifically attack white racism or praise the ANC, I almost always have some black participants call me a racist, an apartheid apologist, a white supremacist, or worse, often in very crude terms.

Sometimes I look up those who insult me and more often than not I discover that they're just ordinary, probably mostly decent, citizens with jobs and families and pets. I'm sure I'd be able to have a civil conversation with most of them if I met them face to face. But somehow, sitting behind their laptops or fiddling with their smartphones, they think it's better to respond with a 'Fuck off, you white racist bastard' instead of 'I disagree'.

This 'disinhibition' of black people is sadly matched blow for blow by white people who somehow think it gives them licence to utter their basest racist emotions in public. Many are simply unrehabilitated racists, but others react because they feel attacked or marginalised, and say things they would never say in person.

The big difference is that white people who make racist remarks in public are almost always quickly corrected and often penalised. An established Afri-kaans writer, Annelie Botes, said in an interview that she didn't like black people. She was forced to give back a literary award she had won and no publisher would take her on for years. Similarly, a charity concert featuring Afrikaans singer Sunette Bridges was cancelled because of racist remarks on her Facebook page. A Pretoria University academic, Louise Mabille, was forced to resign and apologise when she wrote that the rape of babies was a black cultural phenomenon.

Nothing happened to Andile Mngxitama when he encouraged blacks to physically attack a white left-wing activist with whom he had had a disagreement. 'Real Bikoists out there, whenever we see that white little bastard called Jared Sacks, we must beat the shit out of him,' he declared. He kept his job (as policy advisor for the Foundation for Human Rights, *nogal*) and is still a regular contributor to several newspapers.

Zuma, president of all South Africans, has never cautioned against this trend, not even when his cabinet colleague Blade Nzimande took part. Another cabinet minister, Lulu Xingwana, commenting on the Oscar Pistorius murder case, made this sweeping generalisation in early 2013: 'Young Afrikaner men are brought up in the Calvinist religion believing that they own a woman, they own a child, they own everything and therefore they can take that life because they own it.' She later issued a lame apology.

Zuma's silly statement about whites and pets didn't help either. Spending money on buying a dog, and taking it to the vet and for walks belonged to white culture and was not the African way, which was to focus on the family, he said in KwaZulu-Natal in December 2012. This statement wasn't only wrong, as many black dog-lovers pointed out after his speech, but was also a dangerous stereotyping of whites as a group of spoilt, rich and selfish people.

It would have been surprising if black South Africans' feelings of resentment towards whites after the humiliations and dispossession of centuries had simply disappeared after 1994. A Truth Commission with limited scope, coupled with unconvincing apologies from white leaders and the vote, could not possibly have been enough to undo the anger built over generations and through the personal experiences of individuals.

It would have been easier if there had been a proper revolution, an overthrow of the white regime and a triumphant march by the MK through the streets of Pretoria, the toppling of the apartheid masters' statues and other acts constituting a psychological release. Of course, this would probably also have triggered a low-level civil war, a lot of bloodshed and the destruction of the economy. We are enjoying the fruits of a peaceful political settlement and transition, but we're also paying the price.

Several factors retarded the expected progress of the soppy Rainbow Nation concept: the continued gross inequalities, mostly along racial lines; the fact that most white South Africans behaved like nothing had changed after 1994; the continued domination of the economy and senior executive positions by whites; the persistence of white racism and arrogance; the rejection of affirmative action and black economic empowerment by many whites and white lobby groups; the denial by so many whites that they had benefited from apartheid, even of the true nature and impact of apartheid; and, last but certainly not least, the failures of the post-apartheid governments and their inability to substantially change the material conditions of most black people.

Advice from Rwanda

In 2007, I participated in a workshop in Kigali attended by victims and perpetrators of Rwanda's genocide. People were reluctant to talk, so to make things easier I told the group what apartheid really meant to its victims. I identified myself as a member of the 'perpetrator class' and asked the Rwandans to advise me on how we should behave in the post-apartheid era and how we should make peace with the black majority.

A woman of about twenty got up and told her terrible story. She had witnessed her family's neighbour killing her parents and brothers during the genocide. The man still lived next door to her in Kigali and his children went to the same school as her. 'I see them every day. I talk to them, you can even call us friends. Most of the time it is okay, but some days the murder of my family comes up in my mind and drives me crazy. Then I tell them to stand against a wall and I shout and insult them. Then I feel better and we go on again.'

Her advice to me? 'I think you white people should sometimes stand against a wall and allow black people to scream at you and insult you to get all their bad thoughts out into the open. When they feel better, you can go on living together again.' Remarkable.

There is some wisdom in her advice, though. The wound is not yet clean. There's still some stuff that needs to come out. Just as the children who had to listen to the young woman's abuse did not commit murder themselves, but had to face her wrath on behalf of their father, so we should face the anger on behalf of what our fathers and grandfathers did. It is hard, I know.

But there is the danger that this anger is not always righteous; that it or some of it has its roots in something other than the evil past. Sometimes it's simply racist abuse. Also, black anger for the sake of black anger is not very productive – black anger will remain forever if we don't remove what is keeping it alive. We need this anger to take us somewhere, or it will never end and will become destructive.

I am a vocal critic of some of the strategies and tactics of the white lobby group AfriForum and its parent body, Solidarity. I think their macho assertiveness and often brash statements on minority rights are being experienced as insults by many in the black community, and I think they are so focused on white protection that they don't have a balanced view of the dynamics of black politics and public opinion. At the same time, I have to concede that AfriForum and Solidarity are very effective and productive civic action groups led by very intelligent and committed people. Their self-help and charity programmes are an example to others working in the wider community. If only their focus wasn't so narrow.

I think there is room for civic groups guarding the rights of minorities in a country with South Africa's demographic make-up. But they have to do a delicate balancing act not to offend the majority, and sometimes AfriForum doesn't get this right. Sometimes its portrayal of whites and Afrikaners as the prime victims of the new order is downright offensive.

Justice, not guilt

The director of the Centre for the Study of Democracy, Steven Friedman, related a fascinating experience recently. He was part of a research team that tested the attitudes of mainly white middle-class people shortly after 1994 to a proposal that they pay more for water because they had benefited from apartheid and so should subsidise black households. The interviewees reacted abusively, says Friedman, with many accusing black people of wanting to sponge off minorities. In a later survey, the same people were asked whether they would be prepared to pay more for water so poorer people would be able to afford to use more water. This time everyone agreed that it was a good idea. Friedman concludes: 'So, if proposals for a fairer distribution of our resources are framed in terms of racial guilt, they are fiercely resisted. When they appeal to values most of us claim to share, such as justice and fairness, not only are they taken seriously, people who reject the racial argument may even accept them ... Racial minorities who refused to pay more to atone for apartheid did not resist when they were asked to conserve a scarce resource or to reduce poverty.' Human beings generally don't respond well to pleas based on their sense of guilt, regardless of how valid that guilt is.

I'm not suggesting for a second that the truth be sugar-coated or that the beneficiaries of apartheid be mollycoddled. But perhaps our strategies should be more outcomes-based. Do you want to insult whites or do you want to create a fundamentally new social order in as short a time as possible? What is more important, venting your anger or getting results, punishing whites or achieving a more equal society?

There is also the danger that the white minority could become so demonised through this free-for-all that they could eventually be regarded as evil enough to deserve action taken against them. The Hutu nationalists in Rwanda dehumanised the Tutsis with labels like 'cockroach' long enough that it became possible for ordinary people to kill them without regarding the act as murder.

I had a bruising experience in August 2011 when I was attacked as a racist on Twitter. I had lunch with a well-known black public figure a few days later and mentioned it to her. This is what I wrote in my weekly newspaper column the next day:

Are white South Africans too sensitive about being called settlers or colonialists or non-Africans? A prominent South African challenged me on this during a conversation on the weekend and I'm grappling with the question.

My conversation partner, someone for whom I have the highest possible regard, was reacting to my irritation with the reference by singer Simphiwe Dana, the one who had a Twitter-fight with Helen Zille, to whites as 'the colonial race' in the weekend's *Sunday Times*. Dana also made reference to 'the black nation' as if there exists a South African nation that excludes all minorities.

I tweeted Dana's statements with the remark 'It is so 1940s' on Sunday and was 'twitterstormed' by a number of black people justifying her remark and accusing me of being a 'liberal' and, frankly, an apologist of apartheid and its legacy. As Zille has found out, Twitter is fun and a great way to be updated on events, but it is no place for a debate.

I don't feel personally slighted by being called a settler or a colonialist or even a criminal because of my pale skin. I've been around South African politics long enough to know what kind of person makes these kinds of remarks. I also have no doubt whatsoever in my own mind where I see myself fitting into my society and what role I see myself playing.

But what I do find disturbing is that this kind of talk, this crude racial stereotyping and name-calling, has suddenly become very common and acceptable in decent company, and it is becoming progressively more aggressive and hate-filled. Every imaginable ill in society is now directly blamed on whites. I know how this disturbs, angers and scares the average white citizen – and how it undermines the potential for dialogue.

One sometimes feels tempted to ask these bigots: so what is it that you really want, what would really satisfy you? Should the vote be taken away from whites? Should their property be taken away and given to blacks? Should they pay double tax and shut up, restrict their public utterances to 'white affairs'? Would you want them to go and live in an enlarged Orania so you can't see them, or even better, should they all emigrate? No? Then what?

But this reaction would just be silly and childish, stooping to the level of those who drag our public discourse down to the level of insults.

My friend over Sunday lunch is a sober, reasonable thought leader in the country, but she had little sympathy with whites who feel unloved. Do you have any idea how black people felt over many generations being called non-persons, non-citizens or sub-humans? she asked. Why do white people depend on others to define who they are and to determine whether they are part of the nation or not? She was once the chief executive at a major institution which at the time was overwhelmingly white at the top and asked me if I had any idea how lonely and difficult it sometimes was and what fights she had to fight.

I responded that I could imagine her struggles and how tough it must have been being black under apartheid, but said she was underestimating the insecurity of being a tiny minority in the country; that despite the hardships, the black majority always knew that history and morality – and time, and numbers – were on their side.

This argument made no impression on her. She had no sympathy with whites playing victim, feeling sorry for themselves. Stand your ground, be sure of who and what you really are and ignore the crazies, was more or less her advice. And just sometimes try to understand what the roots of this kind of thinking are.

My friend was of course completely correct. We should spend our energies and resources on other crises … rather than on white insecurities.

White South Africans should realise that they simply have to carry the burden of resentment from many or most of their compatriots because of the past and the continuing inequalities and insecurities. They should protest when they're called criminals as a group, or 'the colonial race', but they should not let that paralyse them. Rather, they should try to live and act in a way that would undermine this resentment, on a personal and a national level. They should also stop paying attention to the bigots and crazies on their side. Our Constitution states that they are full citizens and that should be their reassurance ...

White South Africans have a lot of persuading and healing to do.

End of the rainbow

There are those who charge Mbeki with laying the groundwork for the re-racialising of society that is now blossoming like a noxious weed. But they should be asked this question: was it feasible and realistic for Mbeki to simply continue with Mandela's grand project of reconciliation and nation building, with his vision of the Rainbow Nation?

Had the time not come by 1999, when Mbeki became president, for South Africa to move on from reassuring the minorities to a new black assertiveness, to voicing the frustrations most black South Africans were feeling five years after liberation – namely, that little had changed and the former oppressors were living as if it was business as usual? After all, the main aim of reconciliation and reassurance, stability, had been fully achieved by then.

I don't think Mbeki, even if it was his inclination, which it most certainly wasn't, could have avoided moving from reconciliation to justice and assertiveness. His presidency started a new era for South Africa, the post-honeymoon era, the era of dealing with the past and persistent inequalities.

But I do think that if he had just some of Mandela's confidence, self-belief and magnanimity, he could have given substance to these new goals without obsessively focusing on race. He was the president of all of South Africa, after all. Focusing on restitution did not necessarily mean racial confrontation, abandoning all reconciliation.

I first met Mbeki in Lusaka in 1984, when I attended the annual ANC birthday press conference. The next year, at the same occasion, he told me privately that the ANC was ready to start negotiations with the apartheid government. I thought he wanted me to take the message back home and so I asked my friend Frederik van Zyl Slabbert to communicate as much to P.W. Botha's government (although I was working in the parliamentary press gallery at the time, I had no access to the Nats because they hated and distrusted me). In 1987, I got to know Mbeki better when I went on Van Zyl Slabbert's 'Dakar Safari' to talk with the exiled ANC leadership about the prospects for a negotiated settlement.

I thought Mbeki was an impressive politician. He was more sophisticated, articulate and better informed than any of the National Party politicians I had met. But he was also, as I soon discovered, a Machiavellian of the highest order and far too much under the impression of the magnitude of his own intellect.

Years after he was deposed as president, Mbeki is still highly regarded as an intellectual in the ANC and broader black community, even among those who wanted him out. He gave an intellectual respectability to the growing phenomenon of 'Africa for the Africans', even black chauvinism, and the trend to analyse virtually everything with a racial ruler in the hand. It is perhaps worth looking at some of his utterances that are still quoted.

There is broad consensus that Mbeki's 'I am an African' speech, delivered on 8 May 1996, with the acceptance of the final Constitution, was one of the most memorable political speeches ever made in South Africa. It was beautiful and poetic. I was deeply moved by it at the time. (Read it here to refresh your memory: http://www.info.gov.za/aboutgovt/orders/new2002_mbeki.htm.)

He spoke lyrically about 'owing his being' to the Khoi and the San; about the blood of the slaves coursing through his veins; and about being the grand-child of the great black heroes and struggling masses.

He could not exclude the white settlers from his eulogy, but there was a subtle difference, a little more distance. 'I am formed of the migrants who left Europe to find a new home in our native land,' he said. 'Whatever their own actions, they remain still, part of me.'

He was slightly kinder to the Afrikaners of the old Boer republics: 'I am the grandchild who lays fresh flowers on the Boer graves at St Helena and the Bahamas, who sees in his mind's eye and suffers the suffering of a simple peasant folk, death, concentration camps, destroyed homesteads, a dream in ruins.'

He turned to one of his favourite themes, which he would use in his con-troversial speeches on HIV and AIDS, that whites and Westerners see Africa as barbaric: 'The great masses who are our mother and father will not permit that the behaviour of the few results in the description of our country and people as barbaric.'

Mbeki then addressed the sensitive question of who is entitled to call themselves African. 'We are assembled here today to mark their [the masses'] victory in acquiring and exercising their right to formulate their own defini-tion of what it means to be an African,' he said. The Constitution declares unequivocally 'that we refuse to accept that our Africanness shall be defined by our race, colour, gender or historical origins. It is a firm assertion made by ourselves that South Africa belongs to all who live in it, black and white.'

Two nations

There you have it: white South Africans are also Africans. That settles it, yes? I don't think so. Mbeki said it, but he didn't live it. This is true of most ANC leaders to this day. Fast-forward two years to 29 May 1998, same venue, when Mbeki delivered his other famous speech, the 'two nations' speech.

'This reality of two nations, underwritten by the perpetuation of the racial, gender and social disparities born of a very long period of colonial and apartheid white minority domination, constitutes the material base which reinforces the notion that, indeed, we are not one nation, but two nations. And neither are we becoming one nation. Consequently, also, the objective of national reconciliation is not being realised.

'This follows as well that the longer this situation persists, in spite of the gift of hope delivered to the people by the birth of democracy, the more entrenched will be the conviction that the concept of nation building is a mere mirage and that no basis exists, or will ever exist, to enable national reconciliation to take place.' Strong stuff, especially from someone who was about to become the president, not just a political hothead. Also totally oversimplistic.

He asked: 'Are the relatively rich, who, as a result of an apartheid definition, are white, prepared to help underwrite the upliftment of the poor, who, as a result of an apartheid definition, are black?' He then accused some rich whites of tax evasion.

Okay, so he was making the point that genuine reconciliation or nation building would be hard while gross inequalities continued. No sane person can quarrel with that. Fifteen years after his speech this is still the major challenge facing South Africa, although race has significantly diminished as the determining factor. There are many, many black South Africans today who are 'relatively rich' and quite a number of whites who can't be described as such.

Another struggle veteran, and one with far more radical views on the economy than Mbeki, Beyers Naudé, made the same point a year before Mbeki's speech: 'True reconciliation is only possible when we bridge the economic gulf, for you can't build a society of justice on the increasing gap between rich and poor.'

It brings me back to Steven Friedman's research. If you truly want to move towards greater equality, you appeal to people's sense of justice, fairness and humanity; you don't simply lump them all in one group of evil racists and accuse and insult them. The result is inevitable: they will resist and withdraw.

They will also ask, quite legitimately, why it is not really a scandal in the

ANC's eyes when black fat cats screw the poor and undermine efforts to bridge the economic gulf. They will point to the tragedy faced by workers at the Aurora mines owned (and destroyed) by Zuma's nephew Khulubuse Zuma and Nelson Mandela's grandson Zondwa Mandela. Khulubuse and Zondwa continued to live lavishly while about seven hundred workers, who had not been paid salaries for more than two years, eked out a living as beggars.

As *The Times* editorialised in January 2012: 'The plight of hundreds of mineworkers, whose lives have been devastated, has not stopped either of them from flaunting their wealth. Last month, Zuma was reported to have bought his fiancée, Fikisiwe Dlamini, a silver 2009 model Maserati, which sells for between R1 million and R1.6 million, for Christmas.'

The SACP's Aubrey Ntsako Baloyi had already weighed in on the two mine owners' lifestyles on marxist.com back in November 2010: 'They still live a life of luxury which is paraded every day in the pages of South African newspapers. In September, Khulubuse Zuma attended the wedding of national police commissioner Bheki Cele in a R2.5 million Mercedes-Benz SLS63 AMG gullwing.' He added: 'The scandal of Aurora highlights one of the main issues confronting the workers' movement in South Africa: the end of apartheid has given everyone political rights, but workers are still oppressed by capitalists. The only difference is that some of these are now black, but they are still capitalists, out to make a profit from the exploitation of the working class. The attempt to solve "the race question" without addressing the "class question" has failed miserably.'

African hegemony

Let's return to the 'national question' and see what the ANC position is post-liberation.

The latest document I could find was an official ANC discussion document dated 1 July 1997 called 'Nation-formation and nation building: The national question in South Africa'.

It identifies one of the 'basic principles that should be taken into account in addressing the national question' in South Africa: 'From its characterisation of apartheid colonialism, the ANC was correct in asserting, in the documents on Strategy and Tactics from the Morogoro and Kabwe Consultative Conferences, that the main content of the NDR [National Democratic Revolution] is the liberation of Black people in general, and Africans in particular. They are in the majority, and they constitute even an overwhelmingly larger majority of the poor.

'Related to this is the identity of the South African nation in the making: whether it should truly be an African nation on the African continent, or a clone, for example, of the US and UK in outlook, in the style and content of its media, in its cultural expression, in its food, in the language accents of its children, and so forth. Hence, what is required is a continuing battle to assert African hegemony in the context of a multi-cultural and non-racial society.'

Assert African hegemony. I'm not sure how that fits into the *context of a non-racial society.*

This brings me back to Mbeki. In a lecture on 23 August 2013 at UNISA's Thabo Mbeki African Leadership Institute, he delivered a blistering attack on those who said the 2013 elections in Zimbabwe were flawed. Does the West think Africans are stupid, he asked. He also, for the first time, condoned the violent occupation of white-owned land in Zimbabwe in clear terms, despite the fact that the High Court in Zimbabwe and the SADC tribunal in Windhoek had decided that farmers should have been compensated.

Here are some extracts from this speech:

'Many years ago and as part of the leadership in this region, we engaged the Zimbabwean leadership – President Mugabe and others – in a very sustained process to discourage them from the manner in which they were handling the issue of land reform. We were saying to them, "Yes indeed we agree, the land reform is necessary, but the way in which you are handling it is wrong." We tried very hard, "No, no, you see all of these things about the occupation of the farms by the war veterans, this and that and the other, all of this is wrong", that's what we were saying. But fortunately the Zimbabweans didn't listen to us, they went ahead.'

Fortunately?

Another extract: 'I think we should also ask ourselves the question: why is Zimbabwe such a major issue for some people? Zimbabwe is a small country by any standard, there is no particular reason why Zimbabwe should be a matter to which the *New York Times*, the London *Guardian* and whoever else ... why are they paying so much attention to Zimbabwe? Why?

'I know why they pay particular attention to us, because they explained it, they said, "You have too many white people in South Africa. We are concerned about their future. They are our kith and kin. We are worried about what you would do to them, so we keep a very close eye on what happens." So we understand, we may not agree with the thinking, but we understand.'

Let me interject here. When 'they' told Mbeki that whites were their 'kith and kin', were they talking about the small number of white South Africans who have British or other European passports, who see those countries as their true motherland? I'm certainly not the kith and kin of Europeans or Americans. Mbeki said I am an African, and I claim that identity with the majority of other white South Africans.

I don't think anyone 'explained' that to Mbeki. He just made it up. Not that I'm denying that the presence of white people in Zimbabwe isn't an important reason why Western nations seem to be more interested in Zimbabwe than in, say, Burkina Faso. These nations were also vocal in their criticism when Idi Amin kicked Asians out of Uganda. But another reason is that Zimbabwe was a stable, prosperous country before Mugabe went berserk after 2000 and that now some four million Zimbabweans are economic (and some even political) refugees in South Africa and other neighbouring countries.

Mbeki also talked about Zimbabwe's drive to force all companies doing business in the country to hand over half their shares to Zimbabweans: 'The Zimbabweans now are talking about indigenisation and I can see that there is a big storm brewing about indigenisation. But what is wrong with indigenisation? What is wrong with saying, "Here we are as Africans, with all our resources. Sure, we are ready and very willing to interact with the rest of the world about the exploitation of all these resources, but what is the indigenous benefit from the exploitation of these, and even the control?"

'I am saying that because I can see that there is a cloud that is building up somewhere on the horizon when Zimbabweans say "indigenisation". But we have to, as intellectuals and thought leaders, we have got to address that and say, "Yes indeed as Africans we are concerned about our own renaissance, our own development, and we must as indigenous people make sure that we have control of our development, our future and that includes our resources, and therefore indigenisation is correct." We must demonstrate it even intellectually, which I am quite sure we can.'

The onslaught is actually against all Africans, according to Mbeki. 'That offensive is not in the first instance about Zimbabwe, it's about the future of our continent,' he said. 'So the Zimbabweans have been in the frontline in terms of defending our right as Africans to determine our future, and they are paying a price for that. I think it is our responsibility as African intellectuals to join them, the Zimbabweans, to say, "No!"'

A week after this speech, ANC MP and president of the Congress of Traditional Leaders of South Africa (CONTRALESA) Phathekile Holomisa, writing in the *Sunday Independent*, called himself a Mugabe 'praise singer' and said that Mugabe was a true African hero. He said he 'and other Africans' had a 'secretive envious admiration' for Mugabe's policies of land expropriation and indigenisation.

Perpetual victims

Again, I can associate with much of what Mbeki said, although he was simply dishonest in not making any mention of how Mugabe has damaged the economy and violated the human rights of thousands, and of the millions who have fled that country. (About a quarter of Zimbabwe's population now lives in South Africa, Botswana and elsewhere.) What I'm trying to demonstrate is Mbeki's Africans-versus-the-world mentality; his constant subtext that black Africans are the perpetual victims of every kind of imperialism and racism one can imagine; the signals he always sends that African equals black under threat of those who are not black. I see his thinking reflected in the black intellectual discourse in South Africa today.

Here's the crux, I think. It is as if Mbeki and people who think like him have never truly made peace with the fact that South Africa's history is distinctly different from all other African states. It is as if they have never properly accepted the full reality and all its implications – that there is an important community in this country that is not black but also not settler, temporary citizen or visitor. They don't seem to have made peace with the fact that our political dynamics, the very nature of our society, are fundamentally different from those in Ghana or Zambia or even Zimbabwe, because of our demographic make-up.

South Africa's liberation was thus also liberation of a special type, if you will. Unlike other African states, it wasn't a liberation from European colonialists like Britain, France, Belgium or Portugal, but a liberation from an evil political system, from domination and oppression by an internal ethnic group – a nasty 'tribe' of fellow South Africans, to put it another way.

No other African country needed to put in its Constitution's preamble that the country 'belongs to all who live in it, united in our diversity' or had to put in its founding principles that 'non-racialism' is a core value.

I believe it is important that South African intellectuals read Aimé Césaire, Amílcar Cabral, Frantz Fanon and all the black American Black Consciousness writers, especially on the decolonisation of the mind, but we have to remember our peculiar history when we do. I often wonder what our own Steve Biko would have said of Black Consciousness, non-racialism, Africanness and South African nationhood now, thirty-seven years after he was killed by apartheid policemen.

I suspect that if Mbeki and like-minded black South Africans were brutally honest, they would come out and agree with Simphiwe Dana's statement that white South Africans are 'the colonial race' threatening 'the black nation'.

To some, this 'black nation' also excludes Indian South Africans. In May 2013, the ANC-aligned businessman and head of the Mazibuye African Forum, Phumlani Mfeka, expressed this in crude terms.

His statements relate to an incident in which a black traffic officer insulted the ANC mayor of Newcastle, Afzul Rehman, who then asked him if he knew who he was. The officer told him to 'go back to India' because 'this country belongs to us'. Rehman reported him to his superiors and laid a charge of *crimen injuria*, later withdrawn.

Mfeka wrote an open letter to Rehman, published in the *City Press*: 'Who do you think you are, asking an African whether he knows who you are in his native land? Indians have never been comrades. They don't vote for the ANC and thus have no constituency that can warrant you to be mayor in the first place.'

Mfeka said Africans in KwaZulu-Natal 'do not regard Indians as their brethren and thus the ticking time bomb of a deadly confrontation between the two communities is inevitable and shall be exacerbated by the antagonistic attitude that Indians such as yourself and Vivian Reddy have. The traffic official was absolutely correct in reminding you that India is your home, and you should perhaps begin to embrace India as your home as we Africans embrace South Africa as our home, which we are more than willing to fight and die for.'

An influential political journalist and one-time Zuma confidante, Ranjeni Munusamy, wrote in the *Daily Maverick* that the Mfeka saga brought the ANC and Jacob Zuma's dubious relationships with wealthy Indian businessmen like the Guptas to the fore, because it generated resentment.

But her deeper criticism was that 'despite decades of colonial and apartheid rule that ingrained racial hatred and segregation, there is no ongoing dialogue in society on nation building and racial reconciliation. South Africa was hailed as a model nation for its transformation from a system of statutory racism to the full abolishment of segregation, but abandoned the nation-building project over time.'

She concluded: 'The truth is that in South Africa, way too much is left to chance and social issues are only tackled when they reach crisis proportions … despite racism and prejudice still lurking, there is nothing to actively promote a society that is educated about the past and fosters racial reconciliation.'

Munusamy is right. That effort, at least from the side of the government and the ruling party, ended when Mbeki took over from Mandela.

It is appropriate to remember that Mandela himself struggled with these concepts seven decades ago.

Africa for Africans

When he became politically active in the 1940s, Mandela was strongly influenced by the thinking of the charismatic Anton Lembede, who became leader of the ANC Youth League in 1944. Lembede witnessed the growth of Afrikaner nationalism during the period after the symbolic 'Second Great Trek' in 1938 and formulated his own black nationalist ideology. He was an 'Africa for the Africans' man and believed white and Indian South Africans would always remain settlers.

The young Mandela also proclaimed himself an African nationalist and even on occasion broke up Communist Party meetings because most leading members were white. Asked after his release from jail in 1990 about this time in his life and his reaction to the cry 'Hurl the white man into the sea', Mandela said: 'While I was not prepared to hurl the white man into the sea, I would have been perfectly happy if he had climbed aboard his steamships and left the continent of his own volition.'

But his deeper involvement in the struggle during the 1940s and early 1950s, and his working relationship and friendships with Indian and white anti-apartheid activists, changed his mind. By 1955 he was fully behind the adoption of the Freedom Charter that stated: 'South Africa belongs to all who live in it, black and white.' (The chairperson of the Congress of the People, as the gathering of 26 June 1955 where the charter was adopted was called, was a white man, Piet Beyleveld, and there were 112 white delegates.)

During this time, Mandela started arguing for the ANC's cooperation with 'non-Africans' and formed lifelong friendships with people such as Bram Fischer, Ahmed Kathrada, George Bizos, Ismail Meer and Ruth First. When he stepped out of jail after twenty-seven years, he became the embodiment of the belief that South Africa indeed belonged to all who lived in it. During my first private meeting with him in February 1990, Mandela made it clear that he saw Afrikaners and other whites as an integral part of the South African nation and that he intended to 'liberate' them too.

When I met Mandela then, I was an active supporter of the UDF (I was even a member of the rather short-lived Afrikaanse Demokrate that was affiliated with them). The UDF had a clear aim: to end all forms of apartheid, and to establish an open democracy and a just, equal society. It was clearly understood that black South Africans were not only in the majority, but had borne the brunt of apartheid, more so than coloured or Indian South Africans. It was understood that black South Africans would play the most important role in the leadership then and in the post-apartheid era.

I felt completely at home in the UDF's political culture because it practised, not only preached, real non-racialism. Three years before Mandela was released, when P.W. Botha was at the height of his powers, I started an Afrikaans-language newspaper, *Vrye Weekblad*, with a small group of like-minded colleagues. We published our credo in our first edition: we believed racism and apartheid were the biggest threats facing South Africans, and that Afrikaners should 'classify themselves as part of the majority of indigenous people and join the fight for an open, non-racial democracy rather than seeing themselves as a threatened minority'; and we would fight to expose the real face of apartheid and relay the voices of the real leaders of the people to an Afrikaans audience. I'm happy to say that we did just that for the entire six years of our existence, often at great risk to ourselves (we had to close down after we lost a defamation suit against a police general in February 1994).

To this day, non-racialism is official ANC policy – it is also one of the founding provisions of the Constitution.

It is also the most abused, manipulated and misunderstood political concept in South Africa.

There is no prescribed definition of non-racialism. It means anti-racism, yes, but it means a lot more besides. It means, I think, that we should strive to get to a point where we can stop dividing people into racial categories, and that we should dream of a time when we only see people's humanity and not judge them by the colour of their skin or the language they speak.

My understanding of the doctrine of non-racialism has always been that we have to, at least for the foreseeable future, acknowledge race as a factor and as a legacy of colonialism and apartheid, but simultaneously continue the struggle for the creation of an order in which all South Africans have been emancipated to such an extent that race becomes secondary or even non-existent. Chapter 1(b) of the Constitution groups non-racialism with non-sexism as core values of the republic. Non-sexism certainly can't mean that gender doesn't exist; it means that gender shouldn't determine the value of a person's being.

Many white people, especially those who supported apartheid to the end, protest that affirmative action and black economic empowerment go against the grain of non-racialism. If correctly applied, if not abused for reasons other than *regstellende aksie*, or corrective action, these policies are not against the principle of non-racialism, but rather essential to reaching its eventual goal.

One man who, in my view, understood and embodied non-racialism was Jakes Gerwel, former professor at the University of the Western Cape, former chancellor of Rhodes University and later director-general in President Mandela's office, and a loyal ANC cadre to his death in November 2012. I watched his slightly camouflaged irritation with the growing black chauvinism in the ANC during the last few years of his life as he expressed it in his columns in the Sunday paper *Rapport*.

After his death, Athambile Masola, a Cape Town teacher, remembered her first encounter with Gerwel at Rhodes in a piece written for the *Mail & Guardian*. Gerwel had asked her over lunch: 'When you wake up in the morning, do you think of yourself as black? I tend to think of myself as a writer, a thinker, a husband, a father, but race is not forefront in my mind.' Masola wrote: 'As a teacher who has been battling to talk about the dangers of racial prejudice or "labelling people" to my students, I often quote this conversation with Prof Gerwel as an example of what non-racialism could mean, because I no longer wake up in the morning thinking I'm black. I wake up as a thinker, a lover and a teacher.'

Ferial Haffajee, editor of *City Press*, wrote in her paper in March 2013: 'Non-racialism is the injunction to us by the founding mothers and fathers to find ways to transcend race, not identity, and the congealing ways in which race has divided South Africans. It is an injunction to see ourselves and each other as human beings and brothers and sisters before we see ourselves as racialised holograms. It is the Ubuntu we preach but so often fail to practise. Today, it is almost as hard to find adherents of non-racialism as it is to find whites who benefited from apartheid.'

Dead parrot

As I sit and write these words, my overwhelming feeling is that non-racialism, at least as a principle guiding the majority political party, is dead. Not stunned, not pining for the fjords, but expired, passed on, ceased to be, kicked the bucket, like the Monty Python parrot.

I remember sitting on a stage in front of a hall full of people in Pretoria discussing non-racialism and reconciliation in 1997. The hostility of the other panellists and much of the audience led me to declare, shell-shocked, at the end: 'I have never felt as white, male and Afrikaans in my entire life as you have made me out to be tonight.'

I remember being savaged in letters to newspapers and on talk radio when I wrote a column in 1999 claiming my right to call myself a full-blooded African. Keep your filthy racist paws off our heritage, one black intellectual told me publicly. You have stolen our land, our freedom and our dignity and now you want to steal our identity, said another. Professor Thobeka Mda argued in a newspaper piece that no white had the necessary characteristics of a true African:

By taking that identity I include my history, my nation, my culture, my traditions, my customs and religion. I also take the baggage of drought-stricken, war-torn, cannibalistic, superstitious nations. For me and others like me, there has not been anything before African.

Europeans and their descendants have been deciding for centuries on what peoples of the world should be called, in the process taking and giving nationalities and identities. It is called the 'culture of power'.

In South Africa immigrant Europeans called us kaffirs, then Natives, then non-Europeans, then bantus, then plurals and then blacks.

White people who are unhappy when we call ourselves Africans without including them, are not saying 'We are like you, we share your experiences, your traditions, your language'. They are not insisting on being Africans to claim closeness or nationality with us. They are saying so to claim a piece (huge pieces in fact) of land in this country, and there-fore this continent.

To this day it is standard ANC practice, for President Zuma included, to reserve the term 'African' exclusively for black people. Whites are whites, coloureds are coloureds, Indians are Indians, but black people are Africans. There are coloured townships and there are African townships. The old ANC edict that the task of the liberation movement was to liberate 'blacks in general and Africans in particular' is still in use today.

(I spoke at a seminar for history teachers some time ago and found that several coloured teachers used a different terminology: coloured Africans, In-dian Africans, white Africans and black Africans. I wish that would catch on.)

Of course, I can understand why so many black South Africans cherish their African identity with much emotion. After all, only a tiny percentage of the people of sub-Saharan Africa (because, let's face it, most southern

Africans don't really think of Egyptians, Tunisians, Mauritanians or Libyans when they refer to Africans) are not black. Africa is the most maligned continent. It is still seen by too many outsiders as the Dark Continent, the continent of primitive people, of hunger, disease, corruption and civil war. I also get angry when I encounter this bigotry and stupid stereotyping. So taking the African identity as a badge of honour to say to the world, 'Screw you, we're black and African and proud' is a very natural and legitimate mechanism.

But it has to be tempered with the acknowledgement that there are many different interpretations of Africanness and that there are communities inside South Africa that don't fit in with some people's narrow description of who and what constitutes African, and these should not be excluded. Some of these communities don't claim the African identity up front and that should not make them outsiders.

Black and in charge

I know this is harsh, but I think it needs to be said: too many people use the term 'African' to say, 'We're black and we're now in charge. We're the top dogs now.'

When I claim the right to call myself an African, I'm not being pretentious or fake, I'm not romanticising Africa's past. I'm insisting I'm an African because it means that I'm an indigenous, full citizen of South Africa and that there's no contradiction in me having a white skin and being a native of this continent. It means that I belong.

It also means that I am loyal to and associate with the people and cultures of Africa. I have been for many years, by the way, an ardent student of pre-colonial southern African history and I have published books and academic papers on the subject, and have even made a major television documentary about it.

If the contest is about what continent you're from, well, I'm from this one. It so happens that the ethnic group I was born into and the language I speak were also named after the continent.

But, like Jakes Gerwel, I don't wake up in the morning thinking I'm an African or an Afrikaner. I'm a father and a husband and a writer and a lover of music and nature and a citizen of an awesome country.

One of the rising stars in the DA, Mmusi Maimane, recently wrote: 'There is a temptation to equate Africanness with the one thing that remains constant in our lives: race. But it is a dangerous notion. At one level it might be true, but being truly African is about more than simply being black ... What angers me most is that politicians are increasingly using their "Africanness" as a political shield. It misrepresents what it is to be an African.'

The people who should be most annoyed about being excluded from the term 'African' are those whom apartheid classified as coloured.

In February 2012 I was again called all kinds of nasty names when I wrote in a column that if 'coloured' meant people of mixed blood, then the vast majority of people born in South Africa are coloureds, myself included.

Studies in the 1980s found that white Afrikaners had an average of 7 per cent 'black' blood, mostly because of early relationships and marriages between white settlers and slaves or Khoisan people. Some Afrikaners, like my family, have considerably more than 7 per cent black blood.

The converse is true of black South Africans. Three quick examples: ANC veteran Walter Sisulu's father was a white man; Winnie Mandela's mother had light skin, blue eyes and long hair, and her mother-in-law called her a *mlungu*; Nelson Mandela's mitochondrial DNA was found to be pure Khoisan. There were many runaway slaves from the East Indies and European shipwreck survivors in the sixteenth, seventeenth and eighteenth centuries who became part of the Zulu and Xhosa peoples.

Probably a majority of people classified coloured during the apartheid years were descendants of the aboriginal Khoikhoi and the San or Bushmen, with, of course, some white, slave and black blood. But when the ANC and other so-called Africanists refer to 'Africans', they exclude these people. This is sheer madness: the descendants of the first peoples of southern Africa are excluded from being African? The Khoisan were here thousands of years before the first black farming groups arrived from further north. They are the original Africans.

I explain this further by giving the example of my daughter. Her father is a mixture of seventeenth-century French Huguenot, German and Dutch settlers; slaves from Indonesia and Sri Lanka; and at least one Khoi woman, Pietronella, daughter of Krotoa and materfamilias of the Saayman clan. I had my DNA tested at the National Health Laboratory. They told me that on my father's side, I'm in the E1b1b1c1 haplogroup – 23 per cent of black Ethiopians belong to this small genetic group.

My daughter's mother is a mixture of Mauritian immigrants of Chinese/Indian stock, Afrikaners and Scottish missionaries from Kenya. So how is my daughter European?

In March 2011 I wrote about the poor treatment of coloured people by elements in the ANC and was dragged before the Press Ombudsman by the ANC's chief whip, Mathole Motshekga, who accused me of racism. I was specifically reacting to government spokesperson Jimmy Manyi's statement that there was 'an over-supply of coloureds' in the Western Cape; statements by Blackman Ngoro, then spokesperson for former Cape Town mayor Nomaindia Mfeketo, that 'Africans are vastly culturally superior to coloureds' and that coloureds are drunkards; and a piece by black columnist Kuli Roberts, in which she espoused insulting stereotypes about coloured women, such as that they 'shout and throw plates, have no front teeth and eat fish like they are trying to deplete the ocean and love to fight in public'.

I wrote: 'It now turns out that our much revered liberation movement actually only fought for coloured people to be half-liberated. Because, you see, there's a hierarchy of suffering: blacks first, coloureds and Indians second.'

I made the point that, although coloured people didn't have to carry passbooks and had access to some job opportunities blacks were excluded from during apartheid, their suffering under colonialism and apartheid was no less than that of blacks. Their Khoisan ancestors were subjugated quickly and completely during the first decades of white settlement. They lost all their cattle and, with the exception of a few tiny 'coloured reserves', they lost all their land. Eventually they even lost much of their culture and their languages, and instead spoke Afrikaans.

Many of them were condemned to be farmworkers, and as such were enslaved by the dop system (paid in alcohol for their labour). F.W. de Klerk's ex-wife Marike had a word for coloured people that represented what many whites and others thought of them: *uitskotmense*, or rejects.

In contrast, most black people never lost their culture or language and many still had an attachment to their ancestral village.

'This rootlessness of most coloured people, this sense they got over centuries of not belonging, is the only reason why gangsterism is so rife in that community. Gangsterism is almost always a yearning for a tribe, an attempt to belong,' I wrote.

In his letter to the ombudsman, Motshekga contended that my column violated the Press Code and that it should not have been published as it made 'racially disparaging claims about coloured people'.

But Deputy Press Ombudsman Johan Retief dismissed all Motshekga's charges. He said that he found the statement about 'gangsterism almost always being a yearning to belong, rather interesting and refreshing'. In conclusion, Retief wrote: 'The column makes the point that, while the coloured community once was subjugated by white settlers, they are now, in the new dispensation, only half-liberated. Again, this is an opinion – which, to my knowledge, is shared by many people. On the whole, Du Preez is voicing his sympathy for the coloured community, which is a far cry from putting them in a bad light and racially stereotyping them.'

I have to add that some voices from within the coloured community criticised me for 'trying to speak on our behalf', while others said I was simply perpetuating the existence of a group that doesn't and shouldn't exist. I suppose they have a point.

Building a new community

One of the most revolutionary and uncompromising thinkers on race, identity and nationhood South Africa has ever had was Robben Island graduate Neville Alexander, who died in late 2012. In a book I edited and contributed to in 2011, *Opinion Pieces by South African Thought Leaders*, Alexander posed this critical question: 'Are we building a new historical community?' He rephrased it another way: 'Are we using the historic opportunity that the 1990s made available to us for creating another South Africa, one where race thinking and racial discrimination, among other things, will eventually become as anachronistic and as pitiable as the belief in witches?'

Alexander isn't proposing denialism around race. The inherited racial stain did not disappear on 27 April 1994. 'Most South Africans continue to believe in these racial categories because they have been conditioned to accept them as real,' he wrote. Even though social identities are constructed and not given, they seem to have 'a primordial validity for most individuals, precisely because they are not aware of the historical, social and political ways in which their identities have been constructed'. The unravelling of the Afrikaner identity, once regarded as immutable, is an example of how such identities can be deconstructed and reshaped.

Alexander is saying that we should embark on a process to reimagine our people and our communities. We should make sure that measures such as affirmative action do not have the unintended consequence of entrenching racial or other stereotypes in the consciousness of the people.

'It means, fundamentally and among other things, that we have to see to it that the entrenched inherited racial identities that disfigured the popular consciousness of colonial and apartheid South Africa are changed and eventually eradicated,' wrote Alexander. It must be the goal of 'all creative and thinking people to ensure that labels such as black, white, coloured and Indian become irrelevant as a means of identifying groups of people in post-liberation South Africa'.

That's not what I see going on around me in South Africa today, although the youth of the middle classes seem to be doing it well. Too few 'creative and thinking people' are striving towards a post-racial future. Instead, we have reinstituted official forms that compel you to declare your 'race'. Instead, we attack and defend – and insult – from our separate racial trenches, especially when we're in a group context.

Whiteliness

In the last few years, a lot of column inches have been spent on the 'whiteness' (or 'whiteliness') debate, whiteness being a social construction that explains the material and symbolic privileges white societies enjoy. One definition of whiteliness is that 'the way whites see the world is just the way the world is and the way they get around in the world is just the right way around'.

It is a necessary debate because few white people in South Africa have ever paused to contemplate whether being white doesn't mean a lot more than just being the former oppressors and now simply a racial minority.

Many white South Africans scream 'reverse racism' and argue that bodies such as the Black Lawyers Association and the National African Federated Chamber of Commerce and Industry are a racist phenomenon. An email along these lines by right-wing Americans recently went viral among white South Africans. Black Americans have Black History Month, Black Entertainment Television, Miss Black America and more than sixty black colleges, but if white Americans were to have white versions of these, they'd be called racists, the email says. 'You are proud to be black or brown and you're not afraid to announce it. But when we announce our white pride, you call us racists.' Et cetera.

I see a lot of white South African heads nodding in agreement. Too few white (especially Afrikaans) intellectuals and media outlets with large white audiences or readerships have really bothered to unpack the dynamics of power, privilege and history for them.

I have kept a cutting of a particularly insightful piece by Martin Jacques in the *Guardian* since September 2003, when it was published. In it, he explains the global racial hierarchy that helps to shape the power and the prejudices of each race:

At the top of this hierarchy are whites. The reasons are deep-rooted and profound. White societies have been the global top dogs for half a millennium, ever since the Chinese civilization went into decline. With global hegemony, first with Europe and then the US, whites have long commanded respect, as well as arousing fear and resentment, among other races. Being white confers a privilege, a special kind of deference, throughout the world, be it Kingston, Hong Kong, Delhi, Lagos – or even, despite the way it is portrayed in Britain, Harare. Whites are the only race that never suffers any kind of systemic racism anywhere in the world. And the impact of white racism has been far more profound and baneful than any other: it remains the only racism with global reach.

Being top of the pile means that whites are peculiarly and uniquely insensitive to race and racism, and the power relations this involves. We are invariably the beneficiaries, never the victims. Even when well meaning, we remain strangely ignorant. The clout enjoyed by whites does not reside simply in abstraction – western societies – but in the skin of each and every one of us. Whether we like it or not, in every corner of the planet we enjoy an extraordinary personal power bestowed by our colour. It is something we are largely oblivious of, and consequently take for granted, irrespective of whether we are liberal or reactionary, backpackers, tourists or expatriate businessmen.

Jacques argues that the existence of a de facto global hierarchy helps to shape the nature of racial prejudice exhibited by other races. Whites, he says, are universally respected, even when that respect is combined with strong resentment.

Guilt and shame

I agree with all of the above. But the question we need to ask is if this can all simply be applied to post-apartheid South Africa, where whites are outnumbered ten to one and where the political power resides overwhelmingly in black hands. Is South African whiteliness the same as global whiteliness?

Academic Melissa Steyn elevated the whiteness debate from academic obscurity in her 2001 book *Whiteness Just Isn't What It Used to Be: White Identity in a Changing South Africa* and in academic papers after that. But the debate really came alive in 2010, after an article by Rhodes University philosophy lecturer Samantha Vice, titled 'How Do I Live in This Strange Place?', appeared in the *Journal of Social Philosophy*.

'The theses of habitual white privilege and moral damage are especially helpful in thinking about how it is to be white in South Africa,' Vice writes. 'While it is no longer common for whites to be openly and obviously racist, it is impossibly optimistic to think that the ways of whites who grew up and were educated in this country are not in some way still whitely. Because of the brute facts of birth, few white people, however well meaning and morally conscientious, will escape the habit of white privilege; their characters and modes of interaction with the world just will be constituted in ways that are morally damaging ... There is perhaps some justice, along with much that is morally puzzling, in the fact that feeling uncomfortable is an ineradicable part of white life.'

Vice's advice is for whites to feel guilt and shame, shame differing from guilt 'in being essentially directed toward the self, rather than outwards toward a harm one brought about'. Shame, she says, 'seems an appropriate response to the recognition of one's unavoidable privilege. For white privilege does not attach merely to what one does or how one benefits, but, more fundamentally, to who one is.' Feeling shame would at least fulfil 'a moral emotional duty'. It is unlikely, she says, 'that a white South African will be in a situation in which shame is not called for'.

I'm struggling to get my head around this shame Vice wants me to feel. Perhaps my problem is that English is my second language and this is a very basic human emotion. The Afrikaans word is *skaam*, or *skaamte*. In this context (*skaam* also means 'shy'), the word means 'to feel embarrassed, humiliated or unhappy about something stupid or wrong one has done or something or someone one is associated with'. My English dictionary says shame is 'a painful emotion caused by consciousness of guilt, shortcomings, impropriety or disgrace'.

Many participants in the raging whiteness debate echo the need for whites to feel shame. Columnist and talk-radio host Eusebius McKaiser, for instance, said in a piece in the *Mail & Guardian* in 2011: 'Feeling shame as a white person is a way of acknowledging that you have been living in a world filled with an injustice rooted in your whiteness.'

I have no hesitation in saying, as I have on numerous occasions in my writings, that I have lived in such a world, that my white skin afforded me privileges above others and, more specifically, that I was a beneficiary of apartheid through the accident of my birth.

But do I 'regret' being white, as Vice says she does and as McKaiser wants me to? Do I feel ashamed (*skaam*, embarrassed, humiliated, disgraced) that I was born of white-skinned parents, and Afrikaners to top it all? I cannot say that I do. I obviously did not choose my parents. To ask me to be ashamed of my whole being is to render me mentally and psychologically unwell and useless to my society.

What I can and do say is that I regard the actions of my ethnic group, of my forefathers, towards the black majority in this country as shameful, morally reprehensible, inhumane, cruel and selfish. I also recognise that if they had not oppressed black people like they did, I would not have benefited in the way I have. My life would probably have been vastly different.

At the same time, I have to admit that I do still feel some pride in being the descendant of Transvaal Republic president Paul Kruger; that I think fondly of Boer War heroes such as Christiaan de Wet. Contradictory as it might sound, there was some honour in my tribe's past. I do, though, equally admire and associate with grand heroes not part of Afrikaner history, and I've written extensively about them: figures such as the philosopher Mohlomi; King Moshoeshoe of the Basotho; the brilliant female general Mantatisi; Adam Kok of the Griquas; warrior-prophet Makhanda; chiefs Sekhukhune, Khama and Sobhuza; and others.

So what is it that Samantha Vice offers as remedies to whiteliness? They should, she says, try, 'in a significantly different way to the normal workings of whiteliness, to make themselves invisible and unheard'. She added: 'Making pronouncements about a situation in which one is so deeply implicated seems a moral mistake – it assumes one matters politically and morally beyond the ways in which everyone matters equally. One needs to learn that one does not. One would live as quietly and decently as possible, refraining from airing one's view on the political situation in the public realm, realising that it is not one's place to offer diagnoses and analyses, that blacks must be left to remake the country in their own way.'

I think if I were black, I would see this as an insult, as condescending, at the very least as the soft bigotry of lowered expectations. *Ag* shame, man, leave the poor darkies alone to do as they want. They can't handle whiteys' interference. That's the message I hear. Thabo Mbeki, Joel Netshitenzhe, Pallo Jordan, Njabulo Ndebele, Xolela Mangcu and the hundreds of other bright, confident black intellectuals, some only in their early thirties, can't hold their own when confronted by whites. Come on.

English roots

Vice wants to banish white South African citizens into quiet, miserable little corners where they have to sit and feel quietly guilty and ashamed – to turn themselves into second-class citizens, to go into exile in their heads. It is hard to resist, she says in the concluding sentence of her learned article, 'the thought that for most white South Africans it will be almost impossible to lead a good life'.

(Forgive me, but I can't resist the temptation. Is part of Vice's problem that she lives in the rarefied air of some white English-speaking academics? She writes: '… we are planted on one continent but brought up on the cultural influences and narratives of another; many older white South Africans still identify in some way with their English and European roots.' Say no more.)

But I don't want to rubbish Samantha Vice. Her piece was well argued and she clearly means well. Her article triggered dozens of others and many letters to newspapers and radio discussions, even a conference on whiteness at the University of Johannesburg in early 2013.

I do agree with much of what she says, just not in the shame and shut-up parts. I'm closer to McKaiser's advice to whites: 'You have an unqualified political and ethical right to engage in the political and public spheres of (y)our country, but be mindful of how your whiteness still benefits you and gives you unearned privileges. Engage black South Africans with humility, and be mindful of not reinforcing whiteness as normative.'

Some of the contributions to the whiteness debate are deeply irritating, nauseatingly self-conscious and self-righteous. I hope we can move away from the narrow focus that the concept of whiteness has brought. I'm with Ferial Haffajee when she called it 'obsessive navel-gazing' and referred to 'a fetish of victimology'.

'Whiteness also renders white people as lesser citizens,' Haffajee writes. 'Dotted through its scholarship is an injunction to think twice before speaking out, to know your place because of your previous privilege. Again, this is the politics of subjugation and not an effort to live out the constitutional principles that provide for equality and for redress … I would rather our white compatriots commit fully to employment equity and black economic empowerment than engage in their whiteness inside their communities.'

One of the most valuable contributions to the broader debate was T.O. Molefe's mini-book for mampoer.co.za titled *Black Anger and White Obliviousness*. If you read nothing else on the topic, read that.

'To create room for public dialogue in post-apartheid South Africa to unfold without the country's painful past muddying the issues, the solution is obvious,' Molefe writes. 'Whites, generally speaking, need to open their eyes ... to the source of the privilege they enjoy today and with that hopefully understand the moral and constitutional imperative of committing themselves to seeing this country transform. In turn blacks, again generalising, should see the change in their fellow countrymen and women and seek ways of healing. Blacks and whites must speak their truths and reconcile – for real this time.'

This is not Russia

I apologise if I have offended you in this chapter or if I appear depressed about the way we get on with one another in this country. I have witnessed the suppressed but still tangible tensions in Rwanda and the dark anger, even hatred, among many Serbs, Croats, Albanians and Bosniaks in Bosnia-Herzegovina, Serbia and Kosovo. We are doing splendidly in comparison – at least our anger, frustration, fear and prejudice are in the open and we talk about it.

I always take the advice of my friend John Carlin, one of the best journalists in the world and author of the book on which the Clint Eastwood film about the 1995 Rugby World Cup, *Invictus*, is based. Carlin believes that right now there is rather more to admire than to despise in South Africa.

'This is not Zimbabwe,' he writes in the *Observer*. 'This is not, for that matter, Russia, which arrived at democracy at the same time. Socially, things have changed a lot too. South Africa is a country where ordinary, black and white people treat each other not with the arrogance and resentment of the apartheid era but, overwhelmingly, with cordiality and respect. I know this. I have been to South Africa six times in the past year. An American I know, who has spent some six months in South Africa over the last two years, observed that racial tensions remained significantly higher in the US.

'As to black aspirations and white fears, both remain works in progress. But compared with how things were in 1990 – with black people now in power, white people having not been thrown into the sea and the Afrikaner tiger tamed – there is plenty to be thankful for.'

Indeed.

PART III

What lies ahead?

13

A long winter, or an early spring?

South Africans are like the old Karoo farmer standing on his stoep watching the abundant rain quenching the earth's thirst after a long drought. He does this every day for a week as the water comes down, just stands there, pulling on his pipe. On the eighth day the rain suddenly stops and the sun breaks through. The farmer looks up at the heavens with a scowl: '*Daar begin die volgende donnerse droogte al weer!*' (There the next damn drought starts again.)

Sure, there is a lot more angst now, two decades after the golden era of Nelson Mandela. We have squandered a lot of our opportunities as a nation and we know that crunch-time is fast approaching. The political temperature is rising as the black majority's resentment at the continued inequality in society is building up. Many of us are frustrated that the ANC couldn't make the shift from liberation movement to governing party in an open democracy; that it has produced leaders with little vision and leadership; that it has allowed corruption and nepotism to become institutionalised. There is certainly reason to be angry that corporate South Africa hasn't joined the project of transforming our society with more enthusiasm.

But most of us, even the poor, are better off now than before 1994, materially and in terms of personal freedoms and quality of life.

We have what has become the most valuable commodity in the world today: stability. Stability is more than just the absence of violence and mayhem. Stability means predictability: the knowledge that a state will maintain the rule of law; that the Constitution and the laws of the land will be applied; that the legal system is fair, credible and operational.

Our stability is rooted in our splendid Constitution and the fact that no one has tried to mess with it so far; in our strong institutions; our vibrant civil society; our free and independent media; our basically sound economy; our innovative business community; and our growing black middle class. We may curse and resent one another when we operate in racial or ethnic groups, but most South Africans are actually getting along just fine in our neighbourhoods, boardrooms, offices and churches, and on our factory floors and streets.

We do not have a tradition of military interference in politics such as Egypt, Zimbabwe and other countries have. Thanks to the credibility and efficiency of our Independent Electoral Commission, the legality and credibility of our elections are never in doubt.

We have the most sophisticated road and rail infrastructure in the developing world; the best airports and airlines that run on time; the most advanced banking system; excellent fixed-line and cellular phone connections; and the most print and electronic media outlets.

What about the almost daily service-delivery protests and the often violent strikes by trade unions, I hear you ask. Yes, these are symptoms of serious fault lines in our society and we do seem to be more boisterous in our protests than most other societies. At the same time, these actions also remind us that we do not live in a police state, but in a democracy where dissension and protest are allowed. They do not fundamentally undermine our stability, in the same way recent violent protests in Brazil and Turkey didn't make those countries unstable states.

When confronted by those who predict an imminent collapse and a Zimbabwe-type situation, I always advise an hour on Google. Go and read what is happening with crime, corruption, nepotism, media and personal freedom, and indeed democracy in the powerful state of Russia, a democracy three years older than ours. Look at the crumbling economies and financial instability of old democracies such as Greece, Spain and Portugal. Read about the coup in Egypt and how recent events have fractured that society, supposed to be the most stable in that region. Investigate the perpetual instability in Pakistan, and the bloody civil war in Syria. Even take note of the divisions, lack of social cohesion and occasional government paralysis in the mighty America. And then appreciate the sunny southern tip of Africa a little more.

Many of us fear the same things and ask the same questions we did when the negotiations between the ANC and the National Party government started in 1990, twenty-three years ago. We should learn to understand what could potentially go wrong in our society and what is highly unlikely to go wrong. We tend to overreact so much to negative indicators that we don't even notice the positive ones.

When our president uses public money to fund his private villa at Nkandla or allows his Gupta friends to treat South Africa as their own backyard, we should howl and protest, but to start shouting that we are a banana republic is just silly.

If there were one thing I would like us South Africans to learn from other societies it would be that the president and the government of the day do not define who and what we are as a people and a country.

My lefty friends in New York moaned and bitched about George W. Bush when he was president and called him names that I can't repeat here. But they didn't say America was rotten and start making plans to emigrate. America is still America, but Barack Obama has brought a whole new vision, style and political culture.

We might have a weak and ineffectual government and a rather embarrassing president right now, but our country and our people are as vibrant and strong as we were when we negotiated that unlikely settlement in 1994, and as magnificent as we saw ourselves to be when we won the Rugby World Cup twice and hosted the most spectacular Soccer World Cup in 2010.

Let me be frank: there is a lot more to South Africa and South Africans than Jacob Zuma and his present crop of ANC leaders. In fact, there is a lot more to the ANC than Zuma and Co.

I attended a breakfast briefing by futurologist and scenario mapper Clem Sunter early in 2013. He gave a lively, engaging and entertaining presentation, and I was most impressed. It all sounded so logical.

But on my way home I felt the irritation grow inside me. Sunter had just told me that there was a 25 per cent probability of South Africa becoming a failed state. In fact, he said the failed-state scenario was no longer a wild-card possibility lurking in the shadows: it was now a genuine threat.

Why, I thought, would he even say the words 'failed state' and 'South Africa' in one sentence? Why was he devoting his time and energy to measuring whether we are about to become like Somalia, the Democratic Republic of the Congo or Afghanistan? Okay, 25 per cent is a low mark, but as he himself said, would you board a plane if you were told there was a 25 per cent chance that you would die?

I think it is completely inappropriate and sends an alarmist message. It's doing the same as the predictions that we are facing an imminent Arab Spring, a phenomenon that wreaked havoc in Libya and Egypt and resulted in the Syrian civil war.

If you look hard enough, I'm sure you'll find reasons to say states like Brazil, Greece, Argentina, Turkey, Poland, Italy and Spain should also be on a list of countries with some probability of becoming failed states. If you ask a muckraking journalist to find evidence that Barack Obama was possibly a Muslim socialist, Pope Francis was a gangster and Mother Teresa a money launderer, he'd probably be able to produce it. Statistically it is possible that the national rugby team of Tajikistan could beat the Springboks in 2030, but I'm not planning to switch my loyalties to tenpin bowling any time soon.

A failed state is classically defined as a state with a failed judiciary; an inability to provide public services or enforce its own laws; a state with military interference in politics; a state that has lost the monopoly on the legitimate use of physical force within its borders.

Most countries in the world, excluding only Germany, Austria, the Scandinavian countries, Canada, the Netherlands, Australia, Ireland and Switzerland, experience one or more of these problems and many of them in a far more serious way than we do.

I regard Sunter's dark warnings in the same light as I did a warning from a climate-change fanatic who recently told me I should move from where I live now, because in twenty years the rain will have stopped and it will be too hot to go outside in summer. Well, I suppose there is a 25 per cent chance, I thought as I looked over the beautiful snow-capped Cape mountains in early October.

South Africa is not going to become a banana republic or a failed state in my lifetime, and I hope to be around for at least three more decades. We'll have incidents of social upheaval and a few scary moments, perhaps, but no Somalia or Zimbabwe.

Exactly how, I wonder, do these predictors of doom imagine South Africa is going to 'collapse' or 'fail', to become a Somalia, Afghanistan or the Democratic Republic of the Congo?

Unlike the nations affected by the Arab Spring, South Africans have free speech, freedom of movement and freedom of association entrenched in their Constitution. Our Constitution can only be changed by a two-thirds majority in Parliament, which we're very unlikely to see in the foreseeable future, and a three-quarters majority is needed to change the founding provisions that guarantee the supremacy of the Constitution, the rule of law and regular elections in a multiparty system of government.

We have active, legitimate political parties ranging from the far left, such as the Economic Freedom Fighters, to the far right, such as the Freedom Front Plus, with two very strong, organised parties in between, the ANC and the DA. This means that virtually all citizens have a political channel for their views, fears and anger – and if we're angry enough, we can vote out a regime and choose another. Beyond that, we have civil movements doing the same, such as the shack-dwellers movement Abahlali baseMjondolo; the mostly white trade-union movement Solidarity and its social-activist arm AfriForum; and the Land Access Movement of South Africa, and many others representing black farmers, farmworkers, and so on. And of course there are strong trade unions in every sector of the economy and the public service, and very strong faith communities.

All the above formations have recognised leaders and registered offices and can be held accountable by the authorities. If any of them breaks the law or instigates mass violence, sabotage or civil war, the criminal justice system will deal with them, as the Boeremag and others have discovered. The SAPS might not be very efficient, but they have so far successfully contained all incidents of public violence from spinning completely out of control even without the help of the military.

One of the more serious cases of public violence, besides Marikana, took place in November 2012 when casual workers on fruit and wine farms protested in the De Doorns area. The protests were organised and controlled by an ANC politician and COSATU official, Tony Ehrenreich, and by Nosey Pieterse, the not-so-poor president of the Black Association of the Wine and Spirit Industry and general secretary of the Bawsi Agricultural Workers Union. The protestors were addressed (and given food parcels) by the minister of agriculture, Tina Joemat-Pettersson, and by the Western Cape ANC leader, Marius Fransman, so we have reason to suspect that the subsequent violence had something to do with the bitter fight between the ANC and the DA in the Western Cape.

Ehrenreich and Pieterse announced early in 2013 that the strikes would resume and grow, but they didn't – tens of thousands of job opportunities were lost because of the losses suffered during the protests and the steep increase in the minimum wage for farmworkers.

There are very few examples of spontaneous revolts by the poorest of the poor, the completely marginalised people in any society. Successful uprisings, like those in Egypt since 2011, are mostly planned and organised by people with some education – hence the important role played by social media.

There is no chance of a military coup in South Africa, just as there was no chance of one when F.W. de Klerk annoyed many in the armed forces by announcing he was going to negotiate a democratic settlement with the ANC.

So how do these prophets of catastrophe think we will become a failed state if not through mass uprisings or a coup? How can we possibly get to a situation where our courts suddenly collapse, where the state can't enforce its own laws or provide any services to the public?

The trade unions are out of control and militant, I hear some say, and that's where a national revolt or the catalyst for instability could start. Look at the role AMCU played at Marikana, they say.

The reality is that trade unions and their influence are waning rapidly. According to a labour analyst with Adcorp Analytics, Loane Sharp, trade unions lost R95 million in 2012 due to declining membership. Only 24 per cent of South Africa's workforce of 13.7 million is unionised and only 15 per cent of the private-sector workforce. The average age of a union member is forty-three, while the average age of a job seeker is twenty-seven. In 2012, only 4 per cent of union members turned up on the ninety-nine strikes. 'The picture of trade unions on the rampage is, therefore, incorrect,' says Sharp.

Now consider how countries like Somalia, Chad, Sudan, Afghanistan, the DRC, the Central African Republic and Yemen became failed states: religious fanaticism, foreign intervention, successive coups d'état, military interference, irreconcilable ethnic hostilities, a culture of warlords. Not one of these factors is relevant to South Africa. We don't even have the threat of terrorism, hurricanes or earthquakes.

But perhaps the strongest assurance that our stability and democracy are not in any danger any time soon lies with the people of South Africa. The cliché is obviously true: the worst never happens here. We did not descend into chaos during our most trying time between 1985 and 1993. We did not, for instance, run into the streets to kill one another when the second most popular and charismatic leader in the country, Chris Hani, was assassinated by a white right-winger in April 1993. Every single time in recent history that the political temperature rose to critical levels, political, religious and community leaders stood up and we all calmed down. Most South Africans carry the example of Nelson Mandela in their hearts.

Even the most militant among us have too much to lose if we fail as a state. That is certainly true of the political elite, but also of the five million black people now part of the middle class with spending power of more than R400 billion – and obviously of the white corporate sector and middle classes. The proportion of South Africans living on less than $2 a day is down to 5 per cent from a peak of 17 per cent in 2002.

The question we should ponder is whether we are going to live up to our real potential in the next few decades; whether we are going to develop and prosper; whether we're going to succeed in bringing social and economic justice to all citizens.

I think this is possible. But a lot of things will have to change. Visionary political and business leadership and a lot more civic activism are preconditions. We'll need leaders in all sectors of our society to forge a new social contract that most citizens will buy into.

The National Development Plan could have been – could still be – a large part of that. It does present a vision of what we should and should not be doing to achieve excellence.

Jacob Zuma should get credit for setting the NDP ball rolling, but he should also be blamed for not championing and popularising it with clarity and energy. He should have sold it to his constituency like F.W. de Klerk sold negotiations with the ANC to his constituency between 1989 and 1994.

Once De Klerk had made up his mind that a negotiated settlement was the only way forward, he spent all his energy and persuasive powers to sell the idea to his party, to the military and the police, to the civil service, and to Afrikaners and whites in general. It wasn't an easy product to sell after centuries of white power and privilege and *hardegat* Afrikaner nationalism, of which he had been a proponent all his life. He was despised by many for doing it. He had the guts to put the question to white people in a referendum, which, if he had lost, would have meant the end of his political career and his legacy. He spent weeks and months criss-crossing the country speaking at public meetings and at smaller gatherings with business people, Broederbonders and religious leaders. It paid off: on 17 March 1992, 69 per cent of white voters voted for the negotiations option. That, in my view, is De Klerk's political legacy.

In many ways the NDP is a radical document that would, if implemented properly, achieve far more for the poor and the workers than the nationalisation of mines, banks and industries could ever do. But our political debate is still so stuck in dogma that such a pragmatic approach is quickly shot down by the SACP and elements in COSATU because it doesn't contain the language and the catchwords they are married to.

The position is now that those who see themselves as being on the left regard the NDP as an elaboration of Mbeki's GEAR, or DA policy in camouflage, and as a plan that is more sympathetic to the private sector than to the poor and unempowered. This is completely unfounded, and it is clear that most of these people have never read the five-hundred-page document, not even the executive summary. It's now an issue like abortion – you're either in favour of it or against it.

We will have a better indication after the May 2014 election whether there is a chance that the idea of the NDP can be popularly revived. It need not stay the same in every aspect. There's a lot that can be negotiated so more groups and people can come aboard, but the essence will have to remain the same.

An integral part of the NDP is the ways and means and process of implementing it and creating the capacity to do so. Again, we will only know after May 2014 whether there is going to be the political will to make its implementation possible.

We will need our future political leadership to snap out of the ANC's habit of talking revolutionary talk knowing well that it can never go beyond talk. We need leaders to explain the economic realities of the world to people in simple terms. What would happen, what price would all of us, poor, middle class and rich, have to pay if banks and mines were nationalised and farmland seized? What would be the real and inevitable effects if we showed a middle finger to the IMF, the World Bank, foreign investors and local corporations and big businesses?

Since his re-election in 2013, Zimbabwe's Robert Mugabe has emerged stronger than before, regarded even by otherwise sober people such as Thabo Mbeki as a true hero and African liberator. He has given Africa back to the Africans, they say, but here at home whites are still the top dogs in the economy. Few add that he trampled on the human rights of hundreds of thousands of people and destroyed his country's once vibrant economy in the process, driving out at least three million of his own citizens (who would most certainly have voted against him if they were at home, meaning he would have lost the election).

The ANC leadership should be brave enough to speak the uncomfortable truth about Mugabe. They should tell people how vastly different Zimbabwe's history, demographic make-up and economy are to South Africa's; that superficially attractive options such as the indigenisation process are not viable options here; that Mugabe needed his army and the large-scale theft of diamonds inside Zimbabwe and other minerals in other African states in order to stay in power.

In October 2013, when he opened the annual conference of the Ahmed Kathrada Foundation, ANC veteran Mathews Phosa did have the guts to speak some uncomfortable truths. The South African state must resist the kind of populist rhetoric that has sunk the economies of some post-liberation African countries, he said. It is in the interests of attracting investment and building confidence in South Africa to come to the point where 'we are able to predict what will happen in the next three years', he said. History has shown that there is a price to pay for populism. It might work for a while, but hunger follows and states are 'forced to go back to the IMF for restructuring'.

We need more of this honesty, and we need it from our president.

A harsh winter

We have to accept that Zuma and his inner circle will still be in charge of government after May next year. Can he and his team snap out of their present paralysis and initiate a new growth path, a new commitment to clean and efficient government?

You may have noticed by now that I'm not exactly a Zuma fan. But the question I have to ask myself and others is this: Would we have felt the same about Zuma if he was an educated, 'detribalised' (I hate the word 'tribal'), city slicker who could quote from Yeats and had only one wife and two or three children?

Do most of his critics feel offended by their president not being a man of reading, as Richard Calland says? Are they put off by his dancing in leopard skins and his difficulty in reading from a prepared speech? And do they judge his actions as president differently because of this? I think in many cases the answer is yes, especially in the case of white people, but also some black middle-class urban people.

The other side of that question, of course, is whether most Zulu-speakers, and the majority of rural people and those who recently became urbanised, would adore Zuma as much if he looked and sounded like Thabo Mbeki.

I have to confess that I'm sometimes put off by Zuma's love of dancing in public and that I think polygamy belongs in a culture that most South Africans have outgrown. He is no intellectual, but I don't expect my president to be one – most people who call themselves intellectuals are in any case mediocre bores, in my humble opinion. I don't think for one moment Zuma is unintelligent – nobody who has engaged him in conversation would think that. I find it refreshing that a man in his position can sit on his haunches drinking traditional beer from an old paint tin with the old guys in Nkandla on a Sunday, and on the Monday chair a cabinet meeting in Pretoria wearing a snazzy suit and drinking a double espresso.

But he is not a man of the world. He is not a very modern human being. He is not a great thinker when it comes to economic policy or foreign affairs. He would have been a great chief, but he's out of his depth as a president of a modern country and economy where some two-thirds of the people are urbanised.

I don't think he is much of a democrat either, at least not in the sense of our Constitution. He just believes in majority rule. He struggles to accept that, while he was chosen by the majority of the people to lead them, unelected journalists, some of them much younger than him, can criticise and even mock him, and that unelected judges can overturn his decisions. He appears to be puzzled by the furious public reaction to his use of state money to build his rural homestead and to him allowing his rich friends from India to use an air-force base to land their wedding guests.

I'm told that he privately disapproves of gays and lesbians and thinks that it is unnatural for them to get married, and that he doesn't believe in abortion – he is clearly socially very conservative and a staunch patriarch.

Now put this man in the seat of the president of the most sophisticated country in Africa with the most progressive Constitution, and you have a problem.

He is caught between his instincts as a Zulu traditionalist, an MK soldier, a security and intelligence operative, and a political street fighter on the one hand, and the restrictions and challenges of heading a modern constitutional state, a sophisticated market economy and an open, diverse society on the other.

His secret weapon is his abundance of charm and disarming warmth – Mbeki's greatest shortcomings. And, of course, a cunningly brilliant mind to survive any moves to undermine or sideline him.

Zuma would have been a much better president if he had come to power in a different way than through the Polokwane putsch. He would have had fewer enemies inside his party and he wouldn't have had to rely on those who brought him into power. He would have had the time and freedom to pick his advisors and his kitchen cabinet, and structure his office and its support services better. He needed a right-hand man like Jakes Gerwel and Fink Haysom were to Mandela, and like Joel Netshitenzhe, Frank Chikane and Mojanku Gumbi were to Thabo Mbeki. Zuma's director-general, Cassius Lubisi, is not such a person. Instead, his office is rather unstructured and he is pushed this way and that by people such as SACP leader Blade Nzimande, his old comrade and spin doctor Mac Maharaj, cabinet ministers from his home province, and several wealthy black and Indian businessmen. His chief of staff, Lakela Kaunda, a former journalist (Zuma calls her Ntombinkulu, 'big girl'), and his international advisor, Lindiwe Zulu, are competent people but not heavyweights.

At least Zuma has two new 'ministers in the presidency' to draw advice from: Collins Chabane, head of the Department of Performance Monitoring and Evaluation, and Trevor Manuel of the National Planning Commission. He could do a lot worse than these two men, but they don't have their own strong support bases in the ANC.

What about ANC secretary-general Gwede Mantashe? Some analysts have called him Zuma's de facto prime minister. He certainly hasn't hesitated in recent times, like with Guptagate, to let Luthuli House's voice be heard. University of Pretoria political scientist Mzukisi Qobo was quoted as saying: 'The state is almost fully subordinated to the will of the party at Luthuli House. Unless we clear up the confusion and obscurity in the relationship between the party and the state ... we are unlikely to see decisive leadership in the country or the government moving more swiftly in times of crisis.'

I have heard, though, that the once close relationship between Mantashe and Zuma has cooled off somewhat. Still, Mantashe controls the party machinery and will be key in the coming election campaign. Zuma cannot afford to alienate him.

I do not know how much influence the new deputy president in the ANC, Cyril Ramaphosa, has on Zuma. Since his election in December 2012 he has kept a low profile and not involved himself in any controversy – he has always preferred to operate like that. One thing is certain: Ramaphosa is no pushover, not to anyone. He has the one thing the ANC is very short on: gravitas. Zuma must sense how important Ramaphosa is to the ANC and to the 2014 elections. But it is not clear to me what their personal relationship is like.

The fact remains that instead of uniting the ANC as was the expectation at Mangaung, the movement is as divided as ever. Zuma's popularity is at its lowest ebb, at least in the bigger cities. This was demonstrated by a call by the Gauteng ANC to Thabo Mbeki to help with the election campaign, as he would be more attractive to the black middle classes. The call was slapped down by Mantashe.

The stark divisions between the ANC and its *real* left wing (read: not the SACP) – as represented by Zwelinzima Vavi, recently suspended as general secretary of COSATU, NUMSA head Irvin Jim and others – spell real trouble for the alliance. Vavi was driven out after a long campaign against him spearheaded by COSATU president and Zuma loyalist Sdumo Dlamini, but in the end he made it easy by getting involved in a sex scandal in the COSATU offices.

In October 2013 Vavi told the *Sunday Times* he was not ready to be part of an opposition party, but did not rule out the possibility. He said there was an urgent need for COSATU to safeguard the 'democratic revolution', which was being threatened by the ANC's 'slide towards the right'. The paper quoted him as saying: 'For now, we must contest the ANC as the left, and see where we go. And because COSATU is so divided, so paralysed, it can never stop it, and that is a big concern. We need a COSATU that is able to stop this slide towards the right in government policies.'

Ironically, Mantashe had earlier told a congress of the Police and Prisons Civil Rights Union that, should part of COSATU leave the alliance, the ANC would shift to the right as the influence of more conservative forces in the movement would become more powerful.

If the left does leave COSATU, they will find themselves in the company of Julius Malema's Economic Freedom Fighters and two smaller socialist forma- tions, the Workers and Socialist Party and the Democratic Left Front. They all propose radical economic policies, such as the nationalisation of mines and banks. The members of the trade union that became prominent during the Marikana troubles, the Association of Mineworkers and Construction Union, have also made their dissatisfaction with the ANC known and could find a home in this same camp.

All of these elements will closely examine the possibility of joining Malema's EFF, if not before the election then soon after. They could become a formid- able opponent to the ANC if Vavi and Jim joined Malema in the leadership. (At the time of writing, Vavi denied he was planning to join the EFF.) They would also be a huge headache for the SACP, which is supposed to be the real champion of the poor and the working class, but is safely tucked under Zuma's wing.

It does seem inevitable that the real left will at some point consolidate outside the ANC. This could turn the main body of the ANC into more of a middle force, not too far removed from the Democratic Alliance and Mamphela Ramphele's Agang. That could lead to a fundamental – and healthy – realignment of South Africa's politics. But it probably won't happen any time soon.

A change in season

The ANC also has to contend with a 'new' DA, the DA of Helen Zille. She has transformed the party significantly from Tony Leon's 'Fight Back' style of leadership. She has a far better gut feel for street politics and has not only incorporated dancing and singing into her repertoire, but has borrowed freely from struggle history to style her party as the one standing for real liberation in the post-apartheid era.

The DA has sown up the support of the vast majority of voters in the white, coloured and Indian groups and is now aiming at new black voters. At the last local elections they calculated that some 750 000 black people had voted for them.

The DA does still struggle with its white 'neoliberal' roots and character, and the ANC will never allow it to forget that. But in recent years it has attracted a number of bright, attractive, young black leaders such as its parliamentary leader, Lindiwe Mazibuko, and its Gauteng leader and national spokesman, Mmusi Maimane. As this new black component dug itself into the party establishment, the party transformed even further to become a much more acceptable face to especially the black middle class.

One of the DA's strongest arguments why black people should support them is the party's track record in the local councils it already runs as well as the Western Cape – by government's own testing, the most well-run province in the country. The ANC knows this and is going to extreme lengths to discredit the DA in the Western Cape.

The original idea was for Mamphela Ramphele to take over the leadership of the DA, and later for her Agang party, formed in June 2013, to join the DA in an alliance. But they could not agree on the terms and now Agang is fighting the election on its own.

Ramphele is a formidable woman with a rich history in the struggle against apartheid and work in rural communities. She was a director of the World Bank, vice-chancellor of the University of Cape Town, and a very successful and wealthy businesswoman. I think it is a good thing that she is going to go to Parliament in 2014 on her own steam and untainted by associations with the 'white liberal' DA.

Ramphele could play a very constructive role in Parliament, as well as in any realignment of opposition parties. At the time of writing, it looked likely that Agang would be joined by Bantu Holomisa's United Democratic Movement (UDM) and talks were under way with Mosiuoa Lekota's COPE. Ramphele and Zille are old friends and have worked together before.

If COPE and the UDM stand on their own in the election, they can hardly hope for more than 1 or 2 per cent of the vote combined. The other two small parties in Parliament at the moment, the Freedom Front Plus and the African Christian Democratic Party, are unlikely to improve on their weak performances of 2009.

Agang has been in the field for far too short a period to make any real inroads in the 2014 election. It does have a lot of money and employs some very clever people, so I would guess it wouldn't be impossible for it to get 5 per cent or so of the vote. The bad news for the DA is that many of those votes could come from the same pool of black voters the DA is aiming for.

The DA has by far the best-oiled party machinery of all the parties. This is very important at election time, because parties have to make sure their potential voters have ID books, are registered for the election and make it to the polling booth on election day.

The DA is confident that it can corner at least 25 per cent, possibly as much as 30 per cent, of the national vote and that it will be victorious in at least the Western Cape, although it has also set its sights on Gauteng.

Mangosuthu Buthelezi's IFP is fighting for its survival. It lost a lot of support to the ANC because of Zuma's popularity in KwaZulu-Natal and among Zulu-speakers in Gauteng, and was also hurt by the breakaway National Freedom Party.

The EFF probably has the biggest growth potential of any party in the country because of its appeal to young voters and the poor. But Malema and his comrades are known as politicians who think they can attract support simply by populist rhetoric and militant statements, and at the time of writing there was little evidence of work on the ground. The EFF's problem is that its most natural supporters, the frustrated black youth and the poor in the townships, squatter camps and deep rural areas, are exactly the kind of people that don't bother to get IDs, to register as voters and to go to the polls on voting day.

It is also unclear how many people will be able to forget how Malema flaunted his ill-gotten wealth. They will be reminded of it when he appears in court on charges of corruption, but the case will probably not be heard before May 2014.

If all the opposition parties do as well as they think they will, the ANC could end up with less than 60 per cent of the vote in 2014. This will give them the shivers, because if the trend continues they could dip under 50 per cent at the election in 2019. That is, if the present political landscape looks the same then as it does now, which is highly unlikely.

Still, it is making the ANC very nervous – it was Zuma who said the ANC would rule until Jesus returns. Many South Africans ask what the ANC would do if they were to lose an election – would they accept it, or would they pull a Mugabe and ignore it? Fortunately we don't have to answer that question now. Let's just say I'll probably have to apologise to Clem Sunter if that happened with present attitudes in the ruling party.

In mid-2013 the ANC decided to stick with Zuma as the face on their election posters for 2014. This might change in the months before the election. As I write, Public Protector Thuli Madonsela is toiling hard to get access to all the information in order to complete her report on the spending of public money on Zuma's Nkandla villa. If her findings are damning to Zuma – if she, for instance, finds that he lied to Parliament about it – it could force the ANC into a rethink, especially as it comes on top of the damaging Guptagate scandal.

But more importantly, if the courts decide that the 'spy tapes' on which the NPA based its controversial decision to drop the criminal charges against Zuma should be made public, it could lead to a new trial for Zuma. As I've indicated, the evidence against him is very strong and a conviction likely.

Could this case, if so ordered by the court, start before the 2014 elections? Would voters still flock to support a president who is likely on his way to jail?

Zuma's former confidante and nowadays prominent political journalist Ranjeni Munusamy thinks he'll get away with everything. Writing in *Daily Maverick* on the Guptagate scandal, she said:

> President Jacob Zuma lives by the principle of plausible deniability and information on a need to know basis. If there is anything that occurs that could result in a backlash, Zuma's fingerprints will not be detectable. Apart from the rape trial, when there was no way to deny the sexual encounter with the complainant, it has been impossible to hold Zuma answerable to any of the allegations against him. Every now and then, history produces a resilient, hard-wearing leader whose street-smarts outstrip anything anyone from the same generation can offer; Zuma is such a leader. He rose to the nation's top job without being seen as openly ambitious, he controls the ANC strongly without having to raise his voice and he commands an army of 'friends' without getting his hands dirty. He gets his way but leaves no trace. And while it is not impossible that the 'smoking gun' linking him directly to any of the scandals may finally emerge, it still remains an unlikely prospect. Many have tried, but Zuma is still standing.

I'm not so sure. Zuma's brushes with the courts, on his corruption charges and regarding his efforts to control the criminal justice system, have gone wrong for him in recent times. With the independence of our courts still intact, and with the resilience of civil society and opposition parties, he must know that he can run but one day he won't be able to hide.

Mind you, he and his henchmen seem to have made sure that the arms-deal scandal won't, after all these years, embarrass them. The ongoing commission of inquiry under Judge Willie Seriti has shown all the signs of not actually wanting to get to the ugly truth.

When will the ANC stop and say enough is enough, Zuma is an embarrassment and a liability to the party and the country? If they don't, they will have finally lost their soul. If they do, they'll have to be very concerned about the loyalty of voters in KwaZulu-Natal, the only province where the ANC's support has grown in recent years.

City Press editor Ferial Haffajee wondered about the same things in October 2013. What if the court takes the NPA's decision not to prosecute Zuma on appeal? What if Madonsela's report on Nkandla points the finger at Number One? She asked: 'Will the ANC-led government help to cover it all up again? Or will it call upon Number 2 to become Number 1?'

Consider this. If Zuma is indeed fingered by Madonsela and if the criminal charges go ahead (and/or some other Zuma scandal breaks), the ANC might just decide to get rid of him – softly, mind you, like with a presidential pardon or an excuse of ill health combined with a promise that he could keep Nkandla as it is without paying any of it back. Or they might decide to keep him on as ANC president and make the new deputy president after the 2014 election the president – the old two-seats-of-power idea previously mooted by Mbeki.

Another scenario might be that they stand by him, but his trial goes ahead and he gets sent to jail. This could potentially happen before the end of 2015.

If Zuma does leave office before his term is up in 2019, does that mean South Africa will have Cyril Ramaphosa as its president?

Well, if Ramaphosa did indeed become deputy president after the 2014 elections, probably yes. Or perhaps not.

The ANC in KwaZulu-Natal, the same lot who first proposed Ramaphosa as a candidate for deputy president of the ANC, seems to have had a change of heart – or, perhaps more likely, they only used Ramaphosa to make sure Zuma's slate won at Mangaung.

The ANC heavies in the province apparently feel strongly that the time is not ripe for a non-Zulu president. KwaZulu-Natal is by far the ANC's strongest province. They want the presidency in a Zulu-speaker's hands for at least one more term.

Their candidates for this position would be Nkosazana Dlamini-Zuma, Zuma's former wife, former cabinet minister and now head of the African Union Commission, and Zweli Mkhize, former KwaZulu-Natal premier and now based at Luthuli House as treasurer of the ANC.

Both these candidates would, in my view, make good leaders of the ANC and good presidents of the country – much, much better than the present one. At least we know Dlamini-Zuma is an energetic, honest and highly capable leader and administrator.

But Ramaphosa's opponents shouldn't underestimate him – F.W. de Klerk, Roelf Meyer and Niel Barnard did during the negotiations before the 1994 settlement, and they rued the day. Ramaphosa hasn't returned to politics after sixteen years just to be caught up in Zuma's muck or to be messed around by party officials.

The Ramaphosa I know would be concerned with his legacy. His legacy isn't Shanduka, the company he built. He is a political animal. He wants, I think, to build on his legacy as a pioneering trade-union leader and master negotiator for the ANC, and become the president of South Africa. He was, after all, the man who stood next to Nelson Mandela when the latter made his first public speech after his release in 1990, and the chairman of the constituent assembly that gave us our Constitution in 1996. I'm sure he believes it's his destiny to be president.

A final word

No, I don't think we face anything like an Arab Spring. There is an outside chance that the unity in the ANC could at least temporarily be patched up after the 2014 election, which could translate into more of a sense of urgency and purpose in the ruling party. The ANC leadership is beginning to realise that they will have to clean up their act and govern more efficiently if they don't want to lose power in 2019. It could happen, but don't hold your breath, not as long as the man who laughs in your face while he's harming you is in charge.

I personally can't see Zuma serving out his whole five-year term after 2014. I really can't. That brings the prospect of new blood, be it Ramaphosa, Dlamini-Zuma, Mkhize or someone else (Ramaphosa is top of my own wish list), which could be just the key to a new era of discipline, good leadership and growth.

But there's another development that makes me even more optimistic about the future: the reawakening of civil society.

My weather report says that winter will persist for a while, but there is a promise of an eventual spring. It might be accompanied by a few severe thunderstorms, though.

There is, after all, more to South Africa and South Africans than the president and the government of the day.

Bibliography

Alexander, Neville. *Thoughts on the New South Africa*. Johannesburg: Jacana Media, 2012

Alexander, Peter, Thapelo Lekgowa, Botsang Mmope, Luke Sinwell and Bongani Xezwi. *Marikana: A View from the Mountain and a Case to Answer*. Johannesburg: Jacana Media, 2012

Altbeker, Antony. *A Country at War With Itself: South Africa's Crisis of Crime*. Johannesburg: Jonathan Ball, 2007

Basson, Adriaan. *Zuma Exposed*. Johannesburg: Jonathan Ball, 2012

Biko, Hlumelo. *The Great African Society: A Plan for a Nation Gone Astray*. Johannesburg: Jonathan Ball, 2013

Bloch, Graeme. *The Toxic Mix: What's Wrong with South Africa's Schools and How to Fix It*. Cape Town: Tafelberg, 2012

Booysen, Susan. *The African National Congress and the Regeneration of Political Power*. Johannesburg: Wits University Press, 2011

Butler, Anthony. *Cyril Ramaphosa*. Johannesburg: Jacana Media, 2007

Calland, Richard. *Anatomy of South Africa: Who Holds the Power?* Cape Town: Zebra Press, 2006

———. *The Zuma Years: South Africa's Changing Face of Power*. Cape Town: Zebra Press, 2013

Chikane, Frank. *Eight Days in September: The Removal of Thabo Mbeki*. Johannesburg: Picador Africa, 2012

———. *The Things that Could Not be Said: From Aids to Zimbabwe*. Johannesburg: Picador Africa, 2013

Cohen, Tim. *A Piece of the Pie: The Battle over Nationalisation*. Johannesburg: Jonathan Ball, 2012

Daniel, Hogn, Prishani Naidoo, Devan Pillay and Roger Southall (eds.). *New South African Review 2: New Paths, Old Compromises?* Johannesburg: Wits University Press, 2011

De Klerk, F.W. *Die laaste trek – 'n nuwe begin: Die outobiografie*. Cape Town: Human & Rousseau, 1999

Dlangamandka, Felix, Thanduxolo Jika, Lucas Ledwaba, Sebabatso Mosamo, Athandiwe Saba and Leon Sadiki. *We Are Going to Kill Each Other Today: The Marikana Story*. Cape Town: Tafelberg, 2013

Du Preez, Max (ed.). *Opinion Pieces by South African Thought Leaders.* Johannesburg: Penguin, 2011

Ellis, Stephen. *External Mission: The ANC in Exile.* Johannesburg: Jonathan Ball, 2012

————, and Tsepo Sechaba. *Comrades Against Apartheid: The ANC and the South African Communist Party in Exile.* London: James Currey, 1992

Feinstein, Andrew. *After the Party: A Personal and Political Journey Inside the ANC.* Johannesburg: Jonathan Ball, 2007

Foster, Douglas. *After Mandela: The Struggle for Freedom in post-Apartheid South Africa.* New York: Liveright, 2012

Gevisser, Mark. *Thabo Mbeki: The Dream Deferred.* Johannesburg: Jonathan Ball, 2007

Glaser, Daryl (ed.). *Mbeki and After.* Johannesburg: Wits University Press, 2011

Green, Pippa. *Trevor Manuel: 'n lewensverhaal.* Cape Town: Tafelberg, 2009

Gumede, William. *Restless Nation: Making Sense of Troubled Times.* Cape Town: Tafelberg, 2012

Hagg, Gerard, Francis Nyamnjoh and Udesh Pillay (eds.). *State of the Nation: South Africa 2012–2013.* Cape Town: HSRC Press, 2013

Hartley, Ray (ed.). *How to Fix South Africa: The Country's Leading Thinkers on What Must Be Done to Create Jobs.* Johannesburg: KMM Review, 2012

Harvey, Ebrahim. *Kgalema Motlanthe: A Political Biography.* Johannesburg: Jacana Media, 2012

Holden, Paul, and Martin Plaut. *Who Rules South Africa? Pulling the Strings in the Battle for Power.* Johannesburg: Jonathan Ball, 2012

Johnson, R.W. *South Africa: The First Man, the Last Nation.* Johannesburg: Jonathan Ball, 2005

————. *South Africa's Brave New World: The Beloved Country Since the End of Apartheid.* London: Allen Lane, 2009

Kagwanja, Peter, and Kwandiwe Kondlo (eds.). *State of the Nation: South Africa 2008.* Cape Town: HSRC Press, 2009

Kane-Berman, John, and Lucy Holborn (eds.). *South Africa Survey 2012.* Johannesburg: South African Institute of Race Relations, 2012

Kasrils, Ronnie. *Armed and Dangerous: From Undercover Struggle to Freedom.* Johannesburg: Jacana Media, 2013

Marais, Hein. *South Africa Pushed to the Limit: The Political Economy of Change.* Cape Town: UCT Press, 2011

Mbeki, Moeletsi (ed.). *Advocates for Change: How to Overcome Africa's Challenges.* Johannesburg: Picador Africa, 2011

O'Malley, Padraig. *Shades of Difference: Mac Maharaj and the Struggle for South Africa.* New York: Viking, 2007

Parsons, Raymond. *Zumanomics Revisited: The Road from Mangaung to 2030.* Johannesburg: Jacana Media, 2013

Ramphele, Mamphela. *Laying Ghosts to Rest: Dilemmas of the transformation in South Africa.* Cape Town: Tafelberg, 2008

Roberts, Ronald Suresh. *Fit to Govern: The Native Intelligence of Thabo Mbeki.* Johannesburg: STE Publishers, 2007

Rossouw, Mandy. *Mangaung: Kings and Kingmakers.* Cape Town: Kwela Books, 2012

Shubin, Vladimir. *ANC: A View from Moscow.* Johannesburg: Jacana Media, 2008

Suttner, Raymond. *The ANC Underground in South Africa.* Johannesburg: Jacana Media, 2008

Turok, Ben. *The Evolution of ANC Economic Policy: From The Freedom Charter to Polokwane.* Cape Town: New Agenda, 2008

Van Zyl Slabbert, Frederik. *The Other Side of History: An Anecdotal Reflection on Political Transition in South Africa.* Johannesburg: Jonathan Ball, 2006

Zulu, Paulus. *A Nation in Crisis: An Appeal for Morality.* Cape Town: Tafelberg, 2013

Index